ADOLESCENT LIVES 2

A series edited by Jeanne Brooks-Gunn

WORKING AND GROWING UP IN AMERICA

JEYLAN T. MORTIMER

HARVARD UNIVERSITY PRESS

Cambridge, Massachusetts

London, England

2003

Copyright © 2003 by the President and Fellows of Harvard College
All rights reserved
Printed in the United States of America

Library of Congress Cataloging-in-Publication Data
Mortimer, Jeylan T., 1943–
Working and growing up in America / Jeylan T. Mortimer.
     p. cm. — (Adolescent lives ; 2)
Includes bibliographical references and index.
ISBN 0-674-00923-1 (alk. paper)
    1. Youth—Employment—United States—Longitudinal studies.   2. Youth—United
States—Attitudes—Longitudinal studies.   3. School-to-work transition—United States—
Longitudinal studies.   4. Youth—Employment—United States—Psychological aspects.
I. Title.   II. Series.

HD6273 .M67 2002
331.3′47′0973—dc21   2002027604

To my mother, Roselle Martin Tekiner

CONTENTS

ACKNOWLEDGMENTS

The planning and execution of the Youth Development Study have spanned two decades. Throughout this period, I have been greatly blessed with creative and energetic mentors, collaborators, and students. Mike Finch helped to frame the study conceptually and theoretically and contributed to its fruition in manifold ways. I owe him much gratitude for his intellectual insights, methodological guidance, and friendship through all phases of the research. I would also like to thank my other faculty collaborators, including Christopher Uggen, who guided the study during my sabbatical year, as I was writing this book. The University of Minnesota professors Dennis Ahlburg, Timothy Dunnigan, Douglas Hartmann, Scott Eliason, Erin Kelly, Ross Macmillan, and Brian McCall took part in various phases of the study and influenced my thinking as it progressed.

I also would like to thank the graduate students who worked on this project as research assistants, including Pamela Aronson, Timothy Beebe, Kathleen Call, Ronda Copher, Kathleen Dennehy, Lorie Schabo Grabowski, Carolyn Harley, Monica Kirkpatrick Johnson, Chaimun Lee, Daniel Martin, Miles McNall, Sarah Phillips, Laura Puchtell, Seongryeol Ryu, Kent Sandstrom, Michael Shanahan, Connie Stevens, Deming Wang, and Cathy Wisner. I am especially indebted to Timothy Owens, the first YDS project manager, who established a sound framework for all subsequent surveys; and to Sabrina Oesterle and Jeremy Staff, who conducted many of the data analyses and made valuable suggestions. I am also grateful to the undergraduate research assistants for their continuous tracking of the YDS youth and capable collection of data. They include Jill Adler, Annikka

Anderberg, Paola Bernazzani, Jeremy Blackowicz, Sara Borjkland, Jeff Busch, Heather Driscoll, Stephanie Fox, Julie Gagne, Betsy Gerst, Michael Hacker, Jennifer Halko, John Horvick, John Hurney, Mike Kemper, Jennifer Koback, Jill Koniecki, Carol Krauze, Candyce Kroenke, Stephanie Kukowski, Jimmy Lai, Mary Jo Leece, Sandy Lind, Mary Lowe, Sheri L. Lynn, Sara Manny, Mary McDonald, Christine Mealio, Sara Noble, Virginia Parker, Kelly Reagan, Mike Riley, De-Anna Schuler, Sandra Stai, Oliver Urbanchek, Christopher Wavrin, Sally Webber, Jenny Wolesky, and Carol Zierman.

Since its initiation the Youth Development Study has been generously supported by the National Institute of Mental Health (MH 42843: Work Experience and Mental Health: A Panel Study of Youth). This funding has enabled annual data collection and continuous analysis. The study has received additional resources from the National Center for Research on Vocational Education, the National Institute on Aging, the Northwest Area Foundation, and the William T. Grant Foundation. I am grateful to Neil Smelser and Bob Scott, of the Center for Advanced Studies in the Behavioral Sciences, for facilitating my writing of the first draft during the 1998–99 academic year. This sabbatical fellowship was financed by the Center, the Hewlett Foundation, and the W. T. Grant Foundation. Michael Shanahan, my colleague at the Center, offered insights and suggestions that greatly enhanced the book.

The Saint Paul Public School District allowed us to enter the schools and utilize one hour of the students' time. Dr. Thel Kocher's gracious support and endorsement of the project are much appreciated.

The research would not have been possible were it not for the hundreds of young people who have carefully, year after year, filled out lengthy questionnaires with very little compensation. We have learned from our face-to-face interviews that the knowledge that they were contributing to scientific knowledge sustained their motivation to continue. Most parents of these young people also completed surveys at least once during their children's high school years.

The Department of Sociology at the University of Minnesota provided needed infrastructure in the form of office space, clerical help, and accounting resources. Hilda Daniels offered extremely valuable advice on the financial administration of the project. In the early stages of the research, financial support was provided by the Graduate School of the University of Minnesota and the College of Liberal Arts. During my year at the Center for Advanced Studies, return trips to Minnesota were made possible by the Scholar of the College Award from the College of Liberal Arts. Recent interviews with YDS participants in their mid-twenties were enabled by grants from the College of Liberal Arts and the Hubert H. Humphrey Institute of Public Affairs. Holly Schoonover of the Life Course Center provided invaluable assistance in the final stages of manuscript preparation. In continuous good spirits, she labored over the production and correction of countless drafts.

Elizabeth Knoll of Harvard University Press promoted the clarity and organization of the book. Her astute judgment and editorial guidance enhanced each chapter. I am especially grateful for her perpetual encouragement and for her urging me to allow the youth to speak in their own voices. Camille Smith, Senior Editor, helped me to clarify, tighten, and improve the manuscript.

I would also like to express appreciation to my long-term mentors. Years ago, Melvin Kohn advised me to embark on a new longitudinal study. His research on the social psychology of work and Glen Elder's studies of the life course have been tremendous sources of inspiration. Irving Tallman provided much support and guidance at critical phases of the study.

I am grateful to my son, Kent, for sharing his thoughts and concerns as he traversed the bridge from adolescence to adulthood. His insights stimulated many of the ideas presented here. One of Kent's teenage work experiences, helping me with the YDS, raised my sensitivity to the ways work can contribute to adolescent development. I would also like to thank my husband, Jeffrey Broadbent, whose sympathetic listening through all phases of the project has been greatly appreciated. Finally, I have received constant support and encouragement from my mother, to whom this book is dedicated. Her anthropological eye awakened my interest in the understanding of social life and human development.

WORKING AND GROWING UP IN AMERICA

1

SHOULD ADOLESCENTS WORK?

AT THE BEGINNING of the twentieth century, G. Stanley Hall drew attention to adolescence as a stage of life constituting a "new birth," a time of rapid development and maximal receptivity to environmental influence. Hall depicted this phase of quickened biological growth, expanded cognitive capacity, and heightened emotional expressiveness as critically important for personality formation and vocational development: "In no psychic soil . . . does seed, bad as well as good, strike such deep root, grow so rapidly, or bear fruit so quickly or so surely . . . The whole future of life depends on how the new powers now given suddenly and in profusion are husbanded and directed" (1904, xviii–xv).

In view of what he saw as adolescents' acute responsivity to external influence, Hall worried about whether the modern construction of this life phase was encouraging premature assumption of adultlike behaviors. The threat of precocity, a prominent theme among educators of his era (Kett, 1971, 1978), looms large throughout Hall's two-volume tome: "Our young people leap rather than grow into maturity" (xvi). Hall believed that youth needed time to play, to roam the countryside, to explore their widening social worlds, and to turn inward in solitude to develop their emerging identities. He was especially concerned about youth's acquisition of independence and the work role too soon: "Our vast and complex business organization . . . absorbs ever more and earlier the best talent and muscle of youth . . . but we are progressively forgetting that for the complete apprenticeship to life, youth needs repose, leisure, art, legends, romance, idealization, and in a word humanism, if it is to enter the kingdom of man well equipped for man's highest work in the world" (xvi–xvii).

In fact, semi-autonomy is often considered the hallmark of adolescence. At this time of life, young people are moving beyond their families, forming new relationships, and engaging in a wide range of activities. However, the extent to which adolescents can and should be autonomous, able to make their own decisions and take independent lines of action, and the extent to which they should remain dependent and protected by adults, remain controversial.

Throughout the twentieth century, educators and policymakers continued to debate the appropriate balance of working and schooling for teenagers and youth. Hall thought adolescence should be, ideally, a time of freedom from labor. The possibility of such freedom was a relatively recent phenomenon. For centuries children had toiled alongside their parents or parental surrogates, performing whatever tasks in the field, the household, or the shop they were capable of doing. Thus children began economic activities at a very early age, under the guidance and authority of adults. In medieval France and England, youngsters aged 7–9 would typically be apprenticed in families other than their own, where they would perform menial household tasks, including much hard work, until the age of 14–18 (Ariès, 1962).[1] Given the absence of boundaries between occupational and private life, through apprenticeship an adult transmitted to a child "the knowledge, practical experience, and human worth which he was supposed to possess" (ibid.: 366). In return for labor, the apprentice sometimes learned farming practices or the skills of a trade. After the advent of formal schooling, some children attended school during their period of apprenticeship.

Thus, up to the eighteenth century, a lengthy "childhood" was marked by considerable economic contribution along with economic and social dependence. Chronologically, this stage included the phases we now differentiate as childhood, adolescence, and youth.

In preindustrial America, children (in this age-inclusive sense) similarly performed useful labor in family farms and shops. By the age of 6–8, children in Plymouth Colony were expected to work either in their own households or as apprentices elsewhere (Demos, 1972). Strong presumptions that young men would help their farmer fathers, up to the age of 21, persisted in rural America up to the early nineteenth century (Kett, 1978). Apprenticed children were typically placed with relatives or neighbors, not far from their own families. This usually occurred at age 14 (Kett, 1971), but Graff (1995) notes instances of apprenticeship as early as age 8–9.

As formal schooling became established, pupils were expected to absent themselves from school as the needs of the farm dictated (e.g. Graff, 1995). Kett describes education and work in the early nineteenth century as "interwoven" and seasonal. After the harvest, or as other needs for their labor subsided, children could resume their studies. According to Kett, "The nature of education and labor combined made it difficult to say whether a fifteen-year-old boy was dependent or semi-dependent, a child or a youth, for at different times of the year he was likely to be each" (1971: 294). The long summer vacation in present-day America is a remnant of this earlier pattern.

The involvement of youth in farming diminished substantially as America industrialized. In rural areas, however, children continued to toil on farms. In the 1920s child farm workers became the focus of labor reformers (Zelizer, 1985). But reformers' emphatic distinction between family and nonfamily labor reflected the persistent acceptance of the norm that children in farm families should be part of the family economic strategy. Working on one's own family's farm was considered not merely legitimate but valuable, enabling both skill acquisition and character building. In contrast, children's employment on nonfamily farms, for wages or board, was depicted as exploitative and harmful.

In contemporary farm families, children's work is still an integral part of the family economy (Boulding, 1980). However, advocates of child protection no longer distinguish between family and nonfamily labor, arguing against both (Committee, 1998).

Even as America began to industrialize, the family remained in many circumstances the primary unit of production. In America as in Britain, whole families were recruited to the textile mills as working units, with the male heads of household supervising wives, children, and sometimes other adult family members (Smelser, 1959; Hareven, 1982). Children's wages were considered to be the family's property. In fact, children constituted more than half the textile operators in Rhode Island in 1820, and many worked in southern mills as well (Zelizer, 1985).

Even children considered too young to labor in factories were expected to contribute economically to their families. In late nineteenth-century Manchester, New Hampshire, home of the world's largest textile factory, schoolchildren were paid to carry lunches from the company-owned boardinghouses to the mills (Hareven, 1982). They also did housework, cared for younger siblings, and earned money by doing odd jobs. Often mothers and children did piecework in the home, while still attending to farm and other household chores. Such "industrial homework," typically performed by young girls, was a common form of child labor in late nineteenth-century America (Zelizer, 1985).

After the age of 14, school and workplace competed for youth's time and energies. Many young people of this age joined older family members in the factories, where they learned their jobs from relatives—in what Hareven calls an "informal family apprentice system." Many of those who continued to attend school, postponing full-time employment, worked in the mills during the summer and/or left school temporarily to earn money to pay for further education (Graff, 1995). (The nineteenth-century residential academies accommodated a broad age range, from 7 or 8 to 25; Kett, 1978).

Social historians point out that childhood and youth were coming to assume fundamentally new meanings as America shifted from a primarily rural agrarian to an urban industrial society. With the decline of family farms, the child's role as economic contributor to the household diminished. Kett (1978) observes that children in middle-class families were no longer simply "resources"; instead, they became "representatives," expressing their families' status in the community. Middle-class families gained prestige from their children's educational accomplishments.

Kett describes the "sentimentalization of childhood in early nineteenth-century America" that derived from this fundamental reconceptualization. No longer was childhood considered merely the start of life. Instead, early experiences were now thought to shape a person's later development. Childhood came to be seen, much as Hall would later see it, as a precious, critically formative stage requiring much nurturance and protection. Premature association with adults was thought to have a potentially corrupting influence. Casual unsupervised contact with adults, which could occur in the workplace, was especially feared.

Zelizer (1985) documents the emergence of the "priceless child"—

no longer economically useful but of immense emotional value—between 1870 and 1930. The normative ideal was to excuse the child (and the adolescent, in contemporary parlance), insofar as possible, from labor. This trend was particularly pronounced in the working class—since middle-class children had already become economically "useless" earlier. (This ideal has not yet been fully achieved, as children in poor American families still do not have the luxury of devoting themselves solely to education and leisure; see Newman, 1996.) The changing ideological conception of children meant that even their work in the home, when it did occur, could no longer be justified on instrumental grounds: a rationale based on its developmental benefits had to be constructed.

This period of heightened worries about precocity (1890–1930, for Kett) coincided with legislative initiatives to restrict the employment of children, culminating in the federal Fair Labor Standards Act of 1938 (Smelser and Halpern, 1978). According to educators and labor reformers, young people had to be shielded from exploitation by adults, including their parents, both at home and in the workplace (Modell, 1979; Zelizer, 1985). The reformers feared multiple forms of abuse—physical, economic, and sexual. Children who worked in the streets, such as newsboys and bootblacks, were thought to be exposed to deleterious influences that might draw "them into a life of vice and 'unnatural desires'" (Zelizer, 1985: 81). Instead, children were admonished to attend school, filling places created by the vast expansion of secondary schools in urban areas. "Precocity" in the economic role signified a failure to nurture and protect youth by allowing them to assume their rightful positions in the increasingly age-graded and bureaucratic educational system.

In the urban working class, meanwhile, many older children continued to labor in paid jobs, as their families needed their wages. The mother and children often entered the workforce when the father was unable to work or when the family required additional income (Modell, 1979). But in succeeding years a number of trends—changing labor market needs and production processes, unionization, rising real incomes, the growing prevalence of the family wage, and competition with adult immigrants for unskilled labor—decreased both the opportunity for children to work and the family's need for their labor. With children and parents no longer working together in functional economic units, and with children no longer wanted or so strongly needed in the factories, the problem of "idle and vagrant children" was born (Zelizer, 1985: 61).

Augmenting the force of these changing social and economic conditions, the altered conception of the child provided ideological justification for the restriction of child labor in favor of educating youth in the schools. By prolonging the social, economic, and emotional dependence of young people, schooling could preserve their "childhood" and shield their "innocence" from adverse influences. The school's most significant manifest goal was to prepare youth for adulthood, particularly for adult occupational roles. In this context, students were expected to acquire the basic literacy and numeracy they would need in future jobs. The schools also took on the task of teaching large numbers of immigrant youth a new language, new behaviors, and new skills that would facilitate their assimilation into American society.

The experience of schooling, unlike that in the workplace, was shaped by adults so as to promote optimal socialization and character development. In the process of learning about history and the workings of governmental institutions, children were also expected to internalize norms that would promote informed citizenship in a democratic society (Dreeben, 1968). Extracurricular activities, such as student government, were provided to allow children to participate in adultlike civic activities without having to assume premature responsibility. As long as young people were confined to the social worlds of the school and youth organizations, the "regulated peer group" was thought to be a salutary socializing influence (Kett, 1978). Child labor in the home and the workplace would thus be supplanted by more developmentally beneficial pursuits within the contexts of school, extracurricular activities, and peer friendship groups.

The primary business of the child's life, especially in the middle class, came to be understood as attending, and succeeding in, school. Educators and policymakers continued to worry about children, mainly from the urban working class, who labored in factories and on farms. In early twentieth-century America most parents could still not afford to allow their children to attend school for very long after puberty (Kett, 1978), although high school attendance was becoming more prevalent. By 1930 most children under 14 were attending school and were not employed. Thus "in the first three decades of the twentieth century, the economically useful child became both numerically and culturally an exception" (Zelizer, 1985: 6).

But considerable ambivalence and contradiction were inherent in this new normative conception of youth. Many young people still worked, and even the experts did not uniformly perceive school as an altogether salutary environment for the young. Despite the dominant ideological justification for schooling, critics pointed to its drawbacks. For example, Hall thought children should be protected from encountering the stresses of schoolwork and competition with peers too early: attending school would curtail play and exploration and restrict physical activity (see also Kett, 1978).

Concerns about the isolated character of school, its segregation from the "real world," date back to the early establishment of schools in Western Europe. Ariès describes a current of opinion hostile to formal schooling in the seventeenth century, when many saw apprenticeship as more useful than school for one's future life in society. Some thought schooling would unduly prolong childhood along with "childish nonsense" (1962: 378). This perspective provides stark contrast to the increasingly dominant concern that childhood innocence needed to be safeguarded "against pollution by life."

Through the ages, then, controversy about young people's activities has arisen from contradictory values and contrasting ideals of childhood (Smelser and Halpern, 1978). Should society preserve childhood (and what we now call adolescence) by restricting young people to protected settings designed to promote their salutary development? Or should society promote maturity—referring here to adultlike habits of mind and behaviors—by engaging youth in "real world" environments? This issue stands at the crux of age-old debates about the proper roles of children and youth.

Though school attendance continued to extend to older age groups in the early twentieth century, work was not eliminated. As we have seen, rural children and adolescents continued to work on their families' farms and, especially during the harvest, on other farms as well. Youth in small towns and urban areas assisted in their entrepreneurial parents' shops and small businesses after school, on weekends, and during the summers. As in earlier historical periods, young people could thus learn work habits and skills within the family, as they labored alongside or under the direct supervision of their parents or other relatives.

Urban youth, particularly those from economically pressed families, found many ways of earning money. Zelizer describes a lively informal economy in early twentieth-century America. Young girls cared for children in others' homes and did household chores. Boys did yardwork, shoveled snow, ran errands, sold newspapers, and shined boots. Those who held after-school jobs contributed their paychecks to the family coffer. At older ages, young people's economic activity and "hands on" training took place outside the tutelage of parents and parental surrogates. Informal work was supplanted by more formal, contractual employment outside the network of family and friends. And alternation of formal schooling and paid labor was still common, as family needs and other circumstances dictated.

In his classic work *Children of the Great Depression,* Elder notes that work and domestic tasks were considered "virtuous activity for children" in traditional family cultures (1974: 68). He recounts the manifold ways teenagers contributed to their families in the hard times of the thirties. In this way, adultlike responsibilities "extended downward"—just as they still do in poor families where working children take on the status of what Newman (1996) calls "junior adult." Depression-era boys held a variety of part-time jobs, and girls were babysitters. Girls also worked at household chores—cleaning, preparing food, making clothes instead of buying them, and tending to boarders. These responsibilities were thought to inculcate work habits and skills as well as strength of character. Elder, in fact, empirically documents the gains in confidence and work motivation—and in socioeconomic achievement in adulthood—developed through such work activities in adolescence.

By 1940 half of U.S. 17-year-olds were graduating from high school, and employment during the teen years diminished markedly (see Figure 1.1). Knowledge acquired through formal schooling gained importance because of greater occupational specialization and complexity of occupational tasks. But many youth resented having to go to school, seemingly unconvinced that their "book-learning" would be useful to them in the future.

Three decades later, worries about limiting young people to the childlike role of student persisted. The Panel on Youth of the Presi-

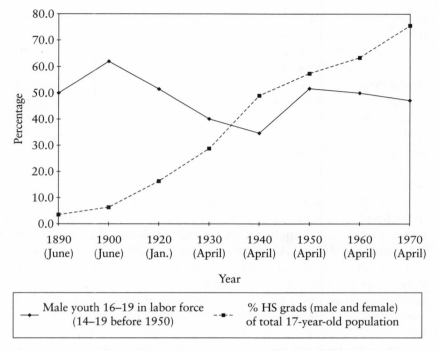

Figure 1.1. Male labor force participation and high school graduation, 1890–1970. *Sources: Historical Statistics of the United States, 1997,* Series D29–41, H598–601; Education Statistics on Disk, 1996, D96, table 98.

dent's Science Advisory Committee was convened to consider what attributes youth needed to become effective adults, and what institutions would contribute to their development. Its report (Panel on Youth, 1974) echoed earlier concerns and articulated major themes that still pervade debates about teenage employment. The panel, headed by the prominent sociologist James Coleman, pointed out that while the school environment fosters cognitive achievement, it also heightens dependency and provides little opportunity to learn self-management skills. The panel questioned whether schooling could fulfill the multifaceted needs of adolescents and youth—to take responsibility, to exercise authority over activities that influenced others, and to experience the consequences of their actions.

The report emphasized the increasing age-segregation of American society. Young people were spending the better part of their days in schools, in close proximity to other youth. They came in contact with only a few adults—their teachers and other school personnel. School separated youth from employed adults and also from so-called real-world problems and work settings. Given the many hours spent in school, and in doing homework, the panel wondered whether young people would have sufficient opportunity to acquire orientations and skills not taught in the classroom but necessary for success in the workplace. Would they be able to apply what they learned in school in productive ways? Would they be fully equipped to assume adult roles?

To address these concerns, the panel recommended closer connections between school and workplace, and more opportunities for young people to be employed while still in school. The panel members anticipated that such employment would bring youth into contact with adults in a wide range of vocations, reduce the social marginality and subjective alienation of youth along with attendant psychological and behavioral problems, and diminish young people's immersion in the leisure-oriented youth subculture, whose influence was seen as antithetical to educational achievement. The panel appears to have been concerned about modern-day equivalents of what Ariès called "childish nonsense."

Consistent with the panel's recommendations, the proportion of youth employed part time during the school year continued to rise, especially among young women (Kablaoui and Pautler, 1991). This growth in employment was caused less by intentional planning than by simple market forces. Young people, desiring a degree of economic independence, entered the labor force in ever larger numbers to meet the needs of America's expanding retail and service sectors, particularly in the shopping malls, retail stores, and fast-food outlets of suburbia.

The Contemporary Context

Today's depictions of adolescence reflect the conceptions of development that emerged a century ago (Kett, 1978; Hall, 1904): this period of life is seen as a critical time for development, and especially for identity formation (Erikson, 1959, 1968). Newly developing self-concepts at this time are seen as highly significant for the future life course. Adolescent self-concepts are believed to influence choices and decisions that have critical impacts upon their future educational, occupational, and family trajectories. Furthermore, adolescents' self-concepts are seen as profoundly influenced by experiences at this time of life.

Current ideals and images of adolescence clearly echo Hall's worries about precocity. But they also reflect Ariès's account of much earlier ambivalence about the relative merits of formal education versus real-world preparation for adulthood. Both scholarly and popular writings continue to express disagreement about the proper roles and activities of young people.

As always, what is expected of adolescents is shaped by conceptions of the difficulties and challenges that await them in adulthood. Today's societal trends and conditions—in the workplace, in the family, and in the connection between school and work—may intensify American adolescents' need to acquire multiple competencies, capacities, and social and psychological resources to help them navigate their paths to adulthood. In modern terminology, experiences that enhance the acquisition of human capital in youth, and those which impart other forms of capital—social, psychological, and cultural—may increasingly matter for future attainment and well-being (Coleman, 1990; Hagan, 1998).

Educators argue that extensive formal schooling is more important today than ever before: that changes in the society, and especially in the economy, place a growing premium on knowledge that is gained most effectively in school. In order to obtain sufficient knowledge and credentials to equip them for the work of the twenty-first century, young people need to be protected from the demands of adulthood for an ever longer period. Early participation in activities and adultlike roles that diminish involvement in education, whether in the labor force or in the family, must be discouraged.

Previous generations, moving into an industrial world, could anticipate a more predictable life sequence: education, considered mainly as preparation for adult work, followed by a career in the line of work for which they had prepared. While young people were not always able to realize this expectation in the past, contemporary youth are even less likely to do so. The rapidly changing economic context necessitates retraining and changes in career paths well after initial entry into the labor force.

Today's young job seekers encounter a highly competitive global economy. Technological change creates new occupations and makes existing ones obsolete. Workers must be able to "adapt, develop, and use leading-edge technology" (Marshall, 1994: 30). In the dynamic, consumer-oriented economy, customized production, responsive to rapidly changing market demands, is replacing the previously dominant system of mass production. Workers are needed who can learn not so much by observation of ongoing processes as through the manipulation of symbols, models, and simulations. Robert Reich (1991), who served as secretary of labor in the Clinton administration, pointed to the growing premium on "symbolic analysis." In view of continual product changes and the complex needs of the global market, workers must be able to put ideas and things together in new ways, to design new products for particular needs and convince customers of their utility, and to link those who identify problems with those who can solve them. In the new marketplace, work skills quickly become obsolete; neither the problems nor the skills and knowledge necessary for their solution are predictable.

Youth's employment insecurity is intensified by organizational transformation—mergers, downsizing, and more tenuous connections between the worker and the employing organization. In fact, one of the most rapidly growing employment sectors in the United States is temporary services; more and more young people are beginning their work lives in various forms of "contingent" employment, as part-time workers, "temps," and self-employed freelancers (Kalleberg and Schmidt, 1996). The need to keep changing jobs and employers places young people in competition, not only with their peers, but also with older workers. Instead of climbing up a bureaucratic job ladder, contingent workers must construct their own careers (Freedman, 1996).

High school students witness youth just a few years older than themselves moving in and out of school and work. They are informed that they can expect to retrain, or "retool," several times during their work lives. Since knowledge gained at any particular time may soon be out of date, they are told that the most important thing for them to learn is how to learn.

How can one acquire the capacities to succeed in this challenging context? Educators emphasize that the foremost place to gain the requisite skills and cognitive capacities is in school. Young people must remain in school, at a minimum, through high school graduation. But for success in the new economy, post-secondary education is increasingly seen as necessary. Most important from our perspective, youth are admonished not to be distracted by part-time jobs.

Ironically, the same economic trends can be seen as a rationale for acquiring work experience before completing formal schooling. No contemporary commentators seriously question the necessity of a high school education, nor do they argue that higher education is not desirable. It is widely understood that earnings differentials between more- and less-educated workers are widening (Heckman, 1996). The debate still focuses on whether formal education should be accompanied by real-world participation in the workplace, not on whether paid employment should supplant education. Like Coleman's Panel on Youth in the 1970s, some social scientists and observers, as well as most parents, continue to see merit in the combination of school and work.

A distinct feature of the American educational system enhances the value of early employment. Youth who leave school in some European countries, such as Germany with its apprentice system (Hamilton, 1990), or in Japan, with its connections between high schools and local employers (Rosenbaum et al., 1990), are provided with well-constructed institutional bridges to the workplace. In contrast, the United States, with its ideology of equal opportunity, reverence for higher education, allowance for "late bloomers," and fear of premature "tracking" into lower-level jobs (Panel on Youth, 1974: 86), provides far fewer formal links between school and work.

Youth in the United States receive general educational credentials. High school and college degrees are not occupationally specific, nor do they provide certification for entry to any particular vocational field. Though substantial numbers of American youth enroll in post-secondary programs that provide vocationally relevant training (Kerckhoff and Bell, 1998), and receive corresponding credentials (licenses, certificates, vocational or associate degrees), these typically lack widespread recognition or legitimacy.

The experience of many European youth is different. In Germany, for example (at least in a more stable era, prior to the recent economic dislocation in that country), two-thirds of young people participate in a coordinated program of formal schooling and vocational training in firms as part of the apprentice system (Heinz et al., 1998;

Hamilton, 1990; Mortimer and Krüger, 2000). Such combined education and training qualifies them to enter a particular line of work with a guarantee of a particular wage. Similar systems are in place in Austria, Denmark, and Switzerland.

The general character of American education and most degree programs may be seen as well adapted to the rapidly changing economic and occupational environment. In such an environment it is ever more difficult to know what skills will be needed to optimize future life chances. Therefore, more general education, equipping youth with basic skills of literacy and numeracy, and, at higher levels, enhancing their capacity to solve complex problems, would appear to be more useful than specific forms of vocational preparation. Moreover, insofar as it is vocationally specific, formal schooling is subject to rapid obsolescence. Indeed, rapid technological change can make it impossible to acquire up-to-date occupational skills anywhere but in the workplace. The general character of formal education thus goes hand in hand with a loosely structured link between school and work.

But, in view of the need for increasing extension of formal education, this very system may enhance the value of early labor force participation. A downside of the American (and Canadian) system is the perilous early course in the labor market, particularly for youth who do not receive four-year college degrees. Most of them attempt to find jobs with little or no help from the school or other institutions. Upon leaving high school, with or without diplomas, they often find that employers do not consider them sufficiently mature or "settled down" to offer them stable, career-like employment, or to invest in training them (Osterman, 1980, 1989). As a result, they flounder from job to job for several years. Those who attend college but do not graduate often face similar circumstances.

Under these circumstances, the job prospects of American youth come to depend not only on their formal educational degrees but also on work experience they obtain while still in school. Employers want recommendations from prior employers, and having relevant work experience may be the very thing that gives a candidate an edge in a competitive marketplace. Even those who graduate from college will benefit from work experience: especially in new and highly technical fields, internships and the vocational experience obtained in cooperative education programs can offer up-to-date training that the class-room cannot match.

Gender Differences

Until fairly recently, the debates about formal schooling versus early work mainly centered on boys' and young men's preparation for adult occupational roles. Boys' and girls' experiences in school and work have differed throughout Western history and continue to be divergent to this day. As schools emerged in Western Europe, boys were the first to attend them, while girls were more likely to persist in apprentice-like arrangements (Ariès, 1962). Such experiences in household work were seen as appropriate preparation for girls' central adult roles of wife and mother. In mid-nineteenth-century America, however, it was the girls who were more likely to attend school; since boys had more job opportunities in commerce and industry, many boys were drawn into the labor force (Kett, 1978). In the twentieth century, changes in the institution of the family have greatly enhanced the importance of girls' preparation for future occupational roles. Hence, whatever balance of formal schooling and work turns out to best facilitate adaptation to the changing economy will pertain to both boys and girls.

The "traditional" family, stable and lifelong, with the husband as economic provider and the wife as homemaker, offered, at least in the ideal and for the middle class, a degree of economic security for women and children. The ideal goal for young women was a life exclusively focused on the family. The "living wage" for men in the early twentieth century enabled many women to give their sole attention to homemaking and motherhood or, as "secondary wage earners," to move in and out of employment as family needs dictated.

Despite the increasing employment of married women in more recent times, normatively the man remains the primary economic provider. In the context of this persistent normative presumption, the declining wage rates of young men, especially those who do not go beyond high school (Bronfenbrenner et al., 1996; Marshall, 1994; Spain and Bianchi, 1996), lessen their desirability as marriage partners and thus decrease both men's and women's opportunities to marry. This problem is especially severe in the minority population

(Wilson, 1987). Young people at lower socioeconomic levels cannot afford to enact the traditional family form—with the husband as earner and the wife as homemaker—even when they desire to do so.

Since World War II there has been steady growth in female employment, furthered since the 1960s by the women's movement. The demise of the "living wage" for men, coupled with enhanced lifestyle aspirations (Schor, 1998), makes a full-time homemaker an unaffordable luxury for the vast majority of families. It is now expected, even normative, for mothers of both school-age and preschool children to be employed outside the home. By 1990 almost three-fourths of married mothers of children under 18 were employed; one-third worked full time, year round. Three-quarters of mothers of preschoolers also worked outside the home (Spain and Bianchi, 1996).

In addition to this fundamental shift in women's roles, other changes have made youth's anticipation of future family life, like that of work, less certain. There is now a multiplicity of family forms and associated lifestyles. Cohabitation, a less stable form of intimate union than marriage, is becoming more prevalent, especially among the young. For those who do marry, divorce is a rather predictable outcome; approximately half of recent marital unions are expected to dissolve. Remarriage following divorce is also declining in frequency. In the 1990s about one-third of births in the United States occurred outside marriage, in comparison to one in ten in 1970. Both normatively and actually, fertility and marriage have been decoupled (Spain and Bianchi, 1996).

These trends, in combination with increasing longevity, diminish the proportion of the life span that young people can expect to spend in legally constituted marital unions. For adolescents who look ahead, the fundamental contours of family life are ever less predictable. Girls watch their mothers and other female relatives alternating periods of more intense childrearing with periods of paid employment. Many youth have experienced parental divorce, remarriage, and even a second separation or divorce. They see their young adult friends and relatives following ever more diverse family paths: cohabiting, marrying, bearing children with or without marriage, separating, divorcing, forming new intimate unions and sometimes "reconstituted" stepfamilies.

Under these circumstances, adolescent girls are wise to plan for economically viable careers, so that they will not have to depend on husbands to support them and their children. Most young women to-day do plan to be employed throughout their lives. Those who anticipate marriage and motherhood foresee a combination of family and occupational roles. In fact, the adult work role is now just as much a part of young women's anticipated futures as it has long been for young men (Johnson and Mortimer, 2000).

As we have seen, changes in both work and family have markedly altered American adolescents' ability to envision their futures with certainty. Still, as Hall pointed out a century ago, decisions made during adolescence have lifelong repercussions. Increasing uncertainty about the future would appear to make it even more essential for young people to develop, early on, a sense of "planful competence" (Clausen, 1993) with which to negotiate a rapidly changing job market and diverse life options.[2]

The historical changes sketched here raise questions about how contemporary adolescents can be prepared for the changes they will encounter in their lifetimes. They will need to acquire various forms of human, social, psychological, and cultural capital to succeed in what may seem to be a bewildering and insecure future. On the one hand, Hall warns about the dangers of "precocity." To what extent do youth still need protection from potential distractions and corruptions of adult society? On the other hand, Coleman admonishes that young people should not be too closely confined and segregated, away from working adults, in the schools. Is there any way that employment in the teenage years, before the onset of "adulthood," may be salutary for American youth?

The Current Controversy

Most young people in America today do not confine themselves exclusively to school or to work. Like their counterparts a century and more ago, most young people combine formal schooling with productive labor. Poor families continue to need the earnings from their children's labor. Newman (1996), who has studied contemporary Harlem, reports that many inner-city youth start to work at the age of 13–15, often "off the books" and paid less than the minimum wage. Their work may mean the difference between household stability and crisis. But these are not the typical teenage workers in the

United States, where paid employment encompasses the vast majority of teenagers.

By the early 1990s, Current Population Survey data showed that about a third of U.S. 16- and 17-year-olds were in the labor force at any particular time during the year. However, it is widely thought that this figure underestimates the extent of adolescent employment. CPS data are based on information from adults who report on the labor force activities of members of their entire households; parents are believed to systematically underreport their children's employment (Committee, 1998).

In contrast, surveys of youth themselves indicate that most high school students hold part-time jobs during at least part of the school year, working after school and on weekends. Of course, the percentage of youth who are counted as "employed" increases with the time interval under observation. Virtually all teenagers, 80 percent or more in recent surveys of youth themselves, are employed at some time during the four years of high school (e.g. Committee, 1998; Steinberg and Cauffman, 1995).

Contemporary youth typically invest substantial time in work. In 1995, 17-year-olds with jobs worked an average of 18 hours per week during the school year (CPS data, Committee, 1998). Moreover, it is not unusual for young people to have the equivalent of a half-time job, 20 hours per week, while school is in session. The National Longitudinal Survey of Adolescent Health, conducted in 1994–95, showed that 50.7 percent of 11th graders who were employed during the school year worked 20 hours or more per week (ibid.).

From the standpoint of both Hall's "adolescent" and Zelizer's "priceless child," who must be shielded and protected from the laboring world, the nearly universal labor force participation of today's teenagers is an ominous trend. In view of the present institutional context, let us now examine the controversy about adolescent work as it has been framed in more recent commentaries—from the mid-1980s to the present.

The Case against Work

The contemporary argument against adolescent work takes two basic forms. First, critics charge that the employment of young people entails massive opportunity costs that override any potential benefits. A fundamental conception of time allocation as a zero-sum game underlies this critique. Indisputably, so the argument goes, the amount of time available to youth (or to people of any age) is limited; by an inexorable rule of logic, what is allocated to paid employment will not be available for alternative pursuits. Second, it is claimed that the characteristic features of contemporary "youthwork" make employment harmful for teenagers. The allegedly poor quality of adolescent work experiences, the often exploitative policies of those who employ and supervise adolescents, and the age-segregated character of young people's workplaces support further restriction, if not banishment, of teenagers from the workplace.

OPPORTUNITY COSTS

Greenberger and Steinberg's highly influential book, *When Teenagers Work: The Social and Psychological Costs of Teenage Employment,* published in 1986, presents a forceful critique of adolescent work. In couching the opportunity cost argument in terms of Erikson's moratorium, their formulation clearly echoes Hall's turn-of-the-century fear of precocity. Given the significance of adolescence for identity formation, Greenberger and Steinberg point out, youth need time: time to reflect on who they are and what they wish to become; time to discover themselves through the give and take of intimate peer relations; and time to seek out, observe, and receive guidance from adult role models.

Greenberger and Steinberg tell us that various clubs and extracurricular activities, many of which are organized and sponsored by the school, give youth opportunities to explore their interests, skills, talents, potential, and values. Participation in athletics, music, and the arts, and immersion in the "adolescent society" of peers and intimate relationships, provide ample occasion for self-exploration. But all this requires a "time out" from the constraints and demands of working life. If teenagers are employed many hours per week, they will have little or no time for such growth-inducing activities.

Greenberger and Steinberg also allege that more beneficial forms of early work are squeezed out by paid work. For example, volunteer work can foster psychological exploration, self-understanding, and reflection on the relation of self to the community (Yates and Youniss, 1996). Volunteering can stimulate prosocial attitudes and behavior (Steinberg and Levine, 1990). It can also give adolescents access to desirable work environments, especially those in the public and nonprofit sectors, where paid employment is less likely to be available to them—for example, in social service agencies, hospitals, shelters, schools, youth camps, charities, and organizations promoting the arts. In such settings adolescents may take the role of assistant under the tutelage of working adults, but have more discretion than in paid jobs over the amount of time invested in work. Thus they can explore their skills and abilities in a setting that is presumably less structured and less coercive than paid employment.

Another form of early unpaid work occurs in the home. Children and adolescents can assist in the daily work of the household by cooking, cleaning, doing laundry, and performing other tasks. Such work not only fosters skills for the future but is also claimed to enhance personal growth and to promote family unity (Elder, 1974; Goodnow, 1988). The adolescent's contribution to household tasks takes on important symbolic meaning, signifying the adolescent's bond to the family. It is plausible to assume that household work augments the sense of attachment to the family and feelings of security, psychological resources that may promote successful transition to adulthood.

Moreover, in the context of family work, many adolescents take care of others, most often younger siblings, but sometimes grandparents and other older relatives. These experiences of nurturance and care can heighten responsibility and conscientiousness and perhaps enhance interpersonal skills. They are widely considered to be developmentally beneficial, increasing resilience (Call et al., 1995; Call, 1996a). Household work might also be considered a kind of familial investment that builds the youth's social capital (Coleman, 1990) in the family, evoking reciprocal, often quite tangible assistance.

As might be foreseen, given the history of controversy over the appropriate balance of school and work, the most prominent opportunity cost of employment in the eyes of the critics is distraction from schooling. This issue has received the bulk of research attention. Youth who are employed are thought to have correspondingly less time to do their homework, to meet with their teachers after school, and to participate in science fairs, debating clubs, and other educational and extracurricular projects. The time and energy invested in employment can diminish an adolescent's psychological engagement with school. Moreover, employment in the evening hours can keep young people from getting enough sleep, so that they have trouble getting to school on time in the morning and staying alert during the school day (Committee, 1998). If educational performance suffers, they may be discouraged from pursuing further education and may even drop out of school.

As noted earlier, the most important manifest purpose of formal education is to impart the knowledge and credentials needed for future jobs. Formal education is also thought to foster the basic cognitive capacities and habits of mind necessary to acquire new information and skills. Consequently, how could reducing the time available for educational investment be anything but detrimental?

A HARMFUL EXPERIENCE IN ITSELF
Aside from the opportunities forgone, critics of teenage employment draw attention to more direct harms that employed youth may incur. Most obviously, many adolescent workers are exposed to noxious work conditions that threaten their physical health. In the late 1990s the National Academy of Sciences convened a panel to investigate the risks of employment to young people's health and development. The Committee on the Health and Safety Implications of Child Labor (1998) documented 100,000 work-related injuries per year among children and adolescents in the United States. These were most frequent on farms, but hazardous conditions were also found in fast-food enterprises and other common youth working environments.

Other harms are seen as equally pernicious but even more insidious because they are less immediately apparent. That is, teenagers may be unprepared for the stress they encounter in the work environment. Some may be unable to manage the multiple demands on their time and energy—from work, families, homework, school activities, and friends. These time conflicts may become overwhelming, inducing a sense of incapacity, withdrawal, depressed mood, and other indications of strain. Such are the potential risks to adolescent mental health, and especially to the development of a healthy identity.

Employed youth are said to face many of the same stressors that confront adult workers: conflicting expectations from supervisors, co-workers, customers, and clients; ambiguity about what they should be doing and about their own authority; unrealistic assignments of too much work to be accomplished in a given amount of time. But young novice workers, in contrast to adults with greater maturity and work experience, may not yet have developed coping skills that enable them to deal with such conflicts and demands.

Some critics argue that when such stressors occur too soon, before a person is developmentally ready for them, the person's subsequent development of coping skills can be severely undermined (Rutter, 1985; Masten and Garmezy, 1985; Simmons and Blyth, 1987). Such early exposure to stressors may increase the person's "sensitivity" so that even low levels of stress trigger negative emotional and physical reactions. If this is the case, the young person may withdraw from future opportunities and challenges.

Other critics argue that early employment imparts orientations and values that impair vocational development. Greenberger and Steinberg (1986) warn that work tasks assigned to adolescents, because of their simple, repetitive, and generally unrewarding character, promote cynicism, negative attitudes toward work, distrust of employers, and materialism. Novice workers may be poorly treated by supervisors; in fact, young workers may observe employers violating the very laws and regulations that have been put in place to protect them. For example, it appears that hours restrictions for minors are frequently violated, and that enforcement of such regulations is variable (Committee, 1998).

Employed youth may come to view the rewards of work as exclusively external to the work itself—the lesson learned is that the occupational role is inherently dissatisfying, a necessary evil that one needs to perform in order to earn money. To these workers, the notion that work is an arena for the gratifying expression of individual interests and potential, for the exercise of abilities and skills, and for the realization of more altruistic motives and goals may be quite foreign. If early employment imparts negative ideas about work and leads to expectations that employers will be uncaring, even exploitative, young workers may later enter adult jobs with attitudes that decrease their readiness to work and lessen their future productivity.

A further concern is that working promotes increased involvement with peers and the peer culture, diminishing young people's identification with and orientation to adults. In the contemporary American context, even Kett's "regulated peer group" is no longer seen as having a salutary influence. Ever since Coleman (1961) drew attention to the "adolescent society," educators have worried that teens' peer culture fosters values that threaten educational activities and goals. Coleman described norms against "excessive" effort in school. The youth culture's emphases on sports, popularity, good looks, dress, immediate satisfaction, and having fun were thought to preclude the development of traits—such as the delay of gratification, self-discipline, and orientation to future goals—that are necessary for high educational and occupational achievement.

The worry that employment increases adolescents' orientation to peers is particularly ironic since Coleman's Panel on Youth (1974) advised that young people be better integrated into the workplace so as to get away from the peer society and to have sustained contact with employed adults. But contrary to Coleman's vision that work settings would bring youth and adults together, Greenberger (1988) depicts the youth workplace as age-segregated and as imparting the values of young people themselves rather than the more mature values of adulthood. She declares that contemporary youth, especially those employed in fast-food establishments, are surrounded by co-workers who are just about their own age. Their supervisors may be contemporaries or only a few years older. This setting is said to encourage behaviors that gain admiration from peers; Greenberger is particularly concerned with activities that connote defiance of adult authority and violation of workplace rules (cheating on time cards, lying to justify lateness or absence, giving food or other products to friends, and other forms of workplace deviance). In this regard, she believes that the workplace has little to recommend it as an arena for teaching good work orientations and habits.

Finally, an influential theme in the contemporary critique of adolescent work, harking back to earlier times, is that this adultlike activity stimulates "precocious maturity" that threatens young people's development. Employed youth are often assigned considerable responsibility, handling money, opening and closing retail stores, and performing other responsible tasks. In doing so, they may come to think of themselves as adults. Relatedly, teenage employment is said to engender "premature affluence" (Bachman, 1983). Not having to pay basic living expenses, adolescents may have a good deal of discretionary income that fosters profligate spending and unrealistic attitudes toward money. Such affluence may further instill a sense of economic independence, encouraging a too rapid movement into adultlike roles.

It is thought that such precociously adultlike youth will want to withdraw from the dependent role of student, curtailing formal education in favor of early full-time work, and may tend to defy adult authority through misbehavior in school. They may prematurely take on adultlike ways of relieving stress and relaxing—smoking, drinking alcohol, and using drugs. In fact, as we shall see in Chapter 6, intensity of employment is often associated with these problem behaviors (see Committee, 1998). Premature family formation is also thought to be stimulated by early work. Early dating and sexual activity, cohabitation, parenthood, and marriage are feared to have negative implications for investment in human capital through education, as well as for future family stability. The threat of precocity still looms large.

The Case for Work

The case against adolescent work has been sufficiently persuasive that today few members of educational policy circles advocate youthwork, unless it occurs under the jurisdiction of the school (as in school-supervised cooperative learning arrangements and internships). In fact, there is evidence that teachers' negative attitudes toward teenage work intensify with their years of experience (Bills et al., 1995). Still, a strong case for teenage employment may be put forward, based on contemporary economic theory as well as empirical evidence concerning economic adaptation and adjustment in early adulthood. Moreover, parents largely approve of employment for teenagers. Again, these contemporary ideas echo themes of the past.

Central to the argument for adolescent employment is recognition that the adult work role is a critical component of adolescents' thinking about the future. Young people project themselves into the future, envisioning their "possible selves" as adult workers, spouses, and parents (Markus et al., 1990). And, as we have seen, working may be considered a key dimension of the adolescent's future "possible self." Virtually all adolescents, both male and female, expect to be employed for major portions of their lives. They come to understand the significance of this adult role for their standard of living, and they may also develop insight about its social and psychological importance.

At the same time, parents, teachers, counselors, and others impress upon youth that adolescence is a time of preparation for adult roles. As young people seek greater autonomy from their parents, they may come to feel constrained by their economic dependence on them. Insofar as having a paid job in adolescence signifies movement toward the desired "possible self" as an independent and autonomous adult, it may be expected to have beneficial consequences, heightening self-esteem and a sense of competence. Having one's own money may take on a great deal of symbolic importance.

Through working, youth do become more economically independent of their parents. As they begin to earn, allowances from parents generally cease, and young people are expected to take over some of their expenses. In doing so, they can acquire valuable money-management skills. Parents may come to view their employed children as more responsible and adultlike in other ways as well (Phillips and Sandstrom, 1990) and supervise them less closely.

Employment experience is a way to acquire human capital, the capacity to be productive in the work setting. Economists recognize that human capital is obtained through education and job training as well as through work experience (Mincer, 1958). Human capital includes a wide range of personal competencies and traits, including knowledge, skills, health, values, motivation, and appearance (Becker, 1993). Work experience may enhance multiple dimensions of "work readiness": knowing how to organize and manage one's time, how to relate to others at work, how to dress and behave in the workplace, punctuality, and other forms of emotional and attentional self-regulation. For youth from the most disadvantaged backgrounds, having a job may entail learning how to function in a more disciplined, structured environment and assuming a new identity as a member of the working world. As Newman (1996: 338) aptly states, "Anything that enhances the draw, the attractiveness, and the normality of working increases the chances that remaining part of the work world will become an integral part of a person's adult expectations." Newman points out that having a track record of employment may be especially important for poor youth attempting to operate in a highly competitive job market of depressed opportunity.

Some youth may feel unable, or be unwilling to exert the effort necessary to succeed in formal education. They may form conceptions of themselves as not very good at or interested in schoolwork. Some may believe they will not be able to afford postsecondary education (Becker, 1993; Heckman, 1996). These views are likely to diminish engagement and effort in high school. Having little expectation of succeeding in school or going on to college, such youth may look to the workplace as the context in which to obtain the work readiness and job skills they will need in the future. Greater investment in work during high school is associated with earlier departure from formal schooling, especially among disadvantaged youth (Tienda and Ahituv, 1996).

Employment gives adolescents, whether college-bound or not, opportunities to acquire social capital—to build relationships and networks that can provide access to information, social support, and diverse other resources when needed (Coleman, 1990). Such networks of association can be helpful in locating future jobs, not only for adult professionals and managers (Granovetter, 1974), but also for inner-city youth facing an unfavorable labor market (Newman, 1996). Mentors in the work setting can also foster the development of orientations and skills for future employment. Young workers will learn about key labor market realities, including pay rates and working conditions, the need for specific experience and credentials for certain jobs, and their own interests and capacities.

Youth who hold a variety of jobs during high school will be exposed to a range of work settings and tasks, and may come to appreciate the diverse rewards that work can bring as well as the kinds of jobs that they do not wish to do in the future. By observing coworkers, adolescents learn about what styles of dress, mannerisms, and speech are appropriate, and inappropriate, in the workplace. Exposure to challenging tasks, instead of being debilitating, may lead to the development of coping skills that promote subsequent problem solving (Shanahan and Mortimer, 1996). Teenagers whose work experiences enable them to demonstrate competence in the world of work may feel more efficacious both in general and with respect to future employment. Though critics point to cynicism and negative attitudes instilled when youthwork is unsatisfying and lacks meaning, employment under more salutary conditions may enhance work-related psychological capital, the motivations and values that are conducive to the acquisition, maintenance, and performance of the work role.

The empirical evidence tends to be consistent with such alleged vocationally relevant gains. Employment during high school has in fact been found to be positively related to a host of indicators of socioeconomic attainment up to a decade later, including earnings, duration of employment and unemployment, and fringe benefits (Ruhm, 1995, 1997).

Finally, the advocates of youthwork contend that employment does not necessarily have opportunity costs (especially if job hours are restricted); many employed adolescents successfully juggle multiple tasks and are involved in a wide range of activities. Thus the allocation of time between working and any other particular activity is not necessarily a zero-sum game. Moreover, undertaking and carrying out diverse activities will teach adolescents time management and other life skills.

All these arguments, pro and con, are intuitively plausible. The proponents of each have brought forth an array of supportive evidence. These contradictory notions and predictions may be confusing for youth themselves, for educators and policymakers, and for parents. Zelizer, in her analysis of the controversy surrounding child labor legislation in the early twentieth century, notes "profound cultural uncertainty and dissent over the proper economic roles for children" (1985: 66). She believes this controversy was resolved by the ascendance of the "priceless" noneconomic child, who was allowed to work only under clearly specified conditions promoting educational betterment. Especially for children under the age of 14, informal work for neighbors, newspaper routes, and small jobs in the home were considered appropriate, while jobs in formal enterprises, and especially the more exploitative and illegal forms of child labor (as migrant workers, drug runners, and so on), were not.

Zelizer describes debates of the early 1980s between those who wanted to enhance children's productive roles in the family and the economic sphere and those who wanted to protect the once progressive but now normatively conventional "sentimental" child. In view of the increasing need for children's work in contemporary dual-worker and single-parent families, Zelizer finds indications of a rapprochement between the economically useful and the sentimental but useless child. That is, children are now seen as having both instrumental and sentimental value.

Writing a decade and a half later than Zelizer, I see evidence of continuing uncertainty and confusion about this question. In fact, Zelizer's account of the controversies of the early twentieth century bears a striking resemblance to the current debates about the pros and cons of adolescent employment (see, e.g., Committee, 1998).

Despite the lasting contention about the appropriate balance of school and work, in comparison to the vast literature on the family, the school, and the peer group, relatively little systematic empirical scrutiny has been directed at work as a domain of adolescent activity. In this book I empirically evaluate the arguments about adolescent employment, primarily by drawing on data from the only long-term longitudinal study of youth that has been specifically designed to assess this issue. Where evidence is available from other empirical research, I refer to these sources as well.

In considering the part that working plays in growing up in contemporary America, I examine the factors that propel youth into the workplace and the influences of work experience on adolescent development. I also address the consequences of early work for the transition to adulthood. The research is unusual in that it treats multiple domains of activity together, that is, the social ecology of adolescent life (Bronfenbrenner, 1979). Much of the contemporary literature on adolescence assesses a singular domain—the family, the peer group, the school. The focus here, by contrast, is on work activities and their meaning, especially in the formal workplace but also in the family, the neighborhood, and volunteer work settings.

The questions I address are vital for an understanding of the fundamental role of work in adolescent development and attainment. Which young people work more, and less, during high school? Are distinct patterns of employment linked to particular strategies of attainment? How do adolescents construct the balance between schooling, working, and other activities? What are the consequences of different patterns of teenage work experience for mental health, psychological development, and early attainment? Do the consequences of paid work depend on its quantity, or upon its quality? What are the benefits (and costs) of adolescent work that takes forms other than paid employment? These are the important questions that lie before us.

THE YOUTH DEVELOPMENT STUDY

THE YOUTH DEVELOPMENT STUDY (YDS) has followed a co-hort of young people for more than a decade. The study began in 1987–1988, when all the panel members were in ninth grade and most were 14–15 years old. My colleagues and I initiated the study at this age to capture the stage of life in which youth in the contemporary United States begin to acquire formal jobs. Our focus is on work experiences during high school, that is, at ages 14–18.

Today's young people, like those of the past, generally become involved in work well before their teens. Children typically have substantial responsibilities in their own homes, doing household chores and caring for younger siblings. In addition, before age 14 most adolescents in the YDS panel had begun to work for pay by performing similar kinds of tasks, especially babysitting and yardwork, for neighbors and relatives. We gathered retrospective data enabling us to gauge the timing and extent of such paid work. While this very early informal work deserves study, it is not at the heart of recent controversies about youthwork. Instead, educators, commentators, and critics express strong reservations about the formal paid employment of teenagers.

The Site of the Research

The YDS is based in St. Paul, Minnesota, a city of approximately 272,000 just across the Mississippi River from Minneapolis (population 368,000). The Twin Cities metropolitan area in 1990 had over 2.5 million residents and was ranked fifteenth in population size among urban areas in the United States. Socioeconomic indicators for the city of St. Paul and for the nation as a whole, as documented by the 1990 Census, are for the most part comparable.[1]

St. Paul had a larger minority population in 1990 (17.7 minority in comparison to the national 7.8 percent). However, young people in St. Paul (and the nation) are more ethnically diverse than the population as a whole. According to the St. Paul Public schools' classification procedures, the minority population for the St. Paul school district was 30 percent in 1985.

Per capita income (in 1989) was $13,727 in St. Paul and $14,420 in the nation. In St. Paul 12.4 percent of families fell below the poverty line, in comparison to 10 percent in the United States. But on some social indicators St. Paul residents appear to be doing very well. Among those 25 or older, 33 percent were college graduates, versus 20 percent of the U.S. population in this age group. As in the Twin Cities generally, the labor market in St. Paul presents good employment opportunities, with relatively low unemployment (4.7 percent in 1990 versus 5.5 percent nationally) and relatively high labor force participation (63 percent versus 60 percent).

Thus employment conditions for youth in the Twin Cities were quite good during the high school years of the YDS participants (fall 1987 to spring 1991). In fact, among those aged 16–19 and enrolled in school, 54.1 percent in the metropolitan area were counted as employed in 1990, as compared with 37.6 percent for the nation at large. Given its vibrant economy, St. Paul might be considered a particularly opportune site for investigating the diversity and the developmental consequences of adolescents' experiences in the labor force.

However, there is great diversity in the prevalence and character of adolescent work within the United States. Some locales offer many more job opportunities than others. Furthermore, it is possible that broad regional differences condition the later effects of youthwork in the life course. Should we be concerned that all the YDS participants resided in one city in the American Midwest? This region was initially settled by Scandinavians and Germans, who are sometimes said to have brought with them from Europe an especially strong work ethic. To the extent that this legacy remains, early work experiences might be more strongly encouraged, as well as having quite positive connotations and benefits.[2]

But it could also be argued that the region in which a study like this is conducted is not the most pertinent contextual consideration. Perhaps investigators should instead focus on socioeconomic advantage and disadvantage and the extent of economic opportunity. The likelihood of finding a job and the meaning of youth employment would be different for a teenager in a depressed rural area, for one in an inner city characterized by severe poverty and unemployment, and for one in a prosperous urban or suburban setting.

Jobs for youth are considerably more plentiful in St. Paul than in Harlem, the site of Newman's (1996) research, where the vast majority of applicants for minimum-wage jobs are turned away. Instead of being sought after by employers, as are Twin Cities youth, teenagers in areas of slow growth and high unemployment generally lose out in the competition for jobs to older, more experienced applicants. Furthermore, as Newman points out, unlike their counterparts in more affluent areas, inner-city youth who do get low-wage jobs, such as those in the fast-food industry, must withstand disapproval, even ridicule, from their peers who receive substantially more money for drug running or other illegal activities.

Newman reports that many inner-city urban youth see employment as a way to escape the danger and turmoil of the streets. For poor young people in Harlem, even a so-called menial job provides entry to a different social world, to people—their fellow workers and employers—who endorse and enact a more conventional way of life. These are surely not key attractions of employment for most employed teenagers in the United States, who come largely from middle-class urban and suburban neighborhoods.

Newman believes that working is a highly formative experience for Harlem teenagers, enabling many of them to eschew the culture of the street and to avoid future trajectories of crime and welfare dependency. Sullivan (1996) also sees conventional employment opportunities as critical in determining whether young people in poor urban areas will desist from adolescent deviance and criminality as they enter adulthood.

Middle-class teenagers are generally free to decide for themselves how to spend their earnings; the situation is quite different for young people whose economic contribution to the household is needed to make ends meet. Shanahan and colleagues (1996) compared the ways adolescents spend their earnings, as well as the consequences of earnings for parent-adolescent relations, in urban St. Paul (using YDS data) and in economically depressed rural Iowa. In the Iowa families the teenagers' employment was much more likely to be an integral part of their families' economic strategy. Newman (1996) discovered a similar situation in depressed areas of New York City. Since multiple earners in a household were necessary for even a minimal standard of living, young people had little choice but to work. Newman notes that the gratitude and respect of other family members, coming with the regular paycheck, offered youth dignity, responsibility, and a sense of maturity.

To be sure, the dramatic differences across various settings necessitate great caution in generalizing beyond the social conditions present in any particular community. Insofar as possible, I will compare the YDS findings with those of similar studies conducted in other locales as well as with large nationally representative surveys. It must be noted, however, that because contemporary debates have centered on the intensity of adolescent work, there is relatively little information available, from either local or national studies, about the quality of the adolescent work experience. In this respect the Youth Development Study is exploring uncharted territory.

Data Collection

A random sample of ninth graders in the St. Paul public school district was selected to participate in the study during the fall of 1987. (For panel selection, consent procedures, and features of the initial sample, see Appendix A.) Comparison of families who agreed to participate in the research with those who did not indicated that the initial panel well represented the population of ninth graders in St. Paul public schools. It included families of diverse ethnic and social class backgrounds reflective of the city of St. Paul. Excepting the Hmong, the initial panel was 74 percent white, 10 percent African American, 5 percent Hispanic, and 4 percent Asian (the remainder did not place themselves in any of these categories or identified themselves as of mixed race). Median household income was in the range of $30,000–39,999; 62 percent of the families had incomes at or below this level. Among the parents, 27 percent of fathers and 19 percent of mothers were college graduates; 59 percent of fathers and 61 percent of mothers had not attained more than a high school education.

Starting with the first wave of data collection, in the spring of 1988, surveys were administered in classrooms each year during high school. We went to great lengths to encourage the young people to remain in the study. If a student was not present for either of the two scheduled administrations, on two separate days in each school, or was no longer attending school, surveys were mailed to the home. A series of reminder postcards and letters, and additional copies of the survey, were sent in a sequence recommended by Dillman (1983). Those who did not respond to the mailings were telephoned. At this time, the adolescents were also offered the opportunity to have their surveys administered in person, and some interviews did take place each year during the high school period (for example, 20 in Wave 1). Staff members tried hard to obtain complete participation (for example, in Wave 1, two surveys were administered in juvenile detention facilities).

The content of the surveys is described briefly here; in subsequent chapters the particular measures (and their sources) will be presented in greater detail. The questionnaires for the high school students covered multiple domains: the family, the school, and peer relationships, in addition to work. Adolescents reported on their experiences, especially those related to autonomy and social support, in each sphere. We also asked about the ways adolescents viewed themselves, and their attitudes and aspirations with respect to the future. The respondents were asked to consider their anticipated involvement, as adults, in multiple roles and relationships (marriage, parenthood, work, friendship, and community); their educational and occupational aspirations and plans; the certainty of their plans; and what they were looking for in future occupations. Indicators of self-esteem and self-efficacy as well as adolescent mood state (depressive affect, sense of well-being) were also included.

The surveys administered to the adolescents contained an extensive series of questions concerning paid work experiences. In the first year of the study the respondents listed, chronologically, all the jobs they ever had. They were asked explicitly to include both formal and informal work, and were given examples of each. They provided basic descriptive information about each job, including the number of hours they worked per week, their wages, and the name of the organization (if applicable) they worked for. These work experience measures will be described more fully in Chapter 3. During each year following, the adolescents gave the same information about current jobs and also described all the jobs they had had since we last surveyed them.

Considerable information was obtained about the jobs held at the time of each survey administration. Panel members were asked about how they had located their jobs, who had helped them, and what search activities they had undertaken. A battery of questions concerned the quality of work experiences, including both intrinsic and extrinsic rewards, stressors, and social relationships in the workplace. We acquired information about initial and continuing training. The adolescents were also asked about the ways work was connected to their family life, peer relations, and school.

During the high school years, parents completed two surveys by mail—the first when the respondents were in ninth grade, the second when most were in the twelfth grade. In Wave 1, 96 percent of the children had at least one responding parent; in Wave 4, 79 percent of the children were so covered. Parents' surveys requested information about family background and context (such as parental education, parental occupation, and work history since the child's birth; household income; marital status of parents and the membership of the household). We also asked parents about their attitudes toward their children's employment and the ways (if any) in which they saw their children changing as a result of working. These data allowed assessment of youth employment and its consequences from a standpoint other than that of the youth themselves.

Finally, the parents were queried about their own work experience as adolescents, the types of jobs they had performed and the quality of their work. Their responses gave us some understanding of intergenerational change in adolescent employment and its consequences for the transition to adulthood (Aronson et al., 1996).

After high school (1992–2000), the respondents continued to be surveyed by mail (with the exception of one year, 1996). Annual life history calendars in these surveys permit monthly tracking of residential arrangements, educational enrollment, and both part- and full-time labor force participation. In these annual surveys, we ask about work experiences and reactions to them as well as aspirations and plans for the future. Four years after high school, many of the questions about psychological states asked during high school were repeated. More detailed information about current work and family activities was also elicited.

Six years after high school (1997), the survey was extended to include more questions about socioeconomic attainment, sources of economic support, and retrospective assessments of experiences and relationships that the participants perceived as having been helpful both during high school and as they moved into adulthood. The 1998 survey included new modules of questions concerning physical and mental health status, environmental attitudes, and rule-breaking behavior.

Though the data collection is ongoing, this book draws mainly on surveys through the tenth wave, 1998, seven years after high school. I focus on the responses supplied by the youth themselves, but also include information obtained from parents. The book also draws on insights derived from qualitative interviews. Forty young women were interviewed during the 1997–98 academic year (Aronson, 1998). Sixty-nine additional interviews were conducted during the 1999–2000 academic year to address the young adults' subjective experiences of transition to adulthood. These interviews, conducted when the respondents were in their mid-twenties, reveal much about how they perceived high school work experiences and the part they played in their vocational development (Mortimer, Zimmer-Gembeck, et al., 2002). In both studies interviewees were selected to represent diverse experiences and pathways to adulthood. Aronson chose young women who emphasized higher education, early motherhood, and work in the years after high school. My colleagues and I selected youth whose survey responses indicated differing patterns and degrees of difficulty in making career decisions.

Panel Retention

Panel retention is the central challenge in a longitudinal study of this kind. To sit down and answer a long series of questions annually may not be a very inviting prospect to many young people. Each year the effective target sample for survey participation consisted of the 1,010 students who had agreed to participate in the study initially.

Immediately upon receipt, each survey was examined closely by

Table 2.1. The Youth Development Study

	Administration in school				Mail survey					
	Wave 1	Wave 2	Wave 3	Wave 4	Wave 5	Wave 6	Wave 7	Wave 8	Wave 9	Wave 10
Year	1988	1989	1990	1991	1992	1993	1994	1995	1997	1998
Age	14–15	15–16	16–17	17–18	18–19	19–20	20–21	21–22	23–24	24–25
No. of adolescent respondents	1,000[a]	964	957	933	816	782	799	780	788	761
Retention rate	96.2%	95.4%	92.7%	81.3%	77.7%	79.6%	77.6%	78.6%	75.9%	
No. of mothers responding	924			690						
No. of fathers responding	649			440						
% of respondents with at least one parent responding	95.9%			79.1%						

a. A total of 1,010 consented to participate in the fall of 1987.

staff members. Some surveys were incomplete. Some young people provided inconsistent information (for example, reported that they were not currently employed, but then described current work experiences). When deemed necessary, the respondents were telephoned to clarify their responses.

As shown in Table 2.1, panel retention remained quite high through the high school period. Of those who completed first-wave surveys, 93 percent did so in the fourth year of the study. After the first four years, all surveys were obtained by mail. Again, we used Dillman's protocol to standardize the survey procedures, and to maximize their effectiveness. Attrition increased, however, despite these efforts and the provision of incentives. This is not surprising, given the geographic mobility and other changes young people experience in the period after high school.

To aid in our tracking efforts, each year we asked the respondents to give us names, addresses, and phone numbers of two people who would be able to find them if they were to move. We also had the names and addresses of their parents, obtained when most of the respondents were still in high school. This information proved invaluable.

To enhance retention after high school, further incentives (in addition to a $10 payment) were offered. Starting with Wave 6 of data collection, two years after high school, we began to provide a ballpoint pen, labeled "The Youth Development Study, University of Minnesota," with the date. The pen was securely attached to the questionnaire. Judging from the greater speed with which the surveys were returned, apparently having the pen right there motivated many respondents to pick it up and start answering the questions immediately. After Wave 4 of the study and again after Wave 8, each respondent was sent a brief report of the findings. Beginning in Wave 8, the annual incentive payment increased from $10 to $20. The tracking and follow-up procedures also intensified.

All these efforts have yielded a fairly high rate of panel retention. In 1997, 78.6 percent of the original panel members were retained; the retention was 75.9 percent in 1998. As is often the case in research of this kind, retention is somewhat higher among young people from more advantaged backgrounds and those who, at least in the early years, were more successful.

Still, the demographic features of the panel have not changed

much over the decade of the study. Socioeconomic background characteristics and some key indicators of ninth-grade achievement are
shown in Table 2.2 for the initial panel and those who remained in
Wave 4, Wave 8, and Wave 10. Means and percentages reflect variables that were collected in ninth grade; numerical changes thus
reflect shifts in sample composition. For example, mean fathers' and
mothers' education, occupational prestige (Stevens and Hoisington,
1987), and income levels (coded from 1 = under $5,000 to 13 =
$100,000 or more) are slightly higher in Wave 8 and 10 than in
Wave 1, but the differences are negligible. Of the Wave 10 respondents, 40.0 percent had at least one parent who had graduated from
college; this was true of 37.3 percent of the Wave 1 panel members.
The percentage in the "some college or more" category likewise increased slightly. The proportion who had lived in two-parent families
(in 1988) increased from 68.4 percent in Wave 1 to 71.7 percent in
Wave 10. The Wave 10 panel also had a larger percentage of whites
(80.0 in comparison to 73.7) and native born (93.8 vs. 92.5 percent)
and a smaller percentage of males (42.7 vs. 47.5). On the whole,
however, the distribution of demographic characteristics appears to
be quite similar despite the loss of approximately one-fourth of the
study participants.

Key psychological and behavioral indicators are also shown in Table 2.2. On the basis of research on younger children and their families, Weinberger and his colleagues (1990) claim that as the degree of
intrusiveness, or the cost of participation in a study, increases, the
more maladjusted children become less likely to participate. The
costs of involvement in the Youth Development Study—requiring
completion of an annual survey—may mount as young people acquire jobs, families, and other adult responsibilities and become more
protective of their time. It is reasonable to expect, extrapolating from
Weinberg's research, that the respondents who showed early signs of
distress, depressed affect, or lack of behavioral control would be
more likely to drop out of the study. But ninth-grade mental health
constructs—self-esteem (Rosenberg, 1965), self-efficacy (Pearlin
et al., 1981), depressive affect and well-being (Ware et al., 1987)—
and substance use (alcohol and tobacco) show few differences between Wave 1 and Wave 10 panel members. (With respect to substance use, both have scores between 1 and 2, signifying between
0 and 1–2 times during the past month for alcohol, and 0 to less than

1 cigarette each day for smoking.) Given our interest in mental health and attainment in adolescence and during the transition to adulthood, these similarities are reassuring.[3]

Furthermore, the first- and tenth-wave respondents have nearly identical indicators of early academic engagement and performance—grade point average in ninth grade (0 = F to 4 = A), intrinsic motivation toward schoolwork (a 4-item scale reflecting interest and engagement in school; see Table 4.1 for three of these), time spent doing homework, and planned level of educational attainment (both indicating mean aspirations between junior college and four-year college degrees). Moreover, they showed similar earlier school problems (propensity to get in trouble in school and to be sent to the principal's office, 0 = never to 3 = 5–10 times or more).

Finally, the distribution of the panel into major work pattern groups, based on employment duration and intensity during high school (this measure will be described in Chapter 3), appeared to be quite similar for the Wave 4 and Wave 10 respondents. We do observe a slight increase in the percentage who followed what appears to be the most favorable, "steady" work pattern, characterized by high duration and low intensity (from 24.9 percent in Wave 4 to 27.8 percent in Wave 10). On the whole, however, the percentage distribution is quite comparable across Waves 4, 8, and 10.

Taken together, the information in Table 2.2 indicates that the Wave 1 panel and the Wave 10 panel were highly similar in socioeconomic background, mental health and substance use, school engagement and achievement, and early labor force involvement. At least with respect to work and its major outcomes (pertaining to mental health, substance use, educational and occupational aspirations, and achievement), the composition of the panel that remained after a decade is not very different from that of the original panel.

There could conceivably be other sources of selection bias, for example, those who stay might be more conscientious or have other personality characteristics (perseverance, altruism, sense of responsibility, compliance) that would increase the likelihood of remaining in a study of this kind. It is not likely, however, that central findings concerning the implications of adolescent work for mental health, values, and attainment are determined by such differences between stayers and leavers.

The Youth Development Study is the only community-based longi-

Table 2.2. Initial background, mental health, substance use, school, and work indicators for retained panel in Waves 1, 4, 8, and 10

	Wave 1 Panel (N = 1000)	Wave 4 Panel (N = 927)[a]	Wave 8 Panel (N = 776)[a]	Wave 10 Panel (N = 759)[a]
Background				
Highest parental education % some college or more	58.9% (951)	60.5% (891)	60.9% (750)	61.2% (740)
Highest parental education: % college graduate or more	37.3% (951)	38.5% (891)	39.9% (750)	40.0% (740)
Family income	5.78 (946)	5.89 (887)	5.98 (747)	6.05 (736)
Father's occupational prestige	42.14 (578)	42.31 (555)	42.92 (480)	42.91 (478)
Mother's occupational prestige	40.54 (721)	40.61 (688)	40.95 (581)	41.02 (579)
Family Composition: % two-parent family	68.4% (996)	70.0% (925)	71.1% (775)	71.7% (757)
Nativity: % U.S.-born	92.5% (980)	93.1% (908)	93.4% (761)	93.8% (746)
Race: % white	73.7% (979)	75.7% (907)	80.0% (760)	80.0% (744)
Gender: % male	47.5% (1000)	46.5% (927)	42.4% (776)	42.7% (759)

	Wave 1 Panel (N = 1000)	Wave 4 Panel (N = 927)[a]	Wave 8 Panel (N = 776)[a]	Wave 10 Panel (N = 759)[a]
Mental health				
Self-esteem	13.56 (973)	13.55 (905)	13.51 (760)	13.50 (746)
Self-efficacy	14.54 (966)	14.55 (902)	14.58 (756)	14.57 (741)
Depressive affect	18.80 (973)	18.74 (903)	18.92 (759)	18.99 (741)
Well-being	16.83 (977)	16.84 (907)	16.79 (763)	16.71 (744)
Substance use				
Alcohol use	1.74 (961)	1.71 (892)	1.75 (749)	1.76 (730)
Smoking	1.22 (953)	1.16 (885)	1.20 (745)	1.21 (724)
School				
Grade-point average	2.48 (963)	2.51 (897)	2.55 (754)	2.56 (740)
Intrinsic motivation toward schoolwork	10.73 (989)	10.74 (916)	10.72 (769)	10.70 (749)
Time spent on homework (minutes per week)	418.10 (992)	420.62 (919)	414.18 (770)	413.90 (753)
School problems	1.23 (991)	1.20 (918)	1.16 (770)	1.18 (753)
Educational plans	3.86 (888)	3.89 (828)	3.90 (690)	3.89 (680)
% planning to complete at least some college	79.7% (888)	80.6% (828)	80.4% (690)	80.4% (680)

Table 2.2. (continued)

	Wave 1 Panel (N = 1000)	Wave 4 Panel (N = 927)[a]	Wave 8 Panel (N = 776)[a]	Wave 10 Panel (N = 759)[a]
Work				
% employed	63.3%	63.9%	64.7%	65.0%
	(817)	(757)	(637)	(626)
Extrinsic work values	13.90	13.90	13.92	13.93
	(984)	(912)	(764)	(747)
Intrinsic work values	18.96	18.93	19.02	18.94
	(979)	(910)	(763)	(744)
Work pattern during high school				
Not working		7.0%	6.4%	6.0%
Low duration–low intensity		23.7%	23.6%	24.4%
Low duration–high intensity		18.4%	17.1%	16.5%
High duration–low intensity		24.9%	27.3%	27.8%
High duration–high intensity		26.0%	25.5%	25.3%
		(886)	(736)	(716)

Note: Number in parentheses is the total valid number of cases.

a. Retained panel, that is, includes Waves 4, 8, and 10 panel members who also responded in Wave 1. The total numbers of respondents in Waves 4 (N = 933), 8 (N = 780), and 10 (N = 761) is somewhat larger because in each wave a small number of persons who consented to participate in the study did not complete a Wave 1 survey.

tudinal study designed explicitly to address the developmental impacts of adolescent work experience. Though several national panel studies enable assessment of employment prevalence and intensity and their consequences after high school, there is no extant data set that contains the variety of work experience measures that have been implicated in adult development. The YDS provides a rich data source with which to examine key questions surrounding early work. In this book I synthesize more than a decade of research, summarizing prior published reports and presenting new analyses and findings. This extensive data archive throws light on the character of teenage work, its consequences for adolescent development and achievement, and the transition to adulthood, issues that have been the focus of great controversy for more than a century.

3

TIME ALLOCATION AND QUALITY OF WORK

WHAT IS YOUTHWORK? Adolescents engage in many worklike activities in diverse settings. Children and adolescents are required to attend school (usually until age 16), and most are assigned at least minimal homework. Virtually all adolescents perform chores at home. Many high school students do volunteer work, contributing their labor to a wide range of community organizations. And many young people engage in these unpaid forms of work and also in paid employment. Before considering the consequences of these diverse activities, it is necessary to survey the "youthwork" landscape.

It is customary to think of the modern life course as composed of three stages, each defined by its relation to paid employment (Kohli, 1985). During the first stage, children and adolescents prepare for the adult work role by attending school; the second stage is the period of occupationally productive activity; the third is retirement, a state of "post-employment" continuing through old age. The prevalence of paid work among high school students calls into question this view of the life course as a sequence of ordered, age-specific role involvements.

As we have seen, in the United States and Canada it has become normative for young people to combine schooling and part-time work. Employment is a major, albeit not necessarily continuous, activity for most secondary school students. No longer is paid work during the teenage years a haphazard, primarily informal pastime that sometimes occurs after school. Instead, the majority of high school students work on a regular basis, for substantial numbers of hours. Even so, little is known about the nature of adolescent work.

It is plausible to think of young people's paid work as very much the same, irrespective of the particular job. The prototypical "hamburger flipper" comes immediately to mind. Greenberger (1988: 30) articulates this point of view: "Most youth-work requires little training: Youngsters already know a good deal about washing cars, mopping floors, and wrapping sandwiches before they come to work." Adolescents, because of their inexperience and their transience in the labor market, are often assigned simple tasks requiring little or no specialized knowledge or skill. As a result, little effort has been directed toward investigating the quality of their work.

The prodigious amount of research on adults' responses to their jobs demonstrates wide-ranging psychological consequences of work experiences (Kohn and Schooler, 1983; Mortimer, Lorence, and Kumka, 1986; see Mortimer and Lorence, 1995, for a review). If, contrary to popular opinion, youth jobs vary in important ways, and if research findings based on adults can be generalized at all to young people, attention to the quality of youth work experience could yield considerable payoff. The longitudinal analyses to be reported in Chapter 6 do, in fact, support this alternative point of view.

Postponing the complexities of the effects of work experience to a later chapter, here I address a simpler question: What are youth jobs like? Given common understandings of what a "good job" or a "bad job" might be, do those typically held by young people conform more to the former or to the latter? Since there are numerous relevant facets of adolescent work, answering this question is not easy.

First, the character of work can be assessed via measurement of "objective" job conditions. Kohn and Schooler (1983) argue that studies of work and personality should focus on occupational tasks—especially their complexity and the worker's discretion in performing them. Features of work tasks are linked to the resources, opportunities, and constraints posed by a person's position in a system of socioeconomic inequality. Kohn and Schooler allege that people respond similarly to the structural imperatives of their jobs regardless of their social locations, values, and other dimensions of their personalities. There is much empirical evidence supporting this position (Mortimer and Lorence, 1995). It therefore is important to examine teenagers' actual conditions of work.

However, a plausible alternative viewpoint is that what distinguishes "good" from "bad" work must be considered subjectively, from the perspective of the person. That is, a job that is challenging and engaging to one job holder may be drudgery to another. Though such reactions are surely connected in some degree to the observable conditions of work, objective structure and subjective perception are hardly identical. Moreover, the character of a person's subjective response to work could have important developmental sequelae.

This alternative view may especially apply to the youngest workers. For as noted in Chapter 1, neophyte workers' reactions to their jobs could be quite different from those of more experienced workers. The extent to which young people perceive merit and value in their early jobs, or, to the contrary, find boredom, tedium, and strain in their initial forays into the occupational world, could strongly influence their developing images of work and their emergent sense of competency.

Because both actual features of the job and subjective responses to it are worthy of attention, this portrayal of teenage work draws on diverse kinds of information. First, *objective* dimensions of work experience are charted through the high school years: rates of labor force participation, amounts of time spent working per week, and cumulative patterns of temporal investment in work. Also assessed are the types of jobs held, wage rates and earnings, and the amount of training supplied by employers.

These objective features of employment could have significant developmental consequences. For example, the labor market may be a more salutary environment if young people occupy a range of different kinds of jobs, indicating diverse work opportunities that promote exploration and vocational development. As long emphasized in the policy debate (Zelizer, 1985), youth may be considered to have "bad jobs" if they work too many hours. But unlike adult employment, jobs for youth may not be evaluated unambivalently on the basis of wage rates. As noted earlier, some commentators (see Bachman, 1983) view high-wage employment as promoting "premature affluence," with quite negative implications.

Learning opportunities at work may be especially important. One prominent argument in favor of youth employment is that schools are not geared to imparting key vocationally relevant skills. Early jobs can foster promptness, correct workplace deportment, and appropriate ways of relating to customers and clients. On their jobs, youth often come in contact with persons from other class, racial, and ethnic groups, people they would not ordinarily meet in their neighborhoods and schools. Such encounters can provide opportunities for both personal and social growth.

Moreover, while the "relevance" of what is learned in school may be somewhat opaque to students, this is not the case for work-based learning. Young workers address concrete, real-world, problems and issues, often with adults who work alongside them. Working can even illuminate the relevance of school-based learning. Jobs that enable the adolescent to apply what is learned in the classroom can enhance educational engagement as well as academic achievement. Tasks that involve reading and writing provide opportunities to practice academic skills. This chapter considers the amount of time adolescents spend on these cognitive activities, as well as dealing with people (a rough indicator of opportunities for developing interpersonal skills), and working with their hands.

An objective indicator of the learning potential of a job derives from the ratings in the *Dictionary of Occupational Titles* (U.S. Department of Labor, 1977, 1986). Using observations by occupational analysts from the Department of Labor, the *DOT* rates the complexity of function with respect to work with data, people, and things. For example, on a scale of complexity of work with people, "persuading" (influencing others) is assigned a higher rating than "speaking-signaling" (to convey or exchange information). Mentoring is at the highest level of people-related task complexity.

The DOT ratings were not constructed to be specific to young workers. In some types of work (such as work in the fast-food industry) adolescents may predominate in particular job categories; they will constitute a small minority of workers in most other jobs. In positions that are typically occupied by adults, it is plausible to assume that young workers would be assigned simpler tasks or would act as assistants to adults. Nonetheless, observing these ratings over time could indicate trends in adolescents' opportunities for learning in the workplace. The amount of training provided by the employer also indicates learning opportunity and job complexity, since lengthier training is likely to accompany more difficult and necessarily self-directed tasks.

A final objective job feature is the extent of supervisory responsibility. The process of supervision involves monitoring, teaching, and correcting others' work. Since supervisors are often called upon to address problems and issues that are not routine, supervisory jobs are likely to involve learning and substantial responsibility.

Besides these objective indicators, the quality of work can be gauged by adolescents' own descriptions of their job activities, and by their subjective responses to their experiences in the workplace. For example, evaluation of whether one's pay is "good" may or may not correspond to prevailing wage rates. A good job may be one that is experienced as interesting or challenging, one that is perceived as offering chances to learn new things, supportive relationships with supervisors and co-workers, and opportunities for advancement. YDS panel members also described distressful circumstances at work, including role overload, role strain, and noxious conditions in the work environment.

These judgments are inherently subjective and depend on many individualistic factors. Teenagers' evaluations of their pay are likely to depend on their perceived need for income, their compensation in previous jobs, their siblings' and friends' wage rates, and a host of other considerations. A person who has never worked as a cashier may find opportunities for learning as a check-out clerk. Perceived strain in the work environment may depend on whether already-acquired job skills are sufficient to perform central job assignments.

Finally, global perceptions and evaluations were elicited about job satisfaction and work commitment. Whereas these multifaceted opinions and reactions might be rejected as measures of work quality in favor of more objective criteria, what is "good" for one young worker may, in fact, be not so good for another.

An understanding of the adolescent work experience must also take into account the intersection of employment with other domains of life. I follow Bronfenbrenner's (1979) dictum that multiple arenas of life must be considered in tandem if we are to comprehend any one sphere's influence on human development. That is, the consequences of participation in any particular domain may depend on the ways it affects experiences in others. A "good" set of work conditions may be offset if employment interferes with other significant parts of an adolescent's life. In an attempt to consider the broad ecology of adolescent experience, employed YDS panel members were asked each year during high school about the effects of their jobs on performance in school and on relationships with their parents and peers.

This investigation of the quantity and the quality of employment in adolescence is attentive to change during this formative period. Whereas much research on youth employment is cross-sectional, allowing only snapshot pictures of adolescent jobs, the YDS reveals changing patterns of work activity as adolescents grow older. Moreover, access to continuous work history data enables construction of a cumulative typology of high school work investment. This classification, as we will see in Chapter 7, has proven to be predictive of early achievement.

This description of employment is also sensitive to gender differences. Despite the changes in women's life patterns during the past half-century, including the tremendous expansion of the adult female labor force, both the sex-typing of occupations (Blau and Ferber, 1985; Reskin, 1993) and gender inequality in attainment are pervasive in adult employment. Men's and women's employment positions are unequal in compensation, opportunities for advancement, autonomy, and many other respects. Rather little is known, however, about gender differences in the earliest work experiences.

Some prior studies (reviewed in Mortimer et al., 1990) indicate that boys and girls have different kinds of work. They also suggest that boys begin working earlier and work longer hours. But such gender differences may be increasingly undermined by adolescent girls' high aspirations for future occupational attainment (Stevens et al., 1992; Dennehy and Mortimer, 1993; Marini et al., 1996), fostered by the women's movement, affirmative action initiatives, and societal concern about gender inequality. Longitudinal study, initiated early in life, is necessary to understand the processes through which males and females are socialized to work and come to have unequal occupational and earnings attainments.

Despite regional differences in types of jobs and opportunities for employment, noted in Chapter 2, the patterns of labor force involvement among YDS participants are quite comparable to those found in representative national samples of teenagers. However, because of the absence of information about the *quality* of youthwork in national studies, there is little basis for evaluating whether work experiences of YDS panel members are similar to those of youth elsewhere.

Finally, to address claims that youth employment was very different in a previous era, the YDS compares the paid work experiences of the panel members with those of their parents. Despite some commentators' impressions that working was a much more salutary experience for teenagers before the expansion of the service industry, parents' retrospective assessments of their work and adolescents' contemporaneous portrayals are actually much alike in their evaluative tone.

Measuring Employment Status

The prevalence of youth employment, as registered by surveys, differs markedly depending on the time span under scrutiny. Some studies ask about teenagers' employment on the day of the survey; others about paid work during the past month or the past school year. When the period covers a year or more, the vast majority of youth are usually counted as working. For example, in the National Survey of Family and Households, initiated at about the same time as the YDS, parents were asked whether their tenth- and twelfth-grade children held jobs *at some time during the school year*. They reported that 61 percent of the tenth graders and 90 percent of the twelfth graders were employed (Manning, 1990). Almost three-quarters of youth surveyed in the National Longitudinal Study of Adolescent Health reported employment during twelfth grade (Committee, 1998: 39). Other national studies, based on teenagers' self-report (e.g. the National Longitudinal Survey of Youth and Monitoring the Future), indicate that about 80 percent of young people are employed at some time while school is in session during their high school years (see Committee, 1998: 35).

Compounding the difficulty of assessing the national prevalence of youth labor force participation, and of comparing estimates across national and local studies, are researchers' varying definitions of what constitutes employment (Kablaoui and Pautler, 1991). For example, larger proportions of youth will be found to be employed if informal work is explicitly included in the definition, or if a threshold criterion of hours or duration of employment does not have to be met.

In the first year of the YDS, the ninth graders were asked, "Have you *ever* had a steady job (at least once a week) for pay outside your own home?" The parenthetical expression was inserted to discourage report of highly sporadic employment. But there could still be definitional ambiguity about what constitutes a "job" or "work." Some young people might discount informal work they do for neighbors, relatives, and family friends; others might include such work. Since babysitting and yardwork are the most common forms of initiation to paid work, we did not want to lose information about these initial jobs. So the question about employment was followed by the instruction: "Include jobs like babysitting and yardwork. Jobs can be for other families and in businesses." Reference to "other families" made a clear distinction between household chores and work performed in settings other than the respondent's own residence. The inclusion of a separate section on "Work at Home" later in the survey gave further emphasis to this conceptual separation of work outside and within the family context.[1]

The ninth graders also completed a chart describing all their jobs, including job title, name of employing organization, number of hours worked per week, wage rate, and month and year of initiating and terminating employment. In the first year of the study, the chart included all paid employment since the teenager's very first job. Subsequent surveys asked about jobs held since the last survey administration. Thus a complete work history has been elicited from each respondent, from the very first job through the mid-20s.

First Paid Work

Many young people hold paid jobs well before ninth grade. Among 11-year-olds in the 1981 National Survey of Children (Furstenberg et al., 1987), half of both boys and girls said they "sometimes work for pay" (Yamoor and Mortimer, 1990). In another study, 13 percent of first graders and 75 percent of seventh graders, two years younger than the first-wave YDS panel, said they held paid jobs outside their homes (Goldstein and Oldham, 1979). Gottfredson (1985) reported that 40 percent of boys and 29 percent of girls from predominantly low socioeconomic and minority backgrounds held regular jobs at some time during grades six to eight.

Of the ninth graders in the first wave of the YDS, 82.5 percent reported that they had *ever* held a steady job. Most (57 percent) of these youth had obtained their first jobs at age 12 or younger. First jobs usually consisted of informal work, such as babysitting (78 percent of girls' first jobs) or work in the neighborhood, especially shoveling snow and mowing lawns (40 percent of boys' first jobs). Boys were also likely to have paper routes or other sales work (28 percent);

only 6 percent of girls started work in these kinds of jobs. A minority (13 percent of boys and 6 percent of girls) held their first jobs in restaurants (mostly fast-food establishments).

Prior studies have indicated that boys begin to work at younger ages than girls (Greenberger and Steinberg, 1983; White and Brinkerhoff, 1981). In the YDS there was no apparent gender difference in the mean age of starting work: 12.2 years. However, information about the age of starting work among students who are 14–15 years old is downwardly biased, because some ninth graders (17.5 percent) have not yet held a steady job. Moreover, a lack of association between age of first job and gender may be misleading if the boys and girls vary in other characteristics (such as socioeconomic background) that influence opportunities for employment. More extensive analysis, taking account of these complexities, indicates that girls, in fact, start to work earlier than boys (see Mortimer et al., 1990).

Girls and boys report similar work hours in their first jobs (averaging 12.7 hours per week for girls and 12.0 for boys, not a statistically significant difference); 9 is the median number of hours reported. As would be expected, the first job's complexity of work with people and with things (as designated by DOT ratings) is very low for both genders; girls' jobs, because of their concentration in babysitting, are rated as significantly less complex than those held by boys with respect to work with data (Mortimer et al., 1994). Despite the substantial similarity in the nature of their first jobs, girls' reported initial wage rates are only 60 percent of those reported by boys—$2.77 vs. $4.63 per hour.

The first-wave work history data enabled assessment of change in job types, hours, wages, and complexity of work for the students who had ever been employed before entering high school (see Mortimer et al., 1990). As noted, the vast majority of the youth, 82.5 percent, had held at least one job. (Of these, 33 percent were current jobs, held at the time of the first-wave survey.) Second jobs were reported by 33 percent; 18 percent had had three jobs; 8.5 percent had had four jobs; and 3.5 percent had already had five jobs before the end of ninth grade.

As the children moved from job to job in this early trajectory, their work became more formal. For example, among students who had two jobs by ninth grade, 57 percent worked in private households as their first job and 39 percent did so in their second job. Third and fourth jobs, for those who reported them, were even less likely to be informal. Complexity of function and work hours also tended to increase as the youth moved from job to job (Mortimer et al., 1992). However, wage rates did not show a similar upward trend. Though the lack of monetary return for labor force experience and for age (and associated increases in maturity) may seem unexpected, it should be recalled that these job histories describe very young children. At the time of the most recent jobs, few were older than 14 or 15.

Paid Work during High School

Unlike "prior" jobs, reported in the first-wave survey but held at different ages and times, "present jobs" were occupied by the respondents when they were approximately the same age and at the same dates. These provide an aggregate portrait of change in jobs during the adolescent period. As in the case of jobs up to ninth grade, we found clear gender differences in labor force participation and in compensation during high school.

Employment, defined as working at least once a week outside the home for pay, was more prevalent among girls than boys, particularly at the beginning of the study, when 63 percent of the ninth-grade girls but only 40 percent of the boys were employed (see Table 3.1). While this difference is undoubtedly linked in the earlier years to the greater opportunity for girls to babysit, girls were also more likely than boys to report holding a paid job during each of the three succeeding years.

Though in past decades teenage boys had higher rates of labor force participation than girls, in 1996 the Current Population Survey reported the same pattern as that found in the YDS: nationally, 16- and 17-year-old girls were more likely than their male age peers to be employed (Committee, 1998). For both boys and girls in the YDS, the prevalence of employment increased over the four-year period, with a dip for girls (from 63 to 52 percent) between ninth and tenth grades, when many outgrow babysitting jobs. In fact, by Wave 4, when most respondents were high school seniors, 58 percent of the boys and 70 percent of the girls reported holding paid jobs.[2]

Table 3.1. Employment and hours of work per week by grade and gender

	Grade 9		Grade 10		Grade 11		Grade 12	
	Boys	Girls	Boys	Girls	Boys	Girls	Boys	Girls
% employed	40%	63%	42%	52%	53%	63%	58%	70%
Hours worked (employed only)								
Median	7.5	9.5	20.0	15.0	20.0	18.0	20.0	20.0
Mean	11.3	11.5	19.6	15.8	21.9	18.6	21.8	19.8
SD	9.7	8.8	10.8	8.3	9.9	8.5	10.6	9.2
Distribution of hours (employed only)								
1–10	61.9	61.3	21.5	32.6	13.2	20.3	15.4	12.9
11–18	19.4	19.9	25.8	34.3	28.2	29.8	21.1	31.9
19–20	5.6	8.6	12.9	12.4	11.8	14.2	20.2	18.1
21–25	5.6	5.0	14.1	7.9	13.6	18.3	12.7	19.3
26–30	2.5	3.0	11.0	9.1	14.5	12.2	14.0	10.7
31–40	3.8	1.3	12.9	2.9	16.4	3.7	12.7	5.8
41–50	1.3	0.7	1.2	0.8	2.3	1.4	0.8	0.8
>50	0.0	0.3	0.6	0.0	0.0	0.0	1.3	0.6
N	160	302	163	242	220	295	228	326

INTENSITY OF WORK

Assessment of the amount of time youth spend working is, like employment itself, subject to vagaries of definition. For example, if certain types of work (such as informal work) are excluded from the definition of employment provided to respondents, they will also not be counted when the temporal investment in paid work is gauged. Nonetheless, national surveys invariably show that employed young people devote substantial time to their jobs (Committee, 1998). In the year of initiation of the YDS, the 1988 Current Population Survey reported that employed 16- and 17-year-olds averaged 21 hours a week at work. But students tend to work fewer hours when school is in session. CPS data show that among 17-year-olds with jobs during the 1995 school year, average hours of work reached 18 per week. Like employment itself, hours of work tend to increase as adolescents get older (Committee, 1998: 39–40).

Employed youth in the YDS appear to be working at about the same level of intensity as has been reported in such national studies. Information about time investment in the "present" job was obtained in two ways. First, the youth indicated the number of hours they were working per week. Second, we asked, "What days of the week, and how many hours each day, do you work?" When there were discrepancies between the answers to these questions, we telephoned respondents to reconcile the differences.

Medians, means, and standard deviations of hours worked in "present" jobs are shown in Table 3.1. Whereas the employed ninth graders devoted only about 11 hours per week to their jobs, hours increased substantially for both genders after ninth grade. The employed boys' mean work hours rose abruptly between ninth and tenth grades, from 11.3 to 19.6 hours per week. The boys' median showed even more dramatic change, from 7.5 to 20 hours. By the time they were surveyed in tenth grade, most youth would have turned 16, the age at which temporal restrictions on work are loosened in Minnesota.[3] The boys' mean work hours approach 22 in eleventh and twelfth grades. Girls showed a smaller increase in hours of work between ninth and tenth grades, from 11.5 to 15.8 hours per week. Their hours of employment continued to increase in eleventh and twelfth grades, so that by Wave 4 they were working almost as many hours as boys (19.8 hours vs. 21.8 hours for boys).

Given the concern about excessive youth employment, it is of interest to identify the proportion of young people who exceed particular hours thresholds. Twenty hours is often considered the dividing line between excessive and acceptable work for teenagers (Committee, 1998). Again, national data suggest that many youth work more than 20 hours per week. In the Monitoring the Future study of high school seniors, 46.5 percent of employed boys and 38 percent of working girls exceeded 20 hours per week (Bachman and Schulenberg, 1992). Among employed seniors surveyed in the first year of the National Longitudinal Study of Adolescent Health, 42 percent were working 25 or more hours per week; 30 percent worked 30 or more hours (Committee, 1998: 39).

Younger adolescents are less likely to work so many hours. Only 20 percent of employed tenth graders in the "AdHealth" study worked 25 or more hours per week, and just 13 percent worked 30 or more. Recall that these percentages are calculated for *working* teenagers. Since not all students are employed at any given time, percentages of *all* high school students working excessive hours are considerably lower.

In the YDS, as in national studies, older youth are more prone to work "excessive" hours, and boys are more likely to do so than girls (Table 3.1). In ninth grade, only 13 percent of employed boys and 10 percent of employed girls reported working more than 20 hours per week. Of employed tenth graders, 40 percent of boys and 21 percent of girls exceeded this threshold; of employed seniors, 42 percent of boys and 37 percent of girls did so. But when we consider all respondents, not just those with paid jobs, the proportion working "excessive" hours becomes more limited. That is, in Wave 4 of the YDS, when most respondents were seniors in high school, only a quarter of the panel was working more than 20 hours—25 percent of girls, 24 percent of boys. These differences are important to consider when evaluating the magnitude of the problem of "excessive" youthwork.

TYPES OF JOBS

True to the stereotypes, employed youth nationally are concentrated in retail trade, especially in the fast-food industry. The 1996 Current Population Survey (March supplement) showed that more than half of employed 15- to 17-year-olds were doing retail work, in restaurants, grocery stores, and other establishments. More than one-quarter worked in services, including recreation, health, and education (Committee, 1998).

Still, teenagers hold many kinds of jobs. Bidwell and his colleagues' (1998) study of young workers, chosen to represent varying social class levels and different types of communities, illustrates this diversity. Though surely not typical, some youth developed small businesses and consulting firms, capitalizing on their individual talents and skills. Others, while still in high school, advanced from lower-level to higher-level jobs, for example, from cashier or behind-the-counter food server in a fast-food chain to supervisor in the same establishment. Still others, especially in higher-status communities, relied on relational and other networks to locate paid (and unpaid) internships in diverse settings.

In the YDS, type of job was assessed annually by asking the youth to enter their job titles in the work history chart, along with the names of their employing organizations. The information about employers proved quite useful, since ambiguity in a job title could sometimes be clarified by the employment context. Job titles were coded according to the *DOT* functional classification and later collapsed into a few descriptive categories.

As noted earlier, if youth are concentrated in just a few types of jobs, and if the jobs available to them remain the same throughout adolescence, then there is little rationale for the investigation of variability in work experience. The distribution of job types by gender and wave, shown in Table 3.2, suggests that such a conception of youthwork does not match the reality.

Informal work is preponderant in ninth grade, especially for girls: almost three-fourths of the employed ninth-grade girls indicated that they did informal types of work, most frequently babysitting. But apparently girls outgrow this kind of work rather quickly. Little more than a third of the employed tenth-grade girls reported informal work.

In fact, the slight dip in the prevalence of girls' employment between ninth and tenth grades, shown in Table 3.1, may possibly be attributable to a difficult transition between informal and formal work. Between ages 15 and 16, many girls may come to think of themselves as too old for babysitting but find it difficult to locate formal employment. Though this issue was not explored, parents may well prefer that their daughters do informal work. Babysitting tends

Table 3.2. Job types by grade and gender

Job type	Grade 9		Grade 10		Grade 11		Grade 12	
	Boys	Girls	Boys	Girls	Boys	Girls	Boys	Girls
Informal	36.4%	73.0%	9.4%	36.1%	3.1%	13.9%	3.9%	7.3%
Restaurant/food work	26.6	16.3	46.8	40.4	47.6	32.3	39.0	27.5
Sales	16.8	5.0	12.3	11.8	14.1	33.9	20.3	34.6
Laborers	10.9	2.1	22.2	3.1	23.8	2.6	20.3	3.4
Semi-skilled	3.3	.3	2.3	2.0	4.0	1.3	7.8	2.4
Clerical	3.3	.9	3.5	3.1	.4	5.2	1.3	13.8
Teaching/recreation	2.2	2.1	2.9	3.1	3.1	9.7	5.2	10.1
Others	.5	.3	.6	.4	4.0	1.3	2.2	.9
N	184	337	171	255	227	310	231	327

to occur close to home and for employers who are the parents' friends, neighbors, and acquaintances. If parents perceive that teen-age girls face greater challenges or dangers than boys in formal employment, they may be more restrictive of their daughters' work activity. The proportion of girls doing informal work markedly declined in Wave 3 of the study and was negligible by Wave 4.

Employed boys are less likely than girls to be doing informal work in ninth grade—just 36 percent are so engaged. While girls babysit, boys do yardwork (shoveling snow, caring for lawns and gardens). Like the girls, boys withdraw from such work as they grow older. In tenth grade, less than 10 percent of the employed males reported informal employment; even fewer did so in later grades.

Employment by youth in the fast-food industry is highly prevalent nationally, and much maligned for the highly regulated, routinized character of job tasks (Leidner, 1993; Reiter, 1991). Consistent with national data, employment in what the census calls "eating and drinking establishments"—pizza parlors, lunch counters, drive-through food outlets, and restaurants—is quite common among YDS adolescents. The category "restaurant/food work" includes several jobs, such as waitress or waiter, receptionist, cook, cashier, and dish-washer. This category constitutes the second most frequent type of work activity, behind informal work, for both genders in ninth grade: about 27 percent of the employed boys and 16 percent of the girls. By tenth grade it occupies almost half of the employed boys and 40 percent of the girls. It continues to be the most common job type for boys through the end of high school.

However, youth take on a broader range of employment after tenth grade. The proportion of girls doing restaurant work declines from 40 to 27 percent between Waves 2 and 4. In the last two years of high school, girls are more likely to report sales and clerical work. Some also enter jobs involving various kinds of teaching and recreation, such as assisting in schools, tutoring children, and working as supervisors in playgrounds. Employed boys also exhibit a movement away from restaurant work, though their participation in this job category does not peak until eleventh grade (at 48 percent).

Adolescent employment in sales becomes more prevalent over the years. Among employed girls it increases from 5 percent in ninth grade to 35 percent in twelfth grade. Boys' sales work also shows a general upward trend in these years, from 17 percent to 20 percent,

Table 3.3. Wages and earnings by grade and gender

	Grade 9		Grade 10		Grade 11		Grade 12	
	Boys	Girls	Boys	Girls	Boys	Girls	Boys	Girls
Wages per hour								
Median	$3.5	$2.0	$4.0	$3.8	$4.4	$4.3	$4.9	$4.7
Mean	4.1	2.8	4.4	3.7	4.5	4.3	5.1	4.8
S.D.	3.7	3.2	3.5	3.2	0.9	1.1	1.3	4.3
Earnings in past two weeks								
Median			$112	$75	$150	$120	$160	$140
Mean			123	85	170	127	175	149
S.D.			103	63	112	77	110	82

Note: Empty cell indicates information not obtained.

with a drop between ninth and tenth grades that reflects their departure from newspaper delivery.

Reflecting the sex-typed adult occupational structure, adolescent boys are more likely than girls to hold jobs as laborers in construction or other industries and as semi-skilled workers. Girls are more likely in grade 12 to be in clerical work; clerical jobs are almost nonexistent among older boys. Girls are almost twice as likely as boys to be teachers or recreation workers. The residual "other" category is very small in all four years, indicating that we have effectively captured in seven broad categories the range of jobs held by YDS youth.

Clearly, there is a fundamental shift in job types through the high school years, suggesting the likelihood of major changes in young people's work experiences. After ninth grade there is wholesale movement out of informal work; a large aggregate increase in restaurant/food work; and then dispersal across diverse job categories. Of course, the aggregate distributions of the adolescents' jobs does not describe the employment "careers" of individual youth. Still, young people's movements in and out of the labor force over these years of middle to late adolescence generate these age-specific occupational distributions. A typology to be presented later in this chapter incorporates changes at the individual level in employment patterns over time.

WAGES

Employed youth's wage rates reflect gender differences in occupations (see Table 3.3). The large differential in hourly wages between boys and girls in ninth grade (means of $4.10 versus $2.80) undoubtedly reflects girls' early concentration in informal work and the low compensation of babysitters. Girls earn somewhat lower wages than boys throughout high school, but the gender difference is quite minimal by twelfth grade ($5.10 versus $4.80).

These wage rates are low by adult standards, but they still offer many youth considerable discretionary income. Adolescents report substantial earnings over a two-week period, growing from $123 to $175 for employed boys and from $85 to $149 for girls between tenth and the twelfth grades. Thus both boys and girls have, in absolute terms, fairly large amounts of money at their disposal. Bachman (1983) worries about youth's "premature affluence," but, as we will see in Chapter 6, many young people's spending patterns appear to be quite responsible and "grown up."

TYPES OF TASKS

Three simple questions gauged the predominant tasks adolescents perform on their jobs (adapted from Kohn and Schooler, 1974): (1) "How much time do you spend reading and writing, or dealing with any written materials?" (2) "How much time do you spend dealing with people? (Only include your work with people that is necessary for the job.)" and (3) "How much time do you spend working with your hands on your job, using tools or machines? This includes pumping gas, stocking shelves, typing, etc." A five-point scale followed each question, from 1 for no time at all to 5 for all of the time.

Of the three kinds of tasks, adolescents report the least time spent reading and writing; the means generally reference "hardly any time" to "less than half the time" (means of 2.1–2.3 for boys, 2.4–2.6 for girls). Corresponding to a gender-typical separation between interpersonal and manual tasks, girls spend "most of the time" to "all the time" dealing with people on their jobs (means of 4.3–4.5), while boys spend "most of the time" working with their hands (4.1). Many of the employed girls, 86–92 percent, spend most or all of their work time dealing with people, while for about 80 percent of the employed boys, manual work is the predominant time use across years.

Use of time on the job becomes somewhat more diversified as adolescents grow older. Girls come to spend more time reading and writing, and doing manual tasks (means of 3.4, 3.7, and 3.7 for grades 10–12); boys become more involved with people (3.5, 3.8, and 3.8). These shifts reflect the changes in job types shown in Table 3.2, especially the growing diversity of jobs that adolescents hold in the last two years of high school.

Although *DOT* ratings may not accurately characterize adolescents' jobs, the changes in job types and in time allocation are reflected in these objective measures. All task complexity scores are low in all four years (see Mortimer, Finch, et al., 1994), indicating relatively simple involvement with data, people, and things. For example, both boys' and girls' job complexity scores for data, on the average, fall at the level of "reading instructions," and their scores for work with people and things involve "serving" and "handling."

Still, work with data becomes more complex over time for both boys and girls (especially for girls between ninth and tenth grades, as they shift from babysitting to formal work). The complexity of work with people shows a similar upward pattern. Work with things becomes more complex for girls from ninth to eleventh grade and for boys from ninth to tenth, after which it remains stable. There are few gender differences in these ratings, but girls' work with people is more complex than that of boys in the third and fourth years.

A further objective indicator of learning opportunity, as well as complexity, skill level, and self-direction in the job, is the amount of training provided by the employer. Jobs that are repetitive and have little need for independent decisionmaking require little or no training. The YDS measured both initial and continuing training: "Did your employer give you any training when you began work?" "How long did the training take?" "Is there any continuing training or instruction on your job?"

The common portrayal of novice workers as receiving little or no training does not accurately describe most YDS panel members' experience, especially after ninth grade. Only about one-third of tenth graders and one-fourth of juniors and seniors report no training at all in their current jobs. The amount of initial training increases between ninth and tenth grades for both boys and girls, reflecting the movement out of informal work. The modal amount of time spent in initial job training in eleventh and twelfth grades is between one and ten days. More than one-third of the employed boys and almost half of the girls report this much or more training. Moreover, substantial proportions of employed adolescents (between 30 and 40 percent across genders and years) say they receive continuing training in their jobs.

We also asked the teenagers each year, "How many other workers do you supervise on your job?" Whereas only a minority of employed adolescents have supervisory responsibilities, this experience is not rare. As adolescents gain mastery over their job tasks, many are assigned to supervise others doing the same tasks. As one young woman (in her mid-twenties) noted, "I was a cashier [in a grocery store] when I started and then I became what they call a customer service desk, which meant you still cashiered when it was busy, but otherwise you supervised the other cashiers, took care of all the cash, did the books at the end of the night." Almost a fourth of employed boys had some supervisory responsibility in ninth grade; 29 percent did so in twelfth grade. If so many adolescents report that they supervise other workers, their jobs surely cannot be sweepingly characterized as lacking in responsibility.

Interestingly, in view of the presumption that supervisory experience adds to an employee's human capital, girls are less likely to be supervisors: only 8 percent in ninth grade and 15 percent in twelfth grade had such responsibilities. For the adolescents who did supervise, the average number of workers they supervised increased over the same period (from 4.2 to 5.2 for boys; from 2.8 to 4.7 for girls).

PERCEIVED QUALITY OF WORK

Overall, the YDS adolescents appear to have rather favorable reactions to their jobs, as evidenced by their positive responses to survey questions about the quality of work. There are reasons to view such responses with caution: errors are inherent in all self-report data, even in reports of presumably objective features of work, such as hours, wages, or the number of workers supervised, and descriptions of job quality may be even more prone to individual biases. For example, they may be influenced by item construction—such as the number of response options to survey questions or the particular wording of questions and response options (Schuman, 1995). Various extraneous motivations, such as to give socially acceptable or positive responses, introduce further measurement error.

Though these potential biases indicate reason for caution, YDS panel members seem reluctant to characterize their jobs in negative terms. The data I present here were collected in Wave 3, when the majority of the adolescents were employed. As shown in Table 3.2, in eleventh grade employed YDS youth were concentrated in jobs that most adults would not consider particularly desirable (71 percent of the employed boys were doing restaurant/food work or manual labor; almost half the girls were in restaurant work, informal work, or manual labor). Youth performing other types of work were probably concentrated in low-level positions, involving simpler job tasks than adult workers in similar jobs.

Because youth is so highly confounded with lack of work experience, we might expect to find the greatest divergence between adolescent and adult evaluations of "youth jobs" on the dimension of learning opportunity. An excerpt from one of Aronson's (1998) interviews with a 23-year-old YDS respondent reveals reactions that may be typical of many adolescent workers.

> INTERVIEWER: You said that you . . . worked at Walgreen's for a long time.
>
> RESPONDENT: Yeah, five years.
>
> INTERVIEWER: You said you really liked it, and I was just wondering what about it.
>
> RESPONDENT: Yeah I loved it. The people, the product knowledge that I got to learn, and I'm a quick learner, um . . . when I was seventeen, it was, I loved it . . . I mean, just, I could go back in back and get boxes, catch people stealing, you know I could, I learned so much in retail. I mean, you learn about numbers . . . I was the price administer. I loved my job.

Clearly, this young person experienced the job as providing variety and much learning opportunity.

When the employed eleventh graders were asked whether the job gave them "a chance to learn a lot of new things," 43 percent said this was "somewhat true" or "very true" and another 42 percent said it was a little true. When asked whether the job "uses my skills and abilities," 45 percent responded that this statement was somewhat or very true, and 34 percent said it was a little true. Likewise, 43 percent described their work as very or somewhat "challenging"; only 19 percent said their jobs were unchallenging. Though the percentage giving affirmative responses does not quite reach a majority, many young workers apparently believe they are learning and finding challenge in the workplace.

The vast majority also report that their jobs allow them to be of service. When asked whether the job "gives me a chance to be helpful to others," 70 percent of the employed eleventh graders replied that this was very or somewhat true.

Self-direction in work is much emphasized in studies of the impacts of work on adult personality (Kohn and Schooler, 1983; Mortimer and Lorence, 1995). Because of their inexperience, one might think that young workers would uniformly describe their jobs as having little autonomy or decisionmaking capacity. But when the YDS panel members in Wave 3 were asked about how much control they had over the way they spend their time at work, a third answered "complete control" or "a great deal of control," while only 6 percent answered "no control." Similarly, 36 percent said they had complete freedom or a great deal of freedom to make important decisions at work about what they did and how they did it.

By the same token, we might anticipate that adolescents would be rather closely supervised. But when asked about how their supervisors allotted work tasks, only 16 percent of the employed youth indicated that the supervisor decides "what I do and how I do it," while 60 percent noted either "I have some freedom to decide what I do and how I do it" or "I am my own boss as long as I stay within the general policies of my employer." Also, almost half reported that the supervisor discussed the work with them rather than just telling them what to do, and three-fourths felt somewhat or very free to disagree with their supervisors.

On the whole, respondents reported high levels of support from supervisors. Fully 71 percent noted that their supervisors were "willing to listen to problems and help find solutions" almost always or often. Indeed, 38 percent felt extremely or quite close to their supervisors.

Admittedly, these characterizations of supervisor-employee relations may not be veridical descriptions of what goes on in the workplace. But most young workers themselves experience at least some discretion in their job tasks and do not report close supervision. Many perceive opportunities to make their own decisions about how to solve the problems they encounter at work. Moreover, in the aggregate, the YDS adolescents convey quite positive portrayals of their relationships with their supervisors.

Given the critics' concern that the workplace may subject adolescents to stress for which they have not yet developed sufficient coping capacity, we asked about several potential stressors, including role ambiguity ("Sometimes I am unclear about what I have to do on my job"), role conflict ("To satisfy some people on my job, I have to upset others"), and time pressure ("How often is there time pressure on your job?"). We also inquired about whether adolescents feel that they control the outcomes for which they are accountable at work ("How often are you held responsible for things that are really outside your control?"). We assessed noxious work conditions ("How often are you exposed to excessive heat, cold or noise at work?") and role overload ("I have too much work to do everything well"; "My job requires that I work very hard").

Only a minority of the employed youth reported such stressors. For example, less than one-fifth agreed that "sometimes I am unclear about what I have to do on my job." Only 22 percent reported that it was either somewhat or very true that "to satisfy some people on my job, I have to upset others." Less than a third said that they often or almost always worked under time pressure, and 65 percent reported that they never or rarely were held responsible for things outside their control.

Furthermore, the adolescent workers seemed somewhat satisfied with the extrinsic rewards they received from their jobs. When asked, "Would you consider your pay 'good pay' for the work you do?" one-fourth responded "Yes, definitely" and almost half checked "Yes, it is pretty good." Only 9 percent responded "No, the pay is not good" (the rest were unsure). The majority also perceived that they had chances for advancement in their jobs. Many youth do have such opportunities, moving from junior to senior lifeguard, or taking on supervisory responsibilities in fast-food restaurants or retail stores (Bidwell et al., 1998). In Wave 3, only 16 percent reported that their jobs lacked opportunities for advancement.

Reflecting the strong demand for part-time workers in the secondary labor market, the young job-holders were quite confident about their job security. Fully 71 percent checked "Yes, I can definitely keep this job as long as I want"; only 1.6 percent checked "I could be laid off at any time."

These youth are certainly not unanimously positive; there is cause for concern for the minority of youth who find their jobs completely lacking in learning opportunities or chances to be helpful to others. While most employed youth do not perceive their jobs as stressful, some do. The same can be said for all the qualities we have investigated. Still, it is remarkable, given the widespread characterization of the jobs available to young people as menial or "bad" jobs, how positive young workers are when asked to comment on the qualities of their work.

At the most global level, the subjective response to work may be gauged by the worker's overall evaluation of the goodness of the job and the degree of commitment to it. When asked to locate themselves on a 6-point job-satisfaction continuum ranging from "extremely dissatisfied" to "extremely satisfied," 88 percent indicated some level of satisfaction: that they were somewhat, very, or extremely satisfied. Furthermore, two-thirds of the employed adolescents reported that their work was sometimes, often, or almost always "meaningful and important," and 42 percent characterized the following statement as somewhat or very true: "I am very much involved personally in my job." Surely these global evaluations of their jobs do not suggest wholesale dissatisfaction or disengagement from the work role.

GENDER DIFFERENCES

It is plausible to expect boys' and girls' descriptions of their jobs to differ, given the differences in the types of jobs they hold. Girls' jobs involve more time with people; boys spend more time working with their hands. Girls' jobs more often involve caring for or assisting others, and in the last two years of high school their jobs have higher complexity ratings in relation to work with people.

Gender differences are not apparent on all the reactions to work included in this assessment. However, where we do find them, girls almost always describe their jobs more favorably than the boys (see Mortimer, Finch, et al., 1994). Consistent with indications from the *DOT* ratings that their jobs involve more complex people-oriented tasks (in Waves 3 and 4), girls were more likely than boys to perceive opportunities to help others on their jobs. Girls more frequently reported close and helpful relations with their supervisors, and were significantly more likely than boys to think their jobs provided them with opportunities to learn skills that would be useful in the future.[4] (Interestingly, this occurred despite the fact that employed girls receive less initial training from their employers than boys.) Girls were also more likely than boys to feel mentally challenged at work, a finding consistent with the greater amounts of time they spend reading and writing.

Not surprisingly, boys were more likely than girls (in grades 11 and 12) to report physical challenges at work. Because of boys' greater size and strength, their jobs probably entail more lifting and other physical tasks even when they are employed in the same broad job classes as girls. Significant gender differences on the stress indicators always indicated more strain on the part of boys. For example, boys were more likely in Waves 3 and 4 to say they were unclear about what they had to do on their jobs. They reported more role overload and more noxious work conditions in all years of the study. In Wave 4 they were more likely than girls to say they could not control things that they were held responsible for at work. These stresses may be indicative of greater responsibility, as suggested by boys' greater involvement in supervisory functions.

There appear, however, to be some compensating extrinsic rewards for boys. Boys perceived more opportunities for advancement than girls in Waves 2 and 3. As we have seen, boys' wages were only slightly higher than girls' in the latter years of high school. However, because of their greater time investment in work, they accrue higher earnings (Table 3.3). Nonetheless, boys and girls did not differ in the assessments of the "goodness" of their pay, or in their perceived job security.

One of the great paradoxes in the literature on adults' work attitudes is the absence of gender differences in job satisfaction, despite the higher wages, greater autonomy, and greater advancement opportunity in men's jobs (Mortimer and Lorence, 1995). But in the case of adolescent workers we do find gender differences, with girls generally more positive on measures of work quality. Despite these differences, there were no gender differences in adolescents' job satisfaction in any year during high school. Some evidence suggests that girls showed greater commitment to their work, but only in the first two years of high school.[5]

Let us now turn to young people's perceptions of the links between their jobs and other important aspects of their lives. As noted in Chapter 1, the tension between school and work is uppermost in the policy debate. The question is often posed in dichotomous terms: Should adolescents be working *or* going to school? If they do both at once, the assumption is that working will interfere with learning and school performance.

Echoing the worries of educators, and despite the relative absence of reported stress deriving from the job itself, many young people found combining the roles of worker and student problematic. For example, in eleventh grade 64 percent agreed or strongly agreed that being both a worker and a student was stressful for them. From tenth to twelfth grade, students were increasingly likely to report that the job interfered with their capacity to do their homework, to come to class prepared, and to come to school on time. They also became more likely to report that because of their jobs they came to school tired. These reports of strain did not differ between boys and girls.

Still, and contrary to the expectations of the critics of youth employment, the role of worker was not generally perceived as interfering with family participation, with relations with parents, or with relationships with peers (Mortimer and Shanahan, 1991, 1994).

CHANGES OVER TIME

Given the many indications that youthwork becomes more diversified and complex as young people move through high school, we might expect adolescents to describe their jobs as increasingly interesting and challenging over time. But in fact there were relatively few aggregate shifts across time in responses to work. The ratings of intrinsic job characteristics, such as opportunities to learn new things, chances to be helpful to others, mental and physical challenges, and the degree of variety at work appear, to the contrary, to be rather stable in the aggregate (Mortimer, Finch, et al., 1994).

Surprisingly, despite the very low wages of ninth-grade girls and the growth in girls' wages over time, employed girls were not more likely to report being well paid in the fourth year than in the first year of the study. Also, adolescents perceived similar levels of support from their supervisors across the high school years, there were no consistent trends in the stress measures, and there was little change in job satisfaction. Perhaps as their pay increases and their jobs become more complex and autonomous adolescents' frames of reference or standards of comparison also shift upward. In any case, the evaluative assessments elicited by the YDS questions showed negligible change over time.

PATTERNS OF INVESTMENT IN WORK

Most studies of youth employment assess the amount of time spent working at a particular time, or over a relatively short period (D'Amico, 1984; Schill, McCartin, and Meyer, 1985; Steinberg and Dornbusch, 1991), or on two occasions (Steinberg et al., 1993). Likewise, each wave of YDS data presents a "snapshot" portrait of adolescents' employment at a particular time: their temporal investment in work, their job types, earnings, objective conditions of work, rewards in the work setting, and reactions to the experiences they encounter in the workplace. The first four waves of the study make it possible to construct a cumulative portrayal of adolescent employment during high school.

Because adolescents move in and out of the labor force frequently, hours of work at any particular time may be a poor indicator of their investment in work over a longer period. But such cumulative, long-term work patterns may be far more consequential for development and attainment.

Two fundamental dimensions of time investment—in work or any other activity—are duration and intensity. Using continuous data from the panelists' work history charts, we computed measures of both duration (each student's total months of paid work while school was in session each year) and intensity (each respondent's total cumulative hours of work divided by the total weeks of work).

We constructed a typology of work investment based on experiences during 24 months of high school: the full tenth- and eleventh-grade academic years of nine months each, and the first six months of twelfth grade. Ninth-grade employment was not considered in the typology because so much of the ninth graders' work was informal. (As noted in Chapter 2, retention through the four years of high school was high—93 percent. Because of increased panel attrition in Wave 5, the first year after most students left high school, a complete employment record was obtained for fewer youth after the Wave 4 survey, that is, from March 1991 on.)

The typology also does not take into account summer employment, which is often considered benign because it does not interfere with school work. (Most youth of high school age do work during the summer. For example, by twelfth grade, according to the national Adolescent Health study, only 18.5 percent of respondents report no summer work; Committee, 1998: 39.)

In the typology of youth work investment, we measured duration by a dichotomy, separating those who were employed more and those who were employed less than the median number of months for all panel members (18 months). Similarly, for intensity, respondents whose cumulative hours of work divided by their weeks of work was greater than 20 were considered high-intensity workers; those for whom this measure was 20 or less were considered low-intensity workers.

These break points are somewhat arbitrary, but they offer convenient and intuitively meaningful ways of characterizing youth's cu-

Table 3.4. Patterns of investment in work by gender

	Total	Boys	Girls	Mean months of work		Mean hours of work	
				Boys	Girls	Boys	Girls
Not working	7.0%	9.9%	4.6%	0.0	0.0	0.0	0.0
Occasional	23.7	23.2	24.1	9.8	11.7	578	650
Sporadic	18.4	23.2	14.3	10.4	11.8	1,216	1,376
Steady	24.9	18.2	30.6	22.0	22.0	1,263	1,328
Most invested	26.0	25.6	26.4	21.9	22.2	2,678	2,587
N	887	406	481				

mulative work experience. Twenty hours per week is widely considered a level above which work becomes "excessive" and deleterious for adolescent development. Though there is no particular level of intensity at which indicators of adjustment markedly decline across studies, if youth are in school approximately 30 hours per week and are employed 20 hours, their effective work week, not including other forms of work such as chores and volunteering, is 50 hours, more than the usual full-time work week for most employed adults.

A five-category typology results from cross-classifying these two dimensions of duration and intensity and adding a category for those who did not work at all during the 24 months of observation. Table 3.4 shows the distribution of the panel in these categories, as well as their actual mean cumulative months and hours of work. What is most immediately striking is that less than 10 percent of the boys, and less than 5 percent of the girls, report no employment during this period of high school. These figures again confirm the common combination of school and work during high school.

Approximately a fourth of both boys and girls are "occasional" workers: low on both duration and intensity. In fact these boys and girls were employed for fewer than half the total months of observation—9.8 and 11.7 months, respectively. Another fourth of the boys, but only 14 percent of the girls, are "sporadic" workers, who similarly worked for relatively brief periods—averaging 10.4 months for boys, 11.8 months for girls—but averaged more than 20 hours per week during those months. For "steady" workers, employment is fairly continuous but restricted in intensity. This is the modal category for girls (31 percent), but the least prevalent among boys (18 percent). Finally, the "most invested" teenage workers, comprising approximately one-fourth of both boys and girls, are employed on average during almost all months of observation and, when employed, average more than 20 hours per week.

It is especially pertinent that employment status at any single time, or even at three occasions measured serially, provides a poor indication of the pattern that is revealed by continuous employment data. This may be especially the case for youth because of the transitory and unstable character of their employment. As a case in point, let us consider "high intensity" workers. At all three annual surveys, 87 adolescents were found to be employed at high intensity. Of these 87, 69 were in the "most invested" category. However, 18 respondents,

Table 3.5. Quality of work by pattern of work investment

Quality of work	Work-investment pattern				F
	Occasional	Steady	Sporadic	Most invested	
Learning opportunities	11.31	11.86	12.21	12.39	4.30**
Specific learning	14.63	15.30	15.26	15.51	2.74*
Advancement opportunity	2.46	2.41	2.80	2.70	8.11***
Security	2.60	2.66	2.72	2.71	2.55
Earnings in past 2 weeks	$105.12	$103.81	$182.77	$176.77	58.89***
Good pay	2.82	2.76	2.78	2.70	.64
Supervisory support	5.96	5.91	6.41	6.13	2.33
Psychological engagement	22.77	22.70	23.53	24.40	5.21**
Work stressors	18.90	18.55	20.76	20.80	11.41***
Work and school compatibility	10.08	10.37	11.13	10.88	5.62**
Work-derived status	4.08	4.44	4.88	4.64	9.20***

*$p < .05$; **$p < .01$; ***$p < .001$.

or 21 percent, were in the "sporadic" category, indicating that despite the high intensity of their work at each yearly observation, their cumulative duration of employment over the 24 months was below the median. Whereas 81 percent of the youth who manifested low-intensity employment at each yearly survey were in the "steady" group, 19 percent were in the "occasional" category.

Characterizing youth employment experience in this way represents a marked departure from past tradition. In studying the consequences of youth employment for socioeconomic attainment, investigators have utilized weeks worked in a particular period as the independent variable (Carr et al., 1996), hours worked per week in a given week or year (Carr et al., 1996; Stephenson, 1981; Steel, 1991; Ruhm, 1997; Warren et al., 2000; Chaplin and Hannaway, 1996), or cumulative work hours over the high school years (Marsh, 1991).

One might think that cumulative work hours during high school would be an especially adequate indicator of work investment. However, even this measure does not reflect the distinctive patterns of young people's work. For example, YDS youth in the "sporadic" and "steady" categories both register about the same number of total hours of work over the period under scrutiny (see Table 3.4), although their patterns of employment activity are very different. If working for long periods at limited intensity has different consequences for development and attainment than working short periods at high intensity, these would not be detected if only the cumulative hours of work were taken into account.

Unlike temporal investment in work, continuous indicators of the quality of work experience are not available in the YDS, only the adolescents' contemporaneous portraits of the jobs they held at each wave of data collection. Thus we have only a partial record from which to construct a cumulative portrait of the challenges, rewards, and stressors adolescents experience on their jobs. Still, averaging these descriptions yields measures of work quality that are analogous to the typology of temporal investment. In the absence of continuous measures, we compute the average of multi-item indices reflecting key dimensions of work experience measured each year.[6] Those employed on all three occasions would have three data entries upon which to base this average; others would have only two or one.

Differences in work quality, by work-investment pattern, are shown in Table 3.5. It is evident that those who worked at high intensity reported more pronounced work experiences of both a positive and a negative character. That is, they reported that their jobs had more general learning opportunities (chance to learn a lot of new things, use of skills and abilities, mental and physical challenges, and usefulness of the job for later life), greater advancement opportunity, and, of course (given that they worked more hours), higher earnings. (Interestingly, in view of the actual earnings differences, the four groups did not differ in the extent to which they perceived that they were well paid.)

Differences in the perception of specific learning opportunities (see note 4) appear to increase with the cumulative amount of time spent working: the difference is greatest between the "occasional" and the "most invested" workers. Those whose employment was both intensive and sustained perceived the greatest chance to learn on the job. Not unexpectedly, in view of these differences, the high-intensity workers exhibited stronger psychological engagement in their jobs.[7] Still, they also described their work as more demanding and stressful (time pressured, involving responsibility for things outside their control, exposure to noxious conditions, role overload, lack of clarity regarding job tasks, role conflict, having to work very hard, and feeling drained of energy after work). (There were no significant differences across groups in perceptions of supervisory support or job security.) Apparently a high degree of temporal investment in work enables employers to assign young employees more learning-rich, as well as more demanding, tasks. Such investment thus provides opportunities for learning and engagement that may not be as available to young people who spend less time working.

Paradoxically, those who work at higher levels of intensity during high school think that working and school are more compatible than those who limit their hours of work.[8] The youth who work longer hours do in fact have work schedules that are likely to impinge on their studying time. But, looked at another way, it could be that precisely because they believe their jobs help them to do better in school, they do not restrict their hours of work. Recognizing the potential conflicts between school and work would appear to provide incentive to maintain a lighter work schedule. (Still, there were no significant differences between the four groups in the belief that working interferes with getting good grades.) High-intensity workers are more likely to believe that working gives them status in the eyes of their friends (as gauged by agreement with the statements "Because I have more money, I can go out with my friends more often"; and "Having a job gives me higher status among friends").

These differences in work conditions give rise to intriguing questions. For example, do youth with certain motivations choose to work more hours to achieve different kinds of work conditions and opportunities? The issue of selection to work will be taken up in Chapter 5.

Intergenerational Comparison

In view of historical shifts in the prevalence of youthwork, chronicled in Chapter 1, and in the kinds of jobs available to young people (Aronson et al., 1996), the experience of employment in youth is sometimes thought to have been a more salutary experience for previous generations (Greenberger and Steinberg, 1986). According to Greenberger, "Youngsters' jobs, once a stepping stone to adult employment, are now usually discontinuous with adult employment" (1988: 24). In an earlier era, opportunities for young people to work in manufacturing, in farming, and in apprentice-like positions, as assistants and helpers to skilled adult workers, provided entry to future careers. The adult employers and supervisors of adolescent workers, having an interest in their remaining in the firm, would actively monitor, teach, and advise them. Thus work experience during high school was thought to have clear payoff in terms of human capital accumulation and career development.

In contrast, as we have seen, today's youth of high school age work in part-time jobs that are especially geared to young people, in whom the employer has little long-term interest. In fact, contemporary young workers often have little contact with more experienced adults, as they work with, and often serve, their age peers (Greenberger, 1988). Contemporary youth are therefore said to be unable to learn from adult workers and to benefit from their instruction and mentoring.

To evaluate this argument, we compared the ways adults and adolescents evaluate their early jobs. Lacking data for earlier cohorts comparable to that collected in the YDS, we could not base this assessment on contemporaneous evaluations from different periods. Instead, following a procedure suggested by Rossi (1989), we obtained retrospective reports from the parents of the YDS panel members about the jobs they had held during high school. Of course, such retrospective assessments may be influenced by the evaluative frames established by subsequent work conditions, nostalgic reminiscences of youth, and other biases. Still, the parents' reports are informative.

During Wave 4 of the study, when most of the adolescents were high school seniors, we surveyed the parents about their own early jobs. Instead of obtaining an entire work history, we asked the parents about their first jobs and the "longest jobs" they had held during high school. A full description of this assessment appears elsewhere (Aronson et al., 1996). Suffice it to say here that historical change in youthwork was clearly manifest in this intergenerational comparison. Change over time in young people's labor force opportunities was likewise apparent when older and younger parents were compared (pre–baby boom and baby boom parental cohorts).

Fathers, and especially the older fathers, were more likely than their sons to have been farm workers or semi-skilled workers when they were teenagers. The mothers, and particularly the older mothers, were more likely than their daughters to have done informal work in their longest jobs. Apparently informal work was not something that girls of an earlier generation did before moving quickly to more formal jobs; instead, such work more frequently continued during the high school years. The mothers were also more likely to have performed clerical work in their longest jobs.

Both daughters and sons were much more likely than their parents to have jobs in the food and restaurant industry. In fact, we find steady growth in restaurant/food work as we move from the oldest parents to the children. Only 8 percent of pre-boom fathers and 19 percent of baby boom fathers, but 48 percent of sons reported working in this industry (the corresponding percentages for mothers and daughters are 18, 27, and 32).

But despite these clear intergenerational differences in job types, comparisons of the benefits and costs of working were remarkably similar between the parents and children (Aronson et al., 1996). We do not have directly comparable measures of conditions or quality of work across generations. However, the parents gave quite favorable descriptions and evaluations of their early employment. In their estimation the advantages of employment markedly exceeded any perceived disadvantages. These data provide some indication that young people have had relatively good jobs, at least as gauged by their own reports, for a fairly long time. (For more about parents' and children's assessments of the benefits of working see Chapter 6.)

Conclusion

As young people move through high school, they become more likely to work, to work longer hours, and to receive higher wages. They move from informal work to employment in formal organizational settings. While restaurant work is quite prevalent among teenagers, older adolescents are dispersed among a wider variety of job types than their younger counterparts. With these job changes, adolescent work becomes more complex over time, involves more reading and writing, and provides increasing training and supervisory responsibilities.

The subjective experience of youthwork appears to be largely positive. Many young people find at least some opportunities for learning new things and for using their skills on the job. Most are able to be helpful to others at work. They feel they are paid well, find opportunities for advancement, and feel secure in their work. The majority do not report stress in the workplace. Most appear to be rather satisfied and committed to working. Girls perceive their work even more positively than boys, despite some objective disadvantages in terms of pay (particularly in the earlier years of the study), supervisory responsibility, and training.

The positive character of these reports is in keeping with the fact that, unlike adults, teenagers usually do not have to work to support themselves or to assist their families economically. But despite this generally positive portrayal, substantial minorities of adolescents experience stressful work conditions and do not find their jobs rewarding. Furthermore, adolescents generally perceive that their jobs interfere with their schoolwork (and increasingly so over time), but such interference does not appear to extend to family and peer involvements.

For the YDS panel, combining school and work is a near-universal experience. However, the patterning of employment is quite variable. Almost half the boys and 38 percent of the girls who work during high school do so, on average, for less than half the months under observation. But for the remainder of working adolescents, mean months of work encompasses almost all the months of observation. Greater temporal investment in work is accompanied by more opportunities for learning and advancement, as well as more demanding and stressful work experiences. Substantial evidence points to the conclusion that young people's work is, by many indicators, "good": objective measures suggest greater complexity and responsibility as youth grow older, and most adolescents, like their parents, describe their teenage jobs in favorable terms.

THE ECOLOGY OF YOUTHWORK

THE MEANING OF WORK, and the distinction between work and leisure, have been long debated (Gamst, 1995; Hall, 1969). Unlike purely expressive or consumptive behavior, work has meaning and value that extend beyond the immediate act. This does not mean that work cannot be enjoyable; but its *raison d'être* lies beyond itself. According to Hall (1994: 5), "Work is the effort or activity of an individual that is undertaken for the purpose of providing goods or services of value to others and that is considered by the individual to be work." The last part of Hall's definition indicates a subjective component; the "worklike" character of an act is not inherent in the task itself. Some tasks performed by adolescents, in school or in volunteer settings, may not be generally thought of as work, and yet from the teenagers' point of view they may be exceedingly worklike.

All persons, families, and communities depend on diverse forms of productive activity for their sustenance and well-being. Much of this activity takes place in the home and in other non-occupational contexts. Work whose purpose is to maintain the self, family members, or other intimate associates is part of the daily round for all adults, male and female. Moreover, such labor often extends well beyond the personal and family spheres. Community organizations rely heavily on contributions in the form of volunteer work; these enable the production of important public goods (Coleman, 1990). The balancing of market and nonmarket work is recognized as a critical problem for adult women in modern societies (Hochschild, 1989, 1997). Though adolescents too are involved in a complex balancing act, little attention has been given to the way they select and manage their paid work and their various forms of nonmarket work.

There is no ambiguity about the status of children's and adolescents' paid employment as "work," whether formal or informal. Their service to community organizations is also widely understood to be work, albeit without payment. And few would quarrel with so designating the chores performed by children and adults in their own homes. The status of educational activities is more ambiguous; they are located outside the economy but have a worklike compulsive character and are considered preparatory for market work.

How do these various productive experiences prepare adolescents for the diverse forms of adult work? We saw in Chapter 3 that children begin to do paid work very early in life; among those participating in the Youth Development Study, at about age 12. Even earlier, children's experiences begin to socialize them for work. Children perform chores in the family and do schoolwork. As they grow older, many do volunteer work.

As noted in the Introduction, educators and developmental psychologists have definite opinions about the relative merits of these various forms of work; the ways young people allocate their time among them are thought to be consequential for their development and attainment. Critics of paid work worry that it will divert young people from presumably more valuable activities, especially homework and extracurricular pursuits (many of which are connected to the school).

Time is a fundamental resource, parceled out among numerous social roles in modern societies. The allocation of time is to a large extent constrained, particularly for adults who must take into account their families' economic needs as well as their partners' and children's schedules. Still, time use is a matter of considerable discretion even for adults. Adolescents have more free time than adults, and greater leeway about whether to enter into various roles, some of which may be quite time-consuming, such as being a member of a sports team or a paid worker. As Shanahan and Flaherty (2001) point out, adolescents' widening social networks and increasing geographic mobility pose new opportunities for diverse uses of time, making the study of time allocation at this stage of life especially strategic. Adolescents' expanding social worlds enable them to explore potential, but not yet actualized, identities, social roles, relationships, and life options.

To be sure, adolescents, at least until age 16, are legally bound to attend school. But the ways they spend their time outside the classroom—in market and nonmarket work, in social activities, and in leisure pursuits—are probably a function of more or less rational considerations as well as a host of adventitious circumstances. Adolescents' time allocation may be linked to their long-term goals and aspirations, their developing values, their emergent self-images, immediate economic and social needs, parents' and other family members' preferences, their skills in negotiating with more powerful "significant others," friends' influences, and, of course, their own preferences.

We can now assess paid employment in the broader context of adolescent time use more generally. Do adolescents trade off one set of experiences in favor of another? Of particular interest, does paid work have opportunity costs, undermining activities that may provide greater developmental benefit? Contrary to the critics' concerns, the findings cast doubt on the conceptualization of adolescent investment in employment and other productive activities as a "zero-sum game" (Shanahan and Flaherty, 2001).

Family Work

Family work has clear analogues to paid employment. Schooler and his colleagues (1983: 243) define housework as "work that must be done to maintain a household, work that someone would have to be hired to do if family members did not do it themselves." At least minimal procurement and preparation of food, cleaning, laundry, and repairs are necessary; the amount of such work increases with the number of residents. Caring for persons is another critical component of family work. Demands on adolescents to perform chores and to care for younger siblings (as well as elderly or infirm family members) may heighten when there are few adults available to fulfill these needs.

Just like paid employment, family work may engender "adultlike" conceptions of self. Performance of household chores and other family work may be seen by the child, as well as by other family members, as moving the young person toward desired adult "possible selves," as spouse, parent, and homeowner (Markus et al., 1990; Nurius, 1991). Household work, often performed with little or no supervision, provides much opportunity to act autonomously and to be

self-directed (Schooler et al., 1983), key attributes of "adultlike" behavior in Western societies. Indeed, the capacity to take responsibility
is a quintessential part of being an adult (Arnett, 1997). Household
work may be seen as reflecting both responsibility and maturity
(McHale et al., 1990).

The long-term trend, particularly in middle-class and affluent families, has been to provide adolescents with fewer opportunities to perform household work, as family work is removed from the household
and incorporated into the market economy (Reiter, 1991). Commercial laundries, child care facilities, homes for the aged, restaurants,
and prepared foods are all part of a broad restructuring of family
work. Indeed, the increasing popularity of eating out enables children
and adolescents to replace home-based food preparation (and other
household chores) with functionally similar activities in the marketplace.

In addition to its instrumental value, housework carries symbolic
meaning, expressing membership and solidarity in the communal
household, nurturance and love for family members. As such, there
are limits on the extent to which family work can be delegated to
paid employees or to commercial establishments, even when resources make such delegation economically feasible. Substantial
amounts of work are still performed in the family context, mainly by
adult women (Spain and Bianchi, 1996).

Zelizer (1985) showed that in the twentieth century, as children
became "sentimentalized," child work could no longer be justified by
its instrumental or productive value, and concerns arose about its potentially exploitative character, especially in circumstances that
heightened the need for children's labor. Children's labor in the home
can be imperative when the mother is employed full time, when one
or both parents are absent, under conditions of poverty, or in the
presence of chronic illness or disability of a family member. In rural
areas, farm work is difficult to separate from household chores; the
economic value of children's help remains highly salient in contemporary farm families (Committee, 1998).

With greater sensitivity to potential exploitation, "good" and
"bad" household work came to be distinguished by its purpose.
"Bad" housework was performed to benefit the family, without consideration for the child's welfare. Critics were particularly concerned

about children who had to stay home from school to take care of sib-lings and perform other household chores. "Good" housework had educational value or was intrinsically enjoyable. It built the child's character and promoted family solidarity. If the benefits of house-work rose with the amount of such work performed, there would be little reason to worry about "excessive" household work. But large amounts of such work were thought to preclude other experiences conducive to healthy development. Thus the same kinds of concerns that surrounded the paid employment of minors came to be applied to household work as well.

Despite the decreasing need for household labor and the continu-ing "sentimentalization" of children, adolescents are still called upon to perform chores in their homes. Divergent rationales for this family work continue to be expressed to this day (see Mortimer, Dennehy, et al., 1994). Many contemporary parents provide an allowance in return for such work (Miller and Yung, 1990). The payment of an al-lowance might be considered a form of recognition of the value of housework, or an incentive for the child to do the work. This early, prototypical economic transaction might be seen as acknowledging the benefit of children's work to the family. In contrast, some parents believe that children should not be paid for doing household chores, as payment undermines the symbolic meaning of this activity as sup-portive of the family. Household work is still justified on the grounds that it reinforces children's identity as family members, enhances their sense of responsibility, and prepares them to function effectively in their future households.

The symbolic connotation of family work makes it inextricably tied to gender roles. Women traditionally nurture children and take responsibility for the smooth functioning of their households. Despite the increase in married women's employment in recent decades, and husbands' greater contributions to family work, wives continue to do much more household work than their spouses (Spain and Bianchi, 1996).

Prior studies have shown that girls likewise invest more of their time in household labor than boys (McHale et al., 1990). Adolescent girls' involvement in household chores is thought to be valuable prep-aration for their adult "possible selves" as wives, mothers, and home-makers. Nonetheless, girls' aspirations for educational and occupational achievement now equal or surpass those of boys (Johnson and Mortimer, 2000). These aspirations may make household work less attractive as a means of anticipating a desired possible self.

It is thus pertinent to consider whether the gender-stereotyped, and markedly unequal, division of household labor in adulthood is preceded by contemporary adolescents' work in the home. Is there evidence from the Youth Development Study that household tasks are becoming less gender-specific?

The YDS assessed ten common tasks that are often allocated to adolescents as chores, for example, cooking, shopping, cleaning, and yardwork. We also asked adolescents how much time they spend caring for younger children and elderly relatives. We found that household chores are nearly universal; almost all YDS participants reported doing some household work each year. As shown in Figure 4.1, of the ninth graders who did housework, boys were averaging about 16 hours per week, girls about 17.

As might be expected from adolescents' growing involvement outside the family, participation in housework declines between ninth and tenth grades for both genders. Between tenth and twelfth grades, however, boys spend decreasing amounts of time doing household work, to a low of only about 9 hours in senior year, while girls' housework plateaus at about 14 hours per week after tenth grade and remains at this level through the remainder of high school.

In addition to this gross inequality in time spent on housework, there is a striking degree of sex-typing in the kinds of chores performed. YDS girls spend significantly more time than boys doing traditionally "female" tasks: cleaning, cooking, doing dishes and laundry, and shopping for groceries (Call, 1996). Boys, meanwhile, perform stereotypically male tasks, such as taking out the trash and doing yardwork. Like adult women, girls do chores that are both more time-consuming and more frequent than those done by their male counterparts.

In fact, boys report spending exceedingly little time even on "male" tasks (Call, 1996a; Gager et al., 1999). For example, in twelfth grade, boys reported spending approximately 20 minutes per week taking out the trash and an hour doing yardwork. In contrast, girls spent six hours per week on their "female" tasks, including laundry, washing dishes, grocery shopping, and cleaning (not count-

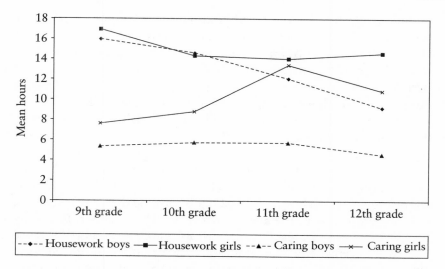

Figure 4.1. Time spent per week on caring activities and household chores, by gender and grade.

ing the hour per week spent cleaning their own rooms, which did not significantly differ by gender).

Adolescents are less likely to care for others than to do these non-personal forms of household work. Whereas chores were nearly universal, only 51 percent of the ninth-grade girls and 43 percent of the boys cared for other family members, and participation declined over the years for both genders. In the senior year, less than a third of the girls and only a quarter of the boys reported this responsibility. Most of the adolescents' caring activities were directed to younger siblings; less than 10 percent of adolescents each year reported caring for older relatives.

Girls were more likely than boys to report caring tasks; those who did so also spent more time engaged in such activity. As shown in Figure 4.1, girls caring increased from an average of 8.8 hours in tenth grade to 13.4 hours in eleventh grade, while throughout high school boys' caring was below 6 hours. Whereas girls' caring activity declined between eleventh and twelfth grades, the gender differential remained large.

Thus the gap between girls' and boys' family labor widens considerably as they move through middle adolescence (Figure 4.1). It is not possible with the data at hand to know whether girls willingly embrace their family work for its congruence with their future "possible selves," or whether, to the contrary, the expectations of parents, and perhaps brothers, pressure girls to persist in their sex-typed tasks. Parents may see boys' growing involvements outside the family—in sports, employment, and even social activities with peers—as more deserving of encouragement, and as better reasons to be excused from chores, than those of girls.

Some limited evidence about such attitudes derives from the parents' surveys. Parents, on average, believed that both boys and girls should be able to have their first paid jobs outside the home at age 12, which corresponds to the average age at which the children actually began to work. But some findings indicated greater support for boys' paid work. Consistent with traditional gender orientations, as boys took on more challenging jobs (jobs that provided greater opportunity to learn skills that would be useful in future employment), they reported feeling closer to their fathers. No such positive effect of work on family relationships was evident for girls. In fact, there was some indication that girls' relationships with their fathers became less close as they worked longer hours. No such change in the quality of relationship to either parent was reported as boys increased their hours of work (Mortimer and Shanahan, 1994).

In sum, the YDS shows that youth do considerable amounts of household labor, and that this labor becomes increasingly sex-typed through the adolescent years. Despite shifts in adult gender roles and related ideologies, boys and girls are being prepared for their adult family lives in remarkably traditional ways.

School Work

Children have their first experiences of work in a formal organizational setting when they go to school. The most salient function of education is to socialize young people for the adult occupational role. In contemporary terms, it is to enhance human capital, increasing productivity as a future worker. This purpose extends the meaning of education well beyond itself, and makes it similar to worklike activities in other settings.

Some, however, might dispute the characterization of educational experiences as work. When an adolescent is fully engrossed in school-work, as in a creative writing or science project, the tasks may be experienced as more like leisure than like work. At its best, education expands the student's horizons in ways that enrich the quality of life in both present and future. But few youth would describe most of their schoolwork in such salutary terms. In fact, when asked to record their emotions in various settings at the sound of a beeper, adolescents are more likely to report boredom, anxiety, and other negative emotions at school than elsewhere (Larson and Richards, 1994). Similarly, Csikszentmihalyi and Larson (1984) found that adolescents manifested significantly less intrinsic motivation when attending class than when socializing with peers. And when Brown and Theobald (1998) asked high school students "What's the best thing about school?" the replies more often referred to friendships ("being with my friends," "spending time with my boyfriend") than to academics. Consistent with these orientations, American youth spend relatively little time doing homework.

Extracurricular activities lack the obligatory character of class attendance and homework. Instead, students engage in them as a consequence of their own intrinsic motivation, and generally report that they are enjoyable (Csikszentmihalyi and Larson, 1984). The vast majority of high school students participate in organized extracurricular programs, such as athletic teams, interest clubs, and the performing arts; substantial proportions report more than one such activity (Brown and Theobald, 1998).

Extracurricular involvement is often depicted as more strongly linked to the peer culture than to the academic administration. At worst, it is thought to distract youth from the serious business of learning. Since Coleman's now classic *Adolescent Society* (1961), sociologists of education have lamented the press of American peer culture away from academic involvement.

But participation in extracurricular activity may be considered educational in the broadest sense—as preparatory for adulthood, including the adult occupational role. Csikszentmihalyi and Schmidt (1998) warn that because sports and other components of the extracurriculum are so much fun they are apt to be "trivialized" as having little to do with future life prospects. But advocates of extracurricular activities believe they provide experiences that enhance citizenship, moral character, and mental discipline, and contribute to young people's social development, interpersonal skills, and ability to cooperate with others.

Moreover, participation in extracurricular activities is widely viewed as indicative, even productive, of a "well-rounded" person with diverse interests and capacities. Extracurricular activities are thought to serve as an antidote to excessive focus on any single interest. Many adolescents themselves recognize that extracurricular pursuits may help them demonstrate to college admissions officers that they have many-faceted interests and abilities. Parents take great pride in their children's athletic, artistic, and other achievements.

Extracurricular activities can engender diverse forms of "social capital," expanding a youth's social network beyond the family and neighborhood in ways that foster socioeconomic attainment (Granovetter, 1974; Furstenberg et al., 1999). Insofar as such activities promote appreciation of the cultural heritage of the performing arts and literature, they enhance "cultural capital," which also may later engender social and economic advantages (Bourdieu, 1977). Thus it would not be difficult to make a case that extracurricular activities have value beyond themselves, and surely greater value than unstructured leisure pursuits, such as watching television, surfing the Internet, or hanging out with friends. Teenagers spend a substantial amount of time watching television; this and other passive activities (computer and video games) are often invoked in commentaries about American young people's low achievement in science and mathematics compared with their peers in other nations (see, e.g., Bronfenbrenner et al., 1996).

With respect to the distinction between work and leisure, extracurricular experiences might be placed in a gray area, containing elements of both. Many contemporary educators attach high value to these activities, considering them "different from—and in many respects superior to—the learning objectives and processes that routinely occur in academic classrooms" (Brown and Theobald, 1998: 115). They sometimes lament students' decreasing participation, brought on by fiscal constraints (Csikszentmihalyi and Schmidt, 1998) or declining student interest. They also worry that teenagers who do paid work will have to restrict their extracurricular involvement.

The YDS inquired about how much time the adolescents spent on homework and on extracurricular activities ("like clubs, band, and sports"). The vast majority claim that they do at least some home-work—more than 90 percent of girls in any year and 80 percent or more of the boys. On the average, between 7 and 10 hours are de-voted to homework each week, which is greater than the national av-erage (Committee, 1998). Though girls appear to spend more hours doing homework, the gender difference is statistically significant only in eleventh grade.

About three out of four adolescents participate in extracurricular activities in ninth grade. While boys' participation remains roughly constant, girls' participation decreases, to only 59 percent, by twelfth grade. Adolescents who take part in these activities do so about 9–12 hours per week, with boys devoting more time to them than girls.

Fears that working draws adolescents away from school are based on the assumption that employed youth will find the workplace a more rewarding and engaging context. The greater opportunity for autonomous action in the work setting is congruent with adolescents' increasing need for self-determination. As Eccles and her colleagues (1996: 277) point out in describing the earlier transition from ele-mentary to junior high school, "the perceived match between the ad-olescents' increasing desire for self-control and the opportunities for self-control is likely to decrease if the opportunities for self-control do not increase at the same rate as the young adolescents' desire for autonomy and more democratic participation in decision making."

It is thus informative to compare working and nonworking adoles-cents' characterizations of school. Do working youth in fact have less favorable perceptions of school than nonworking youth? Twelve variables were chosen—indicating the intrinsic attraction of school, the value of schooling, stressors in the school setting, social support, autonomy, and others. Remarkably, we found virtually no associa-tion between such descriptors of the school and the adolescent's work status. That is, youth appear to evaluate their school experience simi-larly, whether employed or not. In the entire panel, of 96 compari-sons (12 variables × 2 groups [working and not] × 4 years), just 8 are statistically significant, and even these indicate no consistent trend. Similar, mainly null findings occurred for boys and girls. It seems that, for the most part, working youth do not differ from non-working youth in their assessments of the intrinsic merit, the stress-ors, or the opportunities for autonomous action in school.

It is also pertinent to compare young people's characterizations of

Table 4.1. Perceptions of school and work experiences (workers only)

School	Work	Grade 9 School	Grade 9 Work	Grade 10 School	Grade 10 Work	Grade 11 School	Grade 11 Work	Grade 12 School	Grade 12 Work
School has a special meaning to me[a]	Most of my interests are centered around my job	2.89***	1.91	2.93***	1.87	2.99***	1.80	2.98***	1.78
	I am very much involved personally in my job	2.89***	2.52	2.93***	2.45	3.00***	2.35	2.98***	2.29
School helps me to improve my ability to think and to solve problems[a]	I have to think of new ways of doing things on my job	3.18***	2.17	3.09***	2.01	3.00***	2.03	3.00***	1.96
Teachers listen	Supervisor listens	3.29***	2.89	3.39***	2.86	3.44***	2.97	3.46***	2.98
Free to disagree with teachers	Free to disagree with supervisor	3.06**	2.88	3.06**	2.90	3.17***	2.95	3.19***	3.01
Teachers explain why I should do something	Supervisor discusses work	2.03***	1.79	1.91*	1.79	1.91	1.85	1.93	1.87
Freedom to choose own assignments	Freedom to make decisions	2.65	2.69	2.65***	2.33	2.68***	2.15	2.78***	2.12
Schoolwork is repetitive	Work is repetitive	1.60***	2.25	1.75***	2.29	1.85***	2.30	1.77***	2.28
Schoolwork is predictable	Work is predictable	2.59***	2.76	2.64***	2.84	2.77*	2.86	2.87	2.90
Time drags in school[a]	I feel bored at work	3.18***	2.91	3.19***	2.95	3.27***	2.99	3.21**	3.10
Time pressure when doing schoolwork	Time pressure on job	3.04***	2.43	3.06***	2.63	3.19***	2.83	3.13***	2.91

*p < .05; **p < .01; ***p < .001.
a. Items in the Intrinsic Motivation Toward School Scale.

their experiences in work and school settings. Of course, we can assess both only for adolescents who are employed. If employment is perceived as a more favorable environment than school, providing greater opportunity to take responsibility, act autonomously, and receive social support, it may pull youth away from school. However, we find no support for this expectation. Though differences in question wording across school and work settings diminish strict comparability, we find that working youth characterize the school environment in *more* favorable terms than the working environment. This is the case for the total panel (see Table 4.1), for boys, and for girls. (Since response scales across items differ, comparisons should not be made across these experiences.)

For example, each year employed adolescents were more likely to agree with the statement "School has a special meaning to me" than with "Most of my interests are centered around my job" or "I am very much involved personally in my job." They also more frequently endorsed "School helps me to improve my ability to think and to solve problems" than "I have to think of new ways of doing things on my job."

The adolescents were more likely to say their teachers were willing to listen to their problems and help find solutions than to say the same about their supervisors. Likewise, youth felt freer to disagree with their teachers than with their supervisors. Employed adolescents more frequently reported that their teachers explained why they should do something than that their supervisors discussed their job assignments with them (significantly so in the first two years). They were also more likely (in three of the four years) to say that they chose their own assignments at school than that they were free to make decisions at work. Schoolwork is consistently described as less repetitive and less predictable than paid work tasks. Thus in many respects the employed adolescents report more favorable, enriched, and supportive environments at school than at work.

In only two respects was work described more favorably than school: the adolescents reported that they felt more time pressure when doing schoolwork than when working on their jobs, and they reported more boredom in school than at work. These patterns are consistent with earlier reports of low levels of psychological engagement and satisfaction in school (Larson and Richards, 1994).

In sum, assessing homework and extracurricular activities in tandem reveals high involvement in the educational setting throughout the years of high school. There is no indication that school is perceived more negatively by employed adolescents than by those who are not working, or that working adolescents see school as a less favorable context than the job environment. All told, there is little evidence from the YDS that working is associated with disengagement from school. To the contrary, employed youth perceive school to be more meaningful, more promotive of problem-solving ability, and more likely to involve independent decisionmaking than the workplace.

Volunteer Work

The declining civic involvement of adult Americans has been much lamented (Putnam, 1995, 1996), despite continued high rates of volunteering and philanthropic giving (Curtis, Grabb, and Baer, 1992). Young people's civic interest is also thought to be declining. Their lack of interest in elections and voting might be manifestations of a growing self-centeredness and individualism. If so, one might expect adolescent participation in volunteer work to be unusual. However, because most research on volunteering has focused on adults (for a review, see Johnson et al., 1998), much less is known about adolescents' civic involvement.

As in the case of paid work, the proportion of youth who are registered as volunteers is dependent on the time span under consideration, and this varies widely across surveys. Still, the available evidence suggests that adolescent volunteering is prevalent. A national 1991 Gallup poll reported that 60 percent of teenagers had devoted some time to volunteering during the previous year (Raskoff and Sundeen, 1994). In 1995, 72 percent of high school seniors in the nationally representative Monitoring the Future study participated in community affairs or volunteer work at least a few times a year (Oesterle et al., 1998). Approximately 22 percent of ninth and twelfth graders in Minnesota did 1–5 hours of volunteer work in a typical week (Minnesota Department of Education, 1992).

Volunteering is often thought to offer youth many of the same benefits as paid work, such as the opportunity to interact with adult role models, to take responsibility for their work, and to help others, without the disadvantages of market work. Moreover, volunteering is sometimes alleged to be superior to paid employment because both the tasks that are assigned to volunteers and the environments in which they do them are more diverse than in typical "youth jobs."

As we saw in Chapter 3, young people are quite concentrated in particular occupations in a restricted range of settings (especially restaurants and retail stores). In contrast, a wide variety of community organizations seek volunteers. Volunteering may enable youth to gain entry to productive roles in settings that would not be available to them as paid workers, such as schools, hospitals, government agencies, and sometimes even corporations. As a volunteer, adolescents can interact with employed adults in highly diverse occupational and organizational environments, and can learn about what it would be like to enter the same occupations themselves. Volunteer work can, like much paid work, also provide opportunities for youth to relate to persons whose social backgrounds are different from their own, fostering the development of empathy and social skills.

From the perspective of the critics of paid "youthwork," a key advantage of volunteering is that it neither derives from nor reinforces economic motivations. Youth seek jobs to gain money for a variety of goals, including immediate spending. Paid work, by enhancing purchasing power, is sometimes thought to engender a materialistic orientation (Greenberger and Steinberg, 1986). That is, because of their actual or perceived economic needs, young people will be motivated to take paid, but not volunteer, jobs that provide little intrinsic reward or educational benefit. We saw in Chapter 3 that youth describe their paid jobs in quite favorable terms. But because the range of work environments from which they can choose is rather limited, especially in the early high school years, they cannot be too choosy about the type of work they accept. It is assumed that the quality of volunteer jobs must be better than that of paid jobs to offset the lack of monetary return.

Furthermore, the motivation to help others in need is thought to be a primary motivation for volunteering. But given the wide range of environments that are available for youth to express this motivation, many considerations may come into play in the choice of a particular volunteer work setting. The young person looking for volunteer work might plausibly be expected to choose the environment perceived as offering the more intrinsically rewarding experiences, learning opportunities, scheduling flexibility, and other benefits. But even if volunteer work were not intrinsically rewarding or educationally valuable, it makes salient altruistic motives for working, and is believed, through the very process of serving others, to enhance the same motives.

Each year in high school, we asked the adolescents, "Do you currently do any volunteer work (without pay)?" If they answered affirmatively, they were asked how many hours they spent volunteering, and to describe their main volunteer activity. About 13–19 percent of the YDS respondents reported that they were doing at least some volunteer work each year at the time of the data collection; more than 40 percent reported such contemporaneous activity at least once during high school. Thus a substantial minority of youth volunteer. Undoubtedly even more students would be registered as volunteers if the entire year were the unit of observation. Though one might expect that girls' greater nurturance, or interest in helping others (Marini et al., 1996), would make them more likely to volunteer than boys, there were no gender differences in the frequency of volunteering.

Those who did volunteer contributed about 4–5 hours, on the average, each week. The vast majority of the volunteers (between two-thirds and four-fifths of the boys and girls, across years) contributed between 1 and 5 hours per week. Less than a fourth contributed as much as 6–10 hours. National (Fuji Survey, 1992) and statewide (Minnesota Department of Education, 1992) estimates of teenagers' time spent volunteering are quite similar. Thus, although a substantial minority of young people do volunteer work, it does not absorb very much of their time.

Information about volunteer organizations and activities enabled Uggen and Janikula (1999) to code the YDS panel's volunteer experiences into five modes: secular-civic, religious, informal neighboring, private business, and partisan-political. They also plotted change in the prevalence of these volunteer placements over time. Secular-civic volunteering was the most prevalent each year and showed some growth over time. This category of volunteers stocked food shelves, visited the elderly in hospitals or nursing homes, and assisted in other civic organizations. Religious activities tended to be the next most frequent, for example teaching Sunday school or providing child care during religious services.

The category of informal neighboring subsumed tasks that sometimes take the form of informal paid work; however, these were unpaid neighborly activities, such as shoveling sidewalks, raking leaves, or walking neighbors' dogs. Just like informal paid work (as shown in Chapter 3), such activities declined markedly between ninth and tenth grades. Private business volunteers were those who donated their services for activities that would ordinarily be paid, such as answering phones at a pizza place. (Such youth may have hoped that this involvement would eventually yield paid jobs.) Partisan-political volunteering was directed to the policy arena, such as writing letters for Amnesty International or participating in a Gulf War Crisis Hotline. The last two types of volunteering were very rare among ninth graders but showed some increase over time.

It is evident that volunteering allows a sizeable minority of youth to gain entry to a host of organizations and activities. Because the young people devote relatively little time to volunteer work, it might be considered a rather undemanding way of getting acquainted with work in a variety of settings.

A Typology of Time Use

Much of the commentary and controversy about youth employment rests on a largely untested assumption: that work competes for teenagers' time with more beneficial activities. Time allocation is seen as a series of tradeoffs and accommodations to an essentially limited supply, which takes the form of a zero-sum game. Thus educators worry that as teenagers work more hours they will have trouble getting to school on time or receiving help from teachers after school; they will spend less time doing homework; they will withdraw from extracurricular activities; and they will not have time to do volunteer work. Is there evidence that working does "squeeze out" these alternative activities? Having examined investment in each type of productive activity in turn, let us now compare them to one another.

Figure 4.2 presents the mean amount of time spent on each of five activities: paid work, family work, homework, extracurricular activity, and volunteering, by grade. (This figure does not include panel members who do not participate in a given activity.) In the aggregate, as paid work rises, only time spent doing family labor falls markedly. Thus there appears to be some tradeoff between employment and family work. In ninth grade, youth spend more time on chores and

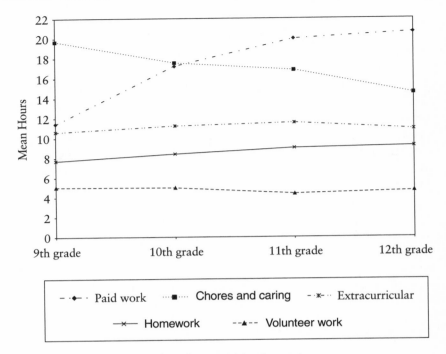

Figure 4.2. Time spent per week in activities, by grade.

caring activities than on paid work. The absolute magnitude of time spent in the other activities, and their ordering vis-à-vis one another, remains relatively constant: extracurricular activities, followed by homework, and then by volunteer work.

But these aggregate data do not speak to the relationships of these activities to one another at the individual level. Does participation in some activities rule out involvement in others altogether? Such a tradeoff could take a variety of plausible forms. Working teens might be permitted to give up, or substantially reduce, their household chores (Manning, 1990). Or they might stop participating in sports or other extracurricular activities, or in volunteer work.

Table 4.2 shows eleventh-grade participation, by work status, in family work, homework, extracurricular activities, and volunteering. Workers and nonworkers are highly similar with respect to these involvements: most youth perform family work and homework, and most do not volunteer, irrespective of their work status. About two-

Table 4.2. Percentage participating in activities, grade 11

Employment	Family work				Homework				Extracurricular activity				Volunteering			
	Yes	No	Row %	Row N	Yes	No	Row %	Row N	Yes	No	Row %	Row N	Yes	No	Row %	Row N
Yes	98.7	1.3	58.2	552	90.4	9.6	59.6	530	67.2	32.8	59.7	528	16.5	83.5	58.2	553
No	98.5	1.5	41.8	397	86.1	13.9	40.4	360	67.8	32.2	40.3	357	12.6	87.4	41.8	397
Column %	98.5	1.4	100.0		88.7	11.3	100.0		67.5	32.5	100.0		14.8	85.2	100.0	
Column N	936	13	949		789	101	890		597	288	885		141	809	950	
	$\chi^2 = .10$ (1 df)				$\chi^2 = 3.88^*$ (1 df)				$\chi^2 = .03$ (1 df)				$\chi^2 = 2.73^\#$ (1 df)			

$^\# p < .10; \ ^* p < .05.$

Note: Row percentages and counts differ across the activities because of missing data on the employment and activity variables.

thirds of both working and nonworking students participate in extra-curricular activities. Contrary to the "squeezing out" hypothesis, those who are employed are slightly more likely to report doing homework than those who are not.

But these cross-tabulations do not bear directly on the degree of investment. Especially when participation is mandatory (or highly encouraged by parents and teachers), the impact of one activity on another may manifest itself more in the amounts of time devoted to each. Gager and her colleagues (1999) report that in the Wave 4 of the YDS, the more time teens spent in paid work, the less time they spent doing household chores. Alternatively, participation in one activity may be conducive to participation in another: for example, in the same study, boys who did more household work were also found to perform more volunteer work. These analyses included both youth who engaged in a given activity and those who did not, so the associations reflect participation as well as level of investment. Table 4.2 shows that many youth do not participate at all in certain domains. Alternatively, if only those who participate in given pairs of experiences (such as volunteer work and housework) were to be examined, the resulting correlations might be based on quite limited numbers of cases.

More revealing is a "person-centered" analysis, enabling identification of common patterns of time use at the individual level. Indeed, the full implications of any given activity may only be fully understood when it is known how that activity fits into the adolescent's complete daily round. For example, for one young person, a substantial amount of paid work could be indicative of a restricted life style. However, another youth who worked a lot of hours might lessen the amount of time in solitary leisure activities (i.e., television and other forms of media use) and "hanging out" with friends, so as to enable participation in sports and other social activities. Identifying persons who exhibit distinct patterns of activities demonstrates variability in the ways paid work intersects with other domains in young people's lives.

Shanahan and Flaherty (2001) performed such an individual-level cluster analysis of patterns of time use by the YDS panel, including the "productive work" variables described in this chapter as well as the amount of time the adolescents spent with their friends. Time with friends was measured not in hours but in number of afternoons and evenings spent with friends during a typical week (zero to ten) and amount of time spent with friends during the weekend (none to all the time). A rough indicator of time with each parent was also included.[1]

Table 4.3 shows the emergent classes of time use for each year, arranged from left to right in order of frequency. The numbers under each class indicate the amount of time spent in employment, doing homework, in extracurricular activities, with friends, doing chores, and with the mother. For each activity, the first number is the median level of participation for persons in the category, and the numbers in parentheses indicate the range about the median in which half the cases fall (semi-interquartile range). (Since time spent doing volunteer work and time spent with father did not differentiate the classes, these variables are not included in the table.)

Each year, two highly prevalent groups are labeled "active"— youth in the active workers class are employed; those in the active nonworkers class are not. It is evident from Table 4.3 that the majority of teenagers, each year, are quite heavily involved in a variety of domains. For example, in ninth grade, students in these two "active" categories spend about as much time as, or more time than, those in other categories doing homework and chores. (They also do volunteer work, not shown in the table.) In ninth and tenth grades, the active youth spend less time than those in the "high leisure" group on extracurricular activities and with friends.

The one mode of time use that separates the two "active" clusters is employment: the active workers' median work time increases from 9 hours per week in ninth grade to 19.5 hours in twelfth grade; the "active nonworkers" are not employed at all. And yet each year the active workers' profile, despite the substantial time invested in paid work, is almost identical in all other respects to the active nonworkers' profile. Apparently, being employed does not prevent the active workers from participating in other productive activities at levels commensurate with their nonemployed peers.

The situation is quite similar across grade levels—the two "active" categories, taken together, comprise 54–64 percent of the youth in any given year. Thus Shanahan and Flaherty find that the majority of YDS youth conform to the American ideal of "well-roundedness." They are involved in a variety of activities, including those widely considered to be the most productive uses of time, whether they are

Table 4.3. Adolescent time use classes, grades 9–12 (median, semi-interquartile range reported)

Wave 1, grade 9

	Active workers	Active non-workers	Work No extra	No work No extra	High leisure	Low engagement
Job hours	9 (5, 15)	0 (0, 0)	10 (5, 18.25)	0 (0, 0)	0 (0, 0)	0 (0, 0)
Homework	2.5 (1.5, 4)	2.5 (1.5, 4)	2 (1, 3.5)	1 (0, 2.4)	0 (0, .1)	2.1 (.8, 5.1)
Extracurricular	8 (4, 14)	7 (4, 12)	0 (0, 0)	0 (0, 0)	14 (5.5, 24)	0 (0, 2)
Friend time	8 (6, 10)	8 (5.5, 10)	8 (6, 11)	9 (7, 12)	10 (8, 11)	1 (0, 1)
Chores	16 (9.3, 27.8)	14.7 (9, 23.5)	15 (6.8, 24)	12 (7, 21.1)	12 (7, 19.9)	14 (5.4, 21.6)
Mother	2 (2, 3)	3 (2, 3)	3 (2, 3)	3 (2, 4)	3 (2, 3)	3 (3, 3)
N / %	360 / 36.0	275 / 27.5	138 / 13.8	124 / 12.4	57 / 5.7	45 / 4.5

Wave 2, grade 10

	Active non-workers	Active workers	No work No extra	Work No extra	Work No homework	High leisure	Productive
Job hours	0 (0, 0)	14 (8, 20)	0 (0, 0)	17 (15, 20)	20 (15, 25.6)	0 (0, 0)	35 (25, 39.3)
Homework	3 (2, 5)	3 (2, 4.8)	1 (0, 2.1)	2.3 (1.5, 3.5)	0 (0, 0)	0 (0, 0)	8.3 (5.6, 9.9)
Extracurricular	9 (5, 15)	9.5 (4, 15)	0 (0, 0)	0 (0, 0)	1 (0, 8)	15 (10, 25)	0 (0, 0)
Friend time	8 (5, 10)	7 (5, 9)	9 (5, 12)	8 (6, 10)	10 (6, 13)	10.5 (8.3, 12)	3 (0, 5.3)
Chores	12 (6.7, 19.5)	11.7 (6.4, 21.6)	11.4 (5.7, 21.1)	11.6 (5.5, 22.1)	6.4 (3, 12.3)	13.2 (9.2, 25)	22 (17.6, 30.3)
Mother	2 (2, 3)	2 (2, 3)	3 (2, 3)	3 (2, 3)	3 (2, 3)	2.5 (2, 3)	2 (1, 3)
N / %	317 / 32.5	256 / 26.3	146 / 15.0	115 / 11.8	64 / 6.5	58 / 6.0	9 / 0.9

Wave 3, grade 11

	Active workers	Active non-workers	No work No extra	Work No extra	Work No homework	Work full-time	Chores
Job hours	17 (12, 25)	0 (0, 0)	0 (0, 0)	20 (15, 21.1)	21 (17.6, 27.4)	40 (24.5, 33.8)	0 (0, 0)
Homework	4 (2.5, 5.9)	3.4 (1.5, 3.9)	1 (0, 3)	2 (.5, 3.6)	0 (0, .5)	0 (0, 0)	3 (1.1, 5.3)
Extracurricular	10 (5, 16.4)	10 (6, 17)	0 (0, 0)	0 (0, 0)	9 (4, 15)	0 (0, 0)	0 (0, 0)
Friend time	7 (5, 10)	8 (5, 10.3)	9 (6, 11)	8 (5, 10.5)	9 (7, 12)	7 (3.5, 12)	0 (0, 1)
Chores	9.3 (5.8, 16.4)	10.3 (6.2, 18.7)	10.8 (6.1, 21.9)	9.5 (5, 16.9)	6.3 (3.4, 12.3)	12 (6.6, 26.4)	13.3 (7, 23.3)
Mother	2 (2, 3)	2 (2, 3)	3 (2, 3)	2 (2, 3)	3 (2, 3)	2 (2, 3)	3 (2, 4)
N / %	294 / 30.8	232 / 24.3	175 / 18.3	171 / 17.9	41 / 4.3	23 / 2.4	20 / 2.0

Wave 4, grade 12

	Active workers	Work No extra	Active non-workers	No work No extra	Chores	Work full-time	Low engagement
Job hours	19.5 (14.1, 24)	20 (16, 21.7)	0 (0, 0)	0 (0, 0)	0 (0, 0)	36.5 (25, 40)	0 (0, 3)
Homework	3 (1.8, 6)	2 (1, 3.5)	3 (1.4, 5.1)	1.5 (0, 2.5)	NA	0 (0, 0)	1.5 (1, 2.4)
Extracurricular	10 (5, 15)	0 (0, 0)	10 (5.8, 15)	0 (0, 0)	NA	NA	.5 (0, 2)
Friend time	8 (5, 10)	8 (6, 10)	8 (6, 10)	9 (6, 12.5)	9 (6, 12.5)	6 (3, 10.75)	0 (0, 1)
Chores	7.7 (4.3, 13.3)	8.8 (4.5, 11.7)	9.4 (5, 18.9)	14.2 (5.4, 15.5)	15 (8, 32.7)	10.7 (6, 19.3)	10 (4.5, 24.8)
Mother	2 (2, 3)	2 (2, 3)	2 (2, 3)	3 (2, 3)	2 (1, 3)	2 (2, 3)	2 (2, 3)
N / %	322 / 34.5	201 / 21.6	183 / 19.6	111 / 12.0	48 / 5.2	46 / 4.9	21 / 2.2

Source: Shanahan and Flaherty (2001: 391). Reprinted with permission.

working at paid jobs or not. In fact, in eleventh grade, the active workers actually spend *more* time on homework than do the active nonworkers.[2]

The YDS data provide no information about solitary leisure activities. Adolescents spend considerable time watching television, listening to music, playing computer games, and so on. Such activities are often more passive than purposive, enabling relaxation and "winding down." Schoenhals and his colleagues (1998) present evidence from the National Education Longitudinal Survey that when young people are employed these other pastimes may be displaced. Among the NELS tenth-grade participants, as hours of work increased, the amount of time spent watching television diminished. Working longer hours, however, did not reduce the time spent doing homework or reading outside of class.

The fact that the active workers and the active nonworkers in Shanahan and Flaherty's typology spent roughly equivalent amounts of time doing homework is quite consistent with Schoenhals and his colleagues' findings. Taken together, these studies suggest that most youth "make time" for work and for the other productive activities that are important to them by reducing the time they spend on more passive activities.

Consistent with the survey findings, the YDS young adult interviewees rarely noted difficulties in scheduling the many activities that interested them. As one young woman put it:

> I don't think I had a hard time balancing things . . . it was a set schedule. Like I had school during the day, after-school activities in the afternoon, and then work was weekends during the day and then weekend evenings would be with-a-friend time. So it was just so scheduled that I don't think I ever really had a balancing problem. And then during finals or crucial moments I would have the weekends off, so again, one of the important things was . . . for me to be able to just shift my schedule whatever way I needed to, so I didn't have a problem with balancing at all.

When asked about how he had balanced work and other activities during high school, a respondent in his mid-twenties replied:

Work was always to pay for things I wanted to do, extracurricular. I never *had* to have the job and that's always the way I looked at it. If there was something I wanted to do I'd hey, I need this [time] off. I need to do this now. If you don't want to do it, you don't want to give me . . . we need to reevaluate things. And they usually understood that, and I put in enough time that when I asked for something off they usually didn't have a problem doing it.

One female respondent had scheduled other activities, including work, around her high school theater group:

My mom put theater first and I always did, and so there were a lot of times if I had to work, but I had a major test coming up and I had lines to study all at once, I'd call in sick to work . . . and I might do that for a whole week. Just so I could get caught up and get my mind adjusted . . . There was one job I ended up getting fired from and I was like, "Oh, well, I didn't need it anyway, I'm just a teenager."

Shanahan and Flaherty's cluster analysis illustrates the diversity in patterns of time use, even among employed adolescents. That is, not all adolescents who hold jobs exhibit the "well-rounded" profile of the active clusters. A minority of employed adolescents participate little in the social/recreational life of the school. Each year a category emerges (labeled "work, no extra") of employed youth who do not engage in extracurricular activities. These youth, constituting 12–22 percent of the panel, focus on paid work, chores, and socializing with friends; they spend about the same amount of time doing homework as most other students. Though they spend about the same amount of time on paid work as the active workers, they forgo extracurricular activities entirely.

By tenth grade a small cluster of youth (6.5 percent of the sample) is found who are employed but spend no time doing homework; 4.3 percent of the eleventh graders exhibit this pattern. By eleventh and twelfth grades 2.4 and 5 percent of the youth, respectively, work full time, do no homework, and do not spend time in extracurricular activities. Most youth in this small cluster have withdrawn from school.

Shanahan and Flaherty's findings also demonstrate that teens who do not have paid jobs do not necessarily use their time in more "productive" ways. Each year 12–18 percent of the youth fall in a category labeled "no work, no extra." Even though they do not have to juggle a job with school, these youth do not participate in extracurricular activities, and they spend less time on homework than the active workers. About 6 percent of ninth and tenth graders, labeled "high leisure," are not employed, do little homework, and instead spend their time in extracurricular activities and with friends. A "low engagement" pattern, evident in ninth and twelfth grades, comprises 4.5 and 2.2 percent of the youth, respectively. This socially isolated pattern involves little or no market work, no extracurricular activities, and relatively little time with friends.

As we have seen, employment does not necessarily squeeze out the productive activities of homework, extracurricular involvements, and family work. Indeed, the vast majority of employed youth do not sacrifice these activities. Conversely, the absence of employment does not necessarily imply high involvement in productive and other beneficial pursuits. These findings should lay to rest the contention that paid work prevents adolescents from engaging in other salutary behaviors.

Shanahan and Flaherty also investigate the stability of patterns of time use, by examining the likelihood of adolescents remaining in a cluster from one year to the next, and by assessing the extent of movement between clusters. Substantial stability is revealed. For example, of youth categorized as "active workers" in Wave 1, 41 percent remain in the same category in Wave 2; 54 percent remain between Waves 2 and 3; and 61 percent between Waves 3 and 4. The active worker cluster thus shows increasing stability over time. The "work, no extra" pattern also shows increasing stability (29, 47, and 51 percent of those initially in this cluster remain there between the three respective intervals). Corresponding figures for the active nonworkers are 53, 43, and 43 percent.

Some continuity in pattern is apparent even when youth move from one cluster to another. For example, some nonworking youth who do not participate in extracurricular activities one year become employed the following year while maintaining their disengagement from school life. (During the last two intervals, about 25 percent of the youth in the "no work, no extra" cluster adopt a pattern of time use characteristic of the "work, no extra" cluster.)

There is also considerable interchange between the two active groups from year to year. In this situation as well, adolescents are moving between employment states without substantially changing their other time involvements. Thus 29 percent of those in the active workers cluster move into the active nonworkers cluster between Waves 1 and 2, 15 percent between Waves 2 and 3, and 16 percent between Waves 3 and 4. Movement in the reverse direction, from active nonworker to active worker, occurs for 21, 31, and 32 percent of the youth during these intervals.

The high likelihood of remaining in each of the clusters, coupled with the patterns of interchange between them, suggests that an "active" mode of time use is characteristic of the majority of young people throughout the years of high school. The patterns of interchange, like the findings presented in Chapter 3 about the typology of investment in work, show that whether a student happens to be working at the time of a particular survey administration is not very indicative of the overall investment in employment during high school.

In addition to these continuities, Shanahan and Flaherty find movement over time from more focused patterns of time use to more diversified, active ones, but no movement in the reverse direction. They conclude: "Once engaged in many domains, students were not likely to become focused on one domain, although focused students often diversified their use of time" (393). So the more frequent pattern of movement appears to be toward the more positively evaluated, "well-rounded" configurations of time use. These relatively stable patterns of activities, suggesting quite divergent strategies of time allocation, surely challenge simplistic assumptions implying widespread, even universal, tradeoffs between given pairs of activities or zero-sum games.

It is interesting to observe how Shanahan and Flaherty's time-use clusters are distributed across the categories of investment in work. In Table 4.4, the duration/intensity typology, based on continuous work history data from three years of high school, is cross-tabulated with the time-use clusters observed in the fourth year. More than half of those in the "steady" category, which was interpreted as indicating a balance between school and work, are found in the "active workers" cluster. These youth have developed a pattern of moderate employment enabling participation in a variety of other activities. A third of the "most invested" workers are also found in this favorable cluster,

Table 4.4. Cross-tabulation of work investment by grade 12 time use

		Not working	Occasional	Steady	Sporadic	Most invested
Active workers	%		34.8	54.3	26.4	34.6
	N		73	120	43	80
Work, no extracurricular activities	%		15.7	25.8	12.9	38.1
	N		33	57	21	88
Active nonworkers	%	74.2	26.2	8.6	23.9	6.9
	N	46	55	19	39	16
No work, no extracurricular activities	%	16.1	17.1	6.8	14.1	6.9
	N	10	36	15	23	16
Chores	%	4.8	2.9	1.8	9.2	4.8
	N	3	6	4	15	11
Full-time work	%		1.4	1.4	9.8	6.9
	N		3	3	16	16
Low engagement	%	4.8	1.9	1.4	3.7	1.7
	N	3	4	3	6	4
Total	%	100.0	100.0	100.0	100.0	100.0
	N	62	210	221	163	231

χ^2 (291.87 / 24 df), $p < .001$.

but they are more likely than others to work without participating in extracurricular activities. And those who exhibited the "sporadic" pattern of employment are the least likely to be active, well-rounded workers. Again, these findings underscore the fact that paid employment, even when pursued in a sustained manner through high school, does not rule out participation in many other activities.

Conclusion

The portrayal of youth's many forms of participation in work and worklike activities is now complete. This contemporary cohort of adolescents is engaged in a wide variety of productive behaviors: nearly all work in family and school domains; the vast majority participate in paid work and extracurricular activities; and a substantial minority do volunteer work. Girls are more involved in family labor, while boys spend more hours at paid jobs and in extracurricular activities. Trends over time suggest an intensification of gender stereotyping as young people proceed through high school: girls maintain relatively high involvement in housework and family caring tasks, while boys become increasingly likely to pursue paid work and extracurricular activities outside the household. These gender differences would appear to anticipate adult men and women's involvements in familial and extrafamilial spheres. Gender differences in adolescents' configural patterns of activities are also apparent (Shanahan and Flaherty, 2001). For example, boys have a stronger propensity than girls toward the "work, no homework" category.

These findings bear strongly on several assumptions that pervade the criticism of adolescent employment. First, contrary to the notion that paid work leads to disengagement from or dislike of education, employed and nonemployed youth have quite similar perceptions of school. Second, employed teenagers perceive their school experiences as more favorable and beneficial than their work experiences on a variety of dimensions. Third, employed youth are not less likely than nonemployed youth to participate in other productive activities, including family work, homework, volunteering, and extracurricular pursuits.

I have presented further evidence that contradicts the widely held assumption that employment squeezes out more beneficial activities. The prevalence of the "active work" pattern of time use, the lack of meaningful difference between active workers and active nonworkers in engagement in other activities, and the high degree of interchange between these clusters across time all point to the same conclusion: most employed teenagers are able to maintain involvements in a wide range of presumably beneficial activities. Though a minority of employed youth work relatively long hours and restrict other productive activities, this is not the norm. For adolescent YDS participants, employment appears to present little risk that opportunities for growth in other central domains of adolescent development will be sacrificed.

5

PRECURSORS OF INVESTMENT IN WORK

"WHY DID I WORK? Because I think my best friend was working there, but actually, I say that sort of jokingly. I think that was true, but I also think my family really has a strong work ethic: if you're able to work, then you should be working, contributing, and saving money. And I worked partly to save for college, partly to pay for things I'd do in high school, like there were clothes I wanted to buy . . . but a lot just to save . . . you always need to be working, to be thinking about the future."

Why do adolescents manifest greater or lesser attachment to the labor force? Why do teenagers acquire more or less time-consuming, challenging, or demanding jobs? Can teenage investment in work be considered an expression of adolescent agency?

It might be thought that the use of time—for work as well as other activities—is rather adventitious, especially for adolescents, given their susceptibility to peer influence. Sheer opportunity may determine whether teenagers are exposed to certain activities and not others, and whether they invest more or less time in various pursuits. A teenager may come across a help wanted ad, or happen to hear about a job opening or volunteer opportunity. Some live near a shopping mall with plentiful jobs for teenagers; others reside far away from such opportunities. Youth who become fully engaged in their schoolwork may have little time remaining for a job. Some high schools offer an attractive range of extracurricular activities, others present quite meager choices. If adolescents were drawn into different work activities, or to the more comprehensive time use clusters described in

Chapter 4, mostly by such unpredictable circumstances, we might safely ignore the problem of selectivity—that is, the possibility that teenagers who choose to invest different amounts of time in work may be different from one another to begin with.

However, it is plausible to assume that other processes are operating. At least from the standpoint of educators, adolescence involves preparation for the future. This future-oriented conception of this phase of life is probably well understood by most adolescents. As they envision their "possible selves" (Markus and Nurius, 1986) and reflect on how they will move toward them, their current worklike activities may assume considerable significance. Forward-looking adolescents will attempt to realize their desired possible selves through their present activities.

Of course, not all adolescents will plan ahead in this way. Clausen (1991, 1993) identified a key constellation of orientations as "planful competence," including intellectual investment, dependability, productivity, and ambition. Shanahan (2000b: 12) defines this concept as "the thoughtful, assertive, and self-controlled processes that underlie selection into social institutions and interpersonal relationships."

Clausen found that planful adolescents engaged in activities that helped them to make choices among various goals, and to move toward them. These young people were thoughtful and reflective as they attempted to discover their own interests and potentials. They actively sought out information and opportunities that would help them to match their own proclivities and capacities with their future roles. Their hard work and delayed gratification were built on a foundation of confidence that they were able to attain personal goals.

Such early attitudes and expectations regarding competent action may be critical for subsequent success (Mainquist and Eichorn, 1989). Clausen demonstrated that the degree of planfulness in the mid-teen years predicted numerous indicators of adjustment and satisfaction in work and in family life through middle and late adulthood. He emphasized that planfulness should be developed early, by age 15, so that the right choices could be made in school, work, and social relationships. Likewise, Jordaan and Super (1974) found that planfulness, future orientation, and responsibility in adolescence predicted occupational attainment at age 25. The more explorative adolescents, actively engaging with their environments, had the more positive early adult outcomes.

It is likely that key experiences arising from a young person's location in the social structure influence the emergence of planful orientations. Resources and opportunities available to an adolescent will affect the propensity to be planful and either facilitate or constrain the exercise of individual agency. External events and circumstances influence, and often restrict, the likelihood that early efforts will be successful and aspirations attained.

Shanahan and his colleagues (1997) emphasize that the consequences of planfulness are historically variable, dependent on the opportunities available to a cohort at critical junctures of its life course. Cross-national differences in planning orientations are also evident. The institutional connections between school and work influence the ages at which young people become psychologically engaged in planning for their futures, the level of stress and uncertainty they experience as they do so, and the probable outcomes of their efforts (Mortimer and Krüger, 2000). For example, teenagers in Germany who must apply for apprenticeship placement manifest considerable interest in their vocational options; American young people of the same age pay relatively little attention to such matters. Within institutional contexts that establish varying degrees of support and constraint, adolescents will attempt to exercise agency so as to realize their "possible selves," to achieve their aspirations, and to execute their plans for the future.

Such processes of agency are of growing interest (Shanahan, 2000a). Still, the psychological capacities, attitudes, and activities that promote socioeconomic attainment as well as more general adjustment in life may appear to be quite antithetical to adolescents' presumed orientation to peers, excitement, and having a good time. For Hall (1904), the set of interests that constituted the essence of adolescence featured fun, friends, music, and athletics. High school students may perceive the adult work role as quite far away (Schneider and Stevenson, 1999), especially in this era of prolonged adolescence. But even after high school, youth who do not go to college have been characterized as focused on peer relationships, adventure, and travel, and as lacking serious career orientation (Osterman, 1989).

Such is the tension between two contradictory conceptions of adolescence—each of them normative. One might think that the inconsistency between them would pose a quandary for teenagers and foster ambivalence between rather diametrically opposed stances—to the present vs. the future, to fun and enjoyment vs. delayed gratification, to peers and the satisfaction of affiliative needs vs. objective achievements. At the extremes, some youth may immerse themselves in a present-oriented fully "adolescent" social and psychological world, with little thought of their adult futures. For others, preparation for adulthood may take center stage—as they strive to do well in school and to participate in the extracurricular pastimes that seem likely to help them in the future. Probably the majority will fall between, or alternate, these stances. The resulting priorities, whether stable or changing, will guide adolescents' engagement in their potential domains of action. Time use is thus the behavioral embodiment of multifaceted social negotiations and complex psychological processes.

Such ambivalence may lessen the likelihood of serious planning for the future. Furthermore, the dominant ideology of achievement in American society posits that opportunity is open-ended, available at many stages, if not throughout life, and accessible from various points of entry. If, as this image implies, planful activity can always be postponed until later, there may not be much point to thinking about or preparing for the future—and adolescents' goals may bear little relation to their time use patterns or their eventual attainments. Planful strategies toward the achievement of future goals may become more prominent as adolescence nears an end, or in early adulthood, when the young person approaches clearly recognized decision points that affect trajectories of attainment.

This chapter draws on the earliest indications of youth's goals and orientations to the future that are available in the Youth Development Study archive, obtained when most participants were 14 or 15 years old. Primary attention is directed to the domain of paid work. Are young people who acquire jobs in adolescence different from those who do not? Are varying patterns of investment in work during high school predicted by position in the social structure and/or by early orientations that may be considered indicative of planfulness? Is there evidence that prior psychological orientations foster the acquisition of distinctive kinds of work experiences?

Other productive activities also enter the analysis. Are teenagers with various patterns of time use characterized by different socioeconomic backgrounds and early interests? Do patterns of time use, including employment and other forms of work and recreational activity, reflect adolescents' varying strategies of preparation for the years ahead? Which adolescents do more housework and volunteer work?

Why Teenagers Want to Work

As noted in earlier chapters, in nineteenth- and early twentieth-century America adolescent work was strongly determined by the economic needs of the family. Youth resided with their families of origin well into early adulthood, during which time a substantial portion, if not all, of their earnings was turned over to their parents. Even today, many youth from economically hard-pressed backgrounds give at least some of their earnings to their parents or use their earnings in ways that help the family. Shanahan and his colleagues (1996) refer to such communal use of earnings by rural youth as "non-leisure spending." Newman (1996) describes young people in Harlem as using earnings to cover their "marginal cost," that is, what is needed to sustain their livelihood over and above the rent and other basic expenses of the household. Youth thereby contribute to a "pooled income strategy that makes it possible for households—as opposed to individuals—to sustain themselves" (328). According to Newman, this strategy is particularly common among immigrants and minorities who are not supported by welfare. Teenagers in these circumstances may be forced to withdraw from school to work full time.

However, even in impoverished families, adolescents' earnings are sometimes used to support their enrollment in trade school or other vocational schooling. Newman views paid work as promoting the educational attainment of poor youth: "Employment provides a structured, disciplined universe whose values 'spillover' to other realms, including school" (1996: 332). Entwisle and her colleagues (1998) have found similar patterns even earlier: they contend that working during elementary school plays a crucial part in the trajectory of vocational achievement among disadvantaged African Americans.

But most teenage workers in America are not poor. In fact, employed youth come disproportionately from middle-class families. Poor adolescents, who generally live in economically depressed neighborhoods, have fewer opportunities to work; they are also likely to be disadvantaged in competing with their more affluent counterparts for jobs (Committee, 1998). Typically, youth who hold part-time jobs, especially in middle-class urban and suburban areas, give little or none of their wages to their parents.

Clearly, most teenagers no longer work to assist their families. However, this does not mean that those who seek employment are seen by their parents as self-centered or as violating parental wishes. The YDS data show that parents greatly approve of their youngsters' employment (Phillips and Sandstrom, 1990; Aronson et al., 1996). In fact, parents think working fosters a variety of beneficial attributes—including independence, responsibility, and skill in managing time. In the eyes of parents, taking on a paid job demonstrates that a youngster can function in an adultlike role, thereby exhibiting autonomy, reliability, timeliness, and other desirable traits. If parents believe that such personal qualities are fostered by work, teenagers are likely to look upon employment in much the same way. Paid jobs will be seen as moving them toward adultlike "possible selves."

Still, young people's own ostensible motivation for work appears to be much more mundane. When asked why they work, they most frequently respond "for the money" (Greenberger and Steinberg, 1986; Committee, 1998: 25). As one young adult male YDS respondent put it: "I wanted extra money. In high school I got a clothing allowance and it didn't get me the clothes that I felt I needed so it was up to me to supplement that as I felt appropriate." A young man who had become an accountant said: "I got my first job when I started my junior year in high school . . . pretty much because I told my parents I wanted to go to Germany on spring break and my mother said, 'Fine, you got to pay for it' . . . So, it was go out and get a job, which I did as soon as football season was over."

Teenage job seekers appear to be motivated to earn money in an "adultlike" way that increases their economic independence from parents. In fact, there is considerable consensus among contemporary parents that children should have discretion over the ways their earnings are spent (Phillips and Sandstrom, 1990). Teenagers need money to participate in the youth subculture, to meet peer standards of dress, to attend concerts and sports events, to acquire and maintain their cars, and to save for the future.

Thus the motivation to work is clearly linked to social location. The middle-class youth will become employed to obtain spending money for largely discretionary expenses. The poor youth will gain a sense of dignity that comes from contributing to the family

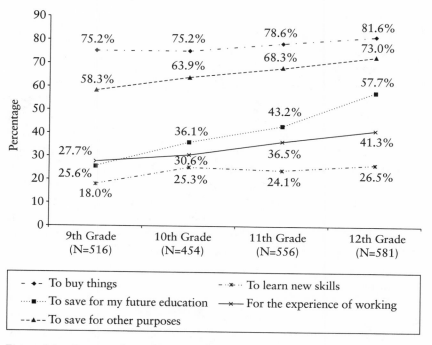

Figure 5.1. Reasons for seeking a job, grades 9–12.

(Newman, 1996). Poor inner-city youngsters may also find that the workplace enables them to escape the stress and violence of the street.

The employed YDS panel members were asked each year about why they had sought their current jobs. Offered a list of possibilities, such as "To buy things," "To save for my future education," "To save for other purposes," "To learn new skills," "For the experience of working," and "To get out of the house," they checked all that applied to them. Despite persistent differences in economic roles assigned to men and women in contemporary society, gender differences in teenage motivations to work are notably absent. Of 34 comparisons of boys' and girls' "reasons" across years, 7 were statistically significant. The failure to find the same significant differences in successive years renders them more chancelike than indicative of robust variation. Therefore, boys' and girls' responses are combined in Figure 5.1.[1]

The vast majority of employed students, three-quarters or more across years, sought jobs because they wanted money to buy things. However, increasing proportions of youth reported that they got jobs so they could save money for future education. By senior year, 73 percent of students sought jobs to save for other purposes. Fewer teenagers checked items that suggest a desire to enhance their human capital—seeking employment for the experience of working (41 percent of seniors) or to learn new job skills (26 percent).

A sizable minority of youth reported other, non-instrumental, reasons for seeking a job (not shown in the figure). Some did it because their parents wanted them to work—less than 15 percent in ninth grade but increasing to more than 25 percent in senior year. After ninth grade, up to a third of the youth reported working because it was "something to do" or "to get out of the house" (these options were not available in the first-year survey). Less than 10 percent in ninth grade, and less than 20 percent in succeeding years, sought their jobs "Because my friends worked there."

Another way of approaching the motivation to work is to examine the ways teenagers actually spend their earnings (see Figure 5.2). Quite small proportions of the youth give any part of their earnings to their families. Entertainment is a highly popular use of earnings. Still, many adolescents spend the money they earn on things that might otherwise be purchased by parents—for example, clothing closely rivals entertainment as the predominant expenditure. Many teenagers use their earnings to cover school expenses. More than a third of the youth, across years, use their earnings to buy food (not shown in the figure). As they advance through high school, growing numbers save at least some of their earnings for future education (almost half by senior year) or for other purposes (not shown).

As they grow older, teenagers increasingly say they use their earnings for their cars. Whereas car ownership on the part of an adolescent may be considered, from an adult standpoint, as a discretionary item, the situation may be perceived quite differently by a teenager who needs the car to go to school, to attend various social activities, and to get to work.[2]

Some critics have disparaged early employment because it allows youth to participate in the materialistic consumer culture (Steinberg and Cauffman, 1995). However, the YDS data suggest multiple motivations for seeking employment, as well as diverse uses of teenagers'

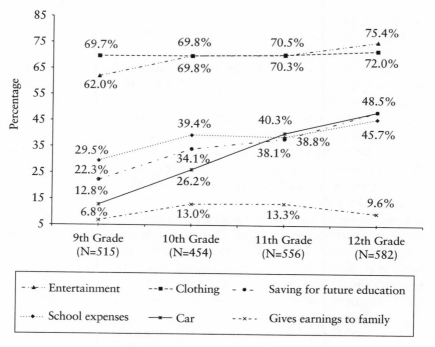

Figure 5.2. Use of earnings, grades 9–12.

earnings. We may reasonably infer from Figures 5.1 and 5.2 that for many teenagers work is an expression of planfulness, a way to realize elements of their present, "adultlike" selves by paying some of their own expenses. Jobs also move adolescents toward future selves—enabling them to save money for college and for other goals, and to become, eventually, economically self-sufficient adults.

Selection to Work Patterns

As we have seen, there is reason to believe that the meaning of work to young people is quite variable. At the extremes, affluent suburban youth and poor inner-city teenagers occupy radically different social worlds. The YDS data do not allow us to examine youth in either of these circumstances. However, there is a substantial range of socioeconomic variation within the YDS panel, making it possible to investigate whether youth from different economic backgrounds select themselves (or are selected by others) into different patterns of employment during high school.

Goals for the future are likely to affect the attractiveness of work in general, as well as specific kinds of jobs. Youth who are motivated to complete college may be more or less aware that their academic performance in high school will influence their chances for college admission (Dornbusch, 1994). Even if they believe they have the ability and can afford to attend college, teenagers may recognize that what they do during high school will affect their chances of getting into, and succeeding in, college. They may learn that their grades, the courses they take, and even their extracurricular activities will be considered by college admissions officers, and will affect their likelihood of receiving financial aid. This knowledge may give ambitious youth, concerned that working may interfere with activities that are more relevant to their educational objectives, considerable incentive to restrict their work hours.

For youth who lack the motivation or the resources—intellectual, dispositional, or economic—to go to college, the picture is altogether different. If they expect to enter the labor market soon after high school, grades and extracurricular activities may seem unimportant. In fact, the prospective employers who hire youth right out of high school are unlikely to ask them for their high school transcripts (Borman, 1991). Students who have limited success in school may find the labor market an alternative venue for achievement. Steinberg and Avenevoli (1998) found that disengagement from school predicts hours of work in their study of students in nine high schools of Wisconsin and northern California. Thus, planful youth with limited educational ambition could reasonably opt for high investment in work. While its effectiveness with respect to actual vocational achievement is yet to be examined, this strategy could be interpreted as an attempt to acquire human capital early on through work experience. For such youth, the appropriate comparison group may be, not middle-class youth who aspire to attend college, but teenagers similar to themselves who do little or no paid work during high school.

Working, at the least, provides experience, something most employers are interested in, as well as a network of contacts and potential references that can be useful in subsequent job-seeking. Newman notes that years of steady work, even in the fast-food business, can provide an advantage for Harlem youngsters: "the reputation—unusual among their peers—of having worked continuously, of sticking with something" (1996: 335).

The YDS data make it possible to compare the reasons for seeking a job among youth who had varying patterns of investment in work during high school. Such attributions, and their association with actual work investment, are surely pertinent to an understanding of adolescent agency. Each year, employed youth were asked about their reasons for obtaining their current job. (This information is not available for those who were not employed at the times of survey administration, even if they worked at some time during the year.)

Here, let us examine the earliest available indicator of employment motivation in the high school surveys, the first expressed reasons for obtaining work.[3] For example, if a teenager gave reasons for seeking employment in both the second and the third surveys, we use the data from Wave 2. Table 5.1 shows the proportion of youth who reported various reasons for seeking employment in each category of work investment (see Chapter 3 for the typology of work investment). Because reasons for working are not mutually exclusive (youth could select multiple options), the percentages do not sum to 100.

In general, youth in the four investment categories appear to pursue employment for quite similar reasons; the overwhelming majority sought work to buy things. Saving is also quite popular across investment categories. However, some differences between groups support a strategic interpretation.

The "steady" pattern of work is the one that appears to be the most balanced, as it involves high continuity of work while at the same time, because work hours are limited, permits the youth to be involved in school activities. Most strikingly, in view of its compatibility with educational achievement, youth who pursue this pattern are especially likely to say they had sought employment "to save for my future education." Still, the majority of youth in three of the four work-investment categories wanted to save at least some of their earnings for future education. Only for those in the "sporadic" category, whose pattern of work investment itself suggests difficulty in maintaining employment, does the proportion who intend to save for future education fall below a majority (to 45.7 percent).

In contrast, the "most invested" workers are the most likely to say

Table 5.1. Reasons for seeking a job by work investment

	Work investment				
	Occasional	Steady	Sporadic	Most invested	F
To buy things	84.5%	93.2%	79.8%	95.7%	10.48**
To save for my future education	58.0%	76.5%	45.7%	65.2%	12.62**
To save for other purposes	75.7%	90.5%	76.7%	91.3%	10.86**
For the experience of working	49.7%	61.1%	45.7%	58.7%	3.73*
To learn new skills	31.5%	42.5%	38.8%	52.6%	6.58**

N = 761; *p < .05; **p < .001.

they sought their jobs because they wanted to learn new skills. Youth who worked for long durations during high school, whether at high or low intensity, were more likely than youth who worked for shorter periods to be seeking "the experience of working." These data are consistent with an agentic interpretation of adolescent investment in work—as a reflection of planful striving to achieve long-term goals.

An agentic understanding of adolescent work construes it as instrumental action directed to optimizing future prospects for attainment. Such an interpretation would be further strengthened by evidence that youth who are likely to have more to gain by working are, in fact, the ones who invest more of their time in working during high school. In the following analyses, predictors of teenage work investment are measured in ninth grade, prior to the assessment of the paid work patterns (which encompass the following three-year period). The rationale for the predictors, along with a description of their indicators, follows.

The general expectation is that disadvantages posing obstacles to the acquisition of higher education will foster attempts to acquire human capital through early intensive employment. Disadvantage may be expressed as features of family background, ethnicity, or motivational and achievement deficits. Socioeconomic background is represented by parental education and family income. Parents of higher educational level will have higher educational aspirations for their children. Annual family income indicates the economic resources that could enable youth to attend college. The numerous advantages of youth from intact families, and their higher levels of socioeconomic attainment, have been well documented (McLanahan and Sandefur, 1994). A variable indicating family structure (coded 1 if intact, 0 if not) is therefore included. Race and nativity reference minority status. Minority adolescents' lesser likelihood of holding paid jobs, documented in many studies (Committee, 1998), could reflect employer discrimination or cultural preferences.

There are two indicators of academic involvement, obtained during ninth grade. As noted, it is reasonable to suppose that youth who are more highly committed to academics will limit their investment in paid work, being more interested in protecting their grade-point averages and allowing time for homework and other school activities. It is also likely that those with lower academic involvement would invest more time in paid work. To what extent do ninth graders find schoolwork meaningful, interesting, worthwhile, and engaging? The respondents were asked to rate (on a 4-point scale from "not at all true" to "very true") four statements, for example, "I put a great deal of myself into some things at school because they have special meaning to me" and "I have little interest in my classes in school" (the other items are indicated in Table 4.1).[4] Self-reported grade point average in ninth grade is measured on a 13-point scale, from F to A+.

This analysis also includes constructs reflecting "problem behavior" and "peer orientation." It is with reference to this set of predictors that notions of "precocious" or "accelerated" development (Bachman and Schulenberg, 1993), "pseudomaturity" (Greenberger and Steinberg, 1986), and "role exit" (Hagan and Wheaton, 1993) become pertinent. That is, youth who are less engaged with their predominant role as students, may become dissatisfied, even rebellious, and act out their frustrations in problem behavior. An additive index of "school problem behavior" addresses rule-breaking in the school setting: "Since the beginning of school this year, how often have you: Gotten into trouble for misbehaving or breaking school rules? Been sent to the principal's office or to detention because of something you have done?"

Furthermore, if educational achievement has low priority in the adolescent peer culture (Coleman, 1961), one might expect adolescents who are more highly oriented to peers to be less engaged with school and more attracted to work. Peer orientation is indicated by time spent with friends: the number of weekday afternoons and evenings, and time during the weekend (from no time at all to all of the time).

Finally, gender is linked to opportunities in the labor market, including access to adolescent jobs as well as the continuity of employment. For example, employers may believe that certain jobs are more appropriate for boys or girls. Because of greater parental restrictiveness of adolescent girls, they may be less likely to be allowed to work at night or to accrue intensive work schedules.

The issue of selection to adolescent work has been given little attention in prior studies; investigators of youthwork have focused primarily on its consequences while controlling "third variable" influences that could influence the propensity to work as well as its presumed effects. For example, nonworking youth may have encountered obstacles to employment. Discrimination by employers, or the need to contribute to family work at home, may restrict their ability to combine school and paid work. In each annual survey the respondents were asked, "Are you looking for a job now?" There are clear differences in job-seeking among youth in the five work-investment categories. In ninth grade, only 22 percent of the nonworkers were seeking a job (in comparison to 40–59 percent of ninth graders in the other employment categories). However, approximately a third of these youth were seeking a job two and three years later, and 44 percent were doing so by Wave 4. Though these teenage respondents do not exhibit an overwhelming desire to work, the nonworking youth are not distinguished by a lack of interest in employment.

The next step is to examine the predictors of adolescent investment in work in a multivariate context. That is, which variables have independent predictive power, controlling the effects of the others?[5] Recall that the work-investment patterns are based on labor force participation in tenth through twelfth grades (see Chapter 3). Since the background variables and the attitudinal and behavioral variables were obtained when the youth were in ninth grade, it cannot be argued that work investment causes what are here considered to be the influences on working.

This analysis designates the variables that affect the likelihood of being in a category, in comparison to a reference group. Here, the "steady" pattern of employment, indicating a persistent balancing of school and work, is the reference. Though nonworkers may appear to be a more natural reference group, the very small size of this category (7 percent of the total sample, less than 10 percent of boys and 5 percent of girls) made it unsuitable as a base of comparison. The "steady" workers, given their relatively advantaged characteristics, make for a useful substantive contrast (see Hardy, 1993, for a discussion of reference group choice). (Preliminary analyses included additional variables that were eliminated to simplify the equations. Only the reduced models are described here.)[6]

Table 5.2 shows that boys are more likely than girls to follow all patterns other than the "steady" reference. The difference in the propensity to pursue high-intensity work during high school reflects stereotypical gender roles in American society—with men assigned major responsibility as breadwinners. However, adolescent boys also show a behavioral propensity to the "occasional" pattern and to the nonworking pattern. The more balanced steady combination of

Table 5.2. Multinomial logit regression coefficients comparing four work pattern groups with "steady" workers

	Occasional		Sporadic		Most invested		Not working	
	b	Exp (b)	b	Exp (b)	b	Exp (b)	b	Exp (b)
Socioeconomic factors								
Gender (1 = male)	.58**	1.79	1.03***	2.80	.50*	1.65	1.26***	3.53
Race (1 = White)	-.56	.57	-1.01**	.36	-.26	.77	-.95*	.39
Nativity (1 = U.S. born)	-.54	.58	.61	1.84	-.78	.46	-.91	.40
Family composition (1 = intact family)	-.63**	.53	-.01	.99	-.30	.74	-.53	.59
Parental education	.07	1.07	.01	1.01	-.23***	.79	.04	1.04
School performance and engagement								
GPA	.11	1.12	-.53**	.59	-.32*	.73	-.12	.89
Intrinsic motivation toward school	-.08	.92	-.06	.94	-.13*	.88	-.19*	.83
Problem behavior and peer orientation								
School problem behavior	-.05	.95	.34**	1.40	.06	1.06	.40*	1.49
Time spent with friends	.10*	1.11	.10*	1.11	.11*	1.12	.10	1.11
N	790							
Log likelihood	-1,111.12							
Chi-Square (df)	187.6*** (36)							

*p < .05; **p < .01; ***p < .001.

school and work is manifest as a distinctly female work pattern, not attributable to school involvement or performance, problem behavior, peer orientation, or social background. Girls' early exposure to a relatively continuous demand for their informal labor—as baby-sitters—may set the stage for a similar, relatively continuous, low-intensity involvement in work after they move into formal employment.

Indicators of disadvantage make it less likely that adolescents will pursue the "steady" pattern. Nonwhite youth of high school age are more likely to be employed sporadically, at high intensity for shorter periods, and to be nonworkers. Being from a non-intact family increases the propensity to enact the "occasional" pattern, which yields relatively little work experience during the high school years. Teenagers whose parents are less well educated are more likely to be in the "most invested" work pattern—working for long periods at relatively high intensity. It is noteworthy that higher levels of parental education appear to reduce only the tendency to pursue the most continuous and intensive work. Well-educated parents are likely to perceive the prolonged, high-intensity pattern as inimical to their children's achievement.

Lower academic performance in ninth grade predicts higher-intensity employment in the succeeding three years. Moreover, as psychological engagement in school increases, young people are more likely to eschew the "most invested" pattern of work. Youth who have greater engagement in school are more likely be "steady" workers than to be nonworkers.

School problem behavior appears to be a key obstacle to subsequent employment. That is, ninth graders who reported getting into more trouble at school were more likely, later in high school, to be nonworkers. However, as we have seen, the nonworkers were not particularly distinguished by lack of interest in acquiring a job.

It is especially interesting that this multivariate analysis reveals differences in the precursors of high-intensity work of high and low duration. In comparison with youth who have the "steady" pattern, youth whose high-intensity employment is of short duration manifest a high degree of early problem behavior. Problem behavior is not characteristic of the most invested high-intensity workers.

Getting into trouble at school and the absence of employment continuity may result from common behavioral propensities. Problem behavior reflects insufficient self-regulation or control. The young person who works sporadically, at high levels of intensity when employed, is clearly not maintaining a consistent course. Whether this reflects a failure of intentional action is not resolvable with the data at hand. What is known is that youth whose pattern of employment is sporadic exhibit substantial interest in working throughout high school.

Turning to the amount of time spent with friends, a clear indicator of peer orientation, there are positive coefficients in three of the four columns of Table 5.2 (but the last, for nonworkers, is not significant). Thus ninth-grade youth in the three other working categories spend more time with their friends than adolescents in the steady or balanced category.

In summary, social location is relevant to youth's early employment. Minority status, having a non-intact family, and having less well-educated parents decrease the likelihood of pursuing the steady work pattern during high school. High-intensity employment of low duration is preceded by relatively poor academic performance, early problem behavior, and strong peer orientation. These precursors suggest restricted attachment to education. Youth who are the most enthusiastic workers in high school, working at high intensity for some part of nearly all the months of observation, also manifest little intrinsic motivation toward schoolwork, low academic performance, and high peer orientation in ninth grade. The steady pattern, in contrast, is clearly characteristic of advantaged youth.

Selection to Work Quality

To be sure, not all jobs are equally desirable in the eyes of teens. Newman found that Harlem teenagers working in fast-food restaurants were ridiculed and taunted by their peers, who viewed their jobs as "servile, requiring deference, obedience to authority, and uniformity in a subculture that prizes the opposite qualities: independence, autonomy, resistance and self-determination" (1996: 333). More advantaged teenagers might be expected to hold much the same attitudes, but because they can view their participation in such jobs as time limited, their aversion to this kind of work may not be so intense. Still, Chapter 3 shows a general aggregate movement of em-

ployed teenagers out of fast-food work into other kinds of employment as they go through high school.

In one of the few attempts to consider how youth come to have
different work experiences, Bidwell and colleagues (1998: 162) emphasize the power of adolescent agency: "Their occupational development depends on the content and clarity of their shorter- and
longer-term life goals, the ways in which they perceive job opportunities, their understanding of ways in which jobs can be found and entered, their conceptions of relationships between present employment
and future prospects, and their consequent motivation to exert energy in job search and subsequent job performance." Some youth in
their study, including those who grew up in quite adverse circumstances, constructed promising sequences of work experiences. Others, in more favorable situations, reacted passively, taking jobs that
were nearby or otherwise convenient.

Some teenagers find jobs that provide exposure to the technical demands and normative environments of "counterpart adult occupations" that they are considering. Bidwell and his colleagues tell the
story of "Jose," whose work experiences indicate a clear progression—from volunteering, to interning, to paid employment in a law
firm (enabling first-hand contact with the legal profession, his occupational objective). Jose's aspirations and motivations toward work
came to be "grounded more in the realities of his paid work experiences," as he moved from wanting to own a law firm to setting up a
legal outreach program.

Bidwell and colleagues emphasize the diverse learning opportunities presented by adolescent paid work: "all kinds of teenage jobs
seem to (a) add to an adolescent's stock of knowledge about the range
of job possibilities and (b) provide opportunities to assess one's sense
of self against the opportunities and constraints of one kind of work
or another" (181). They also speak of "negative learning": acquiring
an understanding of what one does not want to do or what one probably cannot do well. These cognitive evaluations are in keeping with
the multifaceted amalgam of mental processes and activities that
Clausen called planful competence.

It is reasonable to suppose that planful youth who do not do well
in school and those from disadvantaged backgrounds, realizing that
their opportunities to attend college may be limited, will seek learn-

ing experiences relevant to their future occupations. Just as disadvantaged youth pursue extracurricular activities that have a vocational
focus (National Center for Educational Statistics, 1997), the more
planful among them are likely to look for jobs that will help to prepare them for their future work.

Youth who are more oriented to developing their human capital
through employment are likely to be attracted to jobs offering opportunities for advancement. Those who plan to obtain full-time work
shortly after high school may perceive such advancement opportunities as potentially constituting the initial stage of their adult careers.
Higher earnings, which come with advancement opportunity, and
"good pay" are also likely to be attractive to youth who see themselves on initial rungs of an occupational ladder. If their friends are
also primarily oriented toward work, such youth may see jobs as con-
ferring status in the peer group. The YDS adolescents were asked
whether the money they earned from working enabled them to go out
with friends more often, and whether having a job gave them higher
status among their friends.

The perceived general learning opportunities offered by work were
gauged by five items addressing the chance to use skills and abilities,
the opportunity to learn "a lot of new things," the perceived future usefulness of what is learned at work, and the challenges, both
mental and physical, faced at work. Jobs rated high on these dimensions are likely to be the more conducive to human capital development.

Another feature of interest is a job's stressful and demanding character. Though teenagers are likely to avoid distressing and taxing employment, it may be that jobs providing more opportunities for learning, skill development, advancement, and earnings growth are also
more demanding and thus more stressful.

The final qualitative dimension addresses Bronfenbrenner's "mesosystem" or network of inter-context linkages: the connection between
school and work. Compatibility between these two spheres may be
especially important to youth who have high educational ambitions.
One construct, labeled "work and school," references cognitive understanding of the link between the two. (For measures, see note 8 to
Chapter 3.) Positive perceptions of the links between work and
school may facilitate planful competence—by encouraging reflection
about one's own interests and capacities, the kind of work one would

like to do in the future, and the credentials necessary to obtain desirable jobs.

The second construct, titled "work and grades," assessed perceptions of the more performance-related connections between school and job—focusing on the belief that working promotes, or detracts from, grades and the capacity to do homework. Higher scores on this index again reflect positive perceptions—that the job has not detracted from homework, and that working has not had a negative impact on academic performance.

As noted earlier, whereas continuous measures of employment status and work intensity can be derived from the annual work history charts, the YDS has just four "snapshot" pictures of work quality, referencing the current job at the time of each survey administration. As a consequence, this attempt to identify the precursors of qualitative dimensions of work experience during high school is fraught with measurement error. Moreover, the work experiences that are recorded occur at different times and at different numbers of occasions. As in Chapter 3, the work-quality measures reflect the average quality of work (mean scores) at the times the respondent was employed. These variables, unlike the work-investment patterns, do not describe the duration of work. The work-quality variables reference jobs held at one, two, or three occasions (in tenth, eleventh, and/or twelfth grade).

Though it would be useful to assess patterns of change in work quality, such as the determinants of increases or decreases in exposure to work stress over time, the fact that only about half the respondents reported their work quality more than once precludes such refined analysis. (Students who reported no employment in tenth, eleventh, and twelfth grades, 15 percent of the panel, are not included in these analyses.)

Many correlations among the work-quality variables are statistically significant, but most are small in magnitude (under .20). The largest is between the constructs referencing learning opportunities and work-school compatibility; it is positive in direction ($r = .478$, $p < .001$). Thus opportunities for learning and challenge on the job appear to support a positive link between school and work. Work stress, in contrast, is connected to perceptions that work interferes with getting good grades ($r = -.287$, $p < .001$).

Table 5.3 shows correlations between social background variables,

Table 5.3. Correlations of work quality with predictors

	Advancement opportunity	Earnings	Good pay	Work-derived status	Learning opportunities	Work stressors	Work and school	Work and grades
Gender	−.008	.033	−.002	.080*	.035	.011	.065	.060
Race	−.035	−.022	.058	−.027	−.034	−.043	−.088*	−.025
Nativity	.034	.002	.071	.029	.069	.040	−.017	.014
Family composition	−.011	−.057	.001	.006	.020	−.081*	.051	.039
Parental education	−.114**	−.231**	−.021	−.164**	−.026	−.114**	−.113**	−.080*
Family income	−.040	−.183**	.006	−.098*	−.008	−.109**	−.078*	.001
GPA	−.088*	−.244**	.058	−.183**	−.086*	−.147**	−.051	−.121**
Homework	.001	.011	.061	−.033	.030	−.093*	−.041	−.041
Educational plans	−.071	−.215**	.041	−.103**	−.008	−.146**	−.053	−.138**
Intrinsic motivation toward school	.046	−.118**	.051	.019	.083*	−.100**	.053	−.076
Academic self-esteem	−.046	−.161**	.089*	−.107**	−.031	−.075	−.057	−.165**
School problem behavior	−.002	.206**	−.039	.127**	−.031	.099*	.003	.105**
Drinking	−.052	.103**	−.013	.011	.022	.057	.005	.017
Smoking	−.101**	.165**	−.035	.004	.037	.050	.004	.029
Time spent with friends	.086*	.218**	.043	.099**	.003	.084*	.033	.053

*p < .05; **p < .01.

measured in ninth grade, and *subsequent* work experiences. Though there is little bivariate association between the work features and gender, race, nativity, and family composition, it is apparent that the *less advantaged* youth report work experiences that are both more extrinsically rewarding and more stressful. Young people whose parents have less education report more "adultlike" work experiences of both positive and negative character. They have greater access to extrinsic occupational rewards—more advancement opportunities, higher earnings, and greater work-derived status in the eyes of their peers—but their work is also more demanding and stressful.

Adolescents whose parents have *less* education are more likely to think their jobs are compatible with school and with getting good grades. This pattern is not easily interpretable. Teenagers whose parents have less education may find more compatibility between school and work—for example, if they are taking vocationally oriented courses in school and find their job tasks relevant to these subjects. Moreover, youth with less-educated parents may see greater compatibility between working and getting good grades because they are taking less demanding courses and are assigned less homework. Alternatively, parental education may affect the extent to which good grades and homework matter to the teenager. If education, and especially higher education, is assigned less importance in the home, the adolescent may not be very concerned about whether part-time jobs interfere with schoolwork or not. If this is an issue lacking salience, the youth may not be aware of how employment might interfere with getting good grades and doing homework.

Economic resources in the family are also associated with youth's work experiences. Teenagers whose families have lower incomes have higher earnings in their high school jobs, perceive that they obtain more status among their peers from working, and experience greater work demands. Youth whose parents have lower income also tend to see schooling and working as more compatible.

Ninth-grade academic orientations and behavior bear most directly on students' early school engagement, plans for further education, and grade-point average. The most pervasive correlate of high school work experiences is grade-point average in ninth grade. All significant correlations between grades and work dimensions are negative in direction, showing that poorer students have the more pronounced work experiences, whether positive or negative. That is, as ninth-grade academic performance declines, subsequent jobs are perceived as having greater advancement opportunity, higher earnings, more status in the eyes of peers, and greater learning opportunities. But the less academically successful youth also report that their work is more demanding and stressful.

This pattern of correlations would seem to reflect enactment of adolescent agency: those ninth graders who, comparatively speaking, do not perform well in school go on to acquire jobs that involve higher extrinsic rewards as well as greater opportunity for human capital development. We see similar, though more restricted, links with ninth-grade educational goals and academic self-esteem. Ninth graders with more limited educational ambitions and lower academic efficacy have higher earnings in their subsequent jobs and think their jobs give them more status among their peers. They also are more likely to think working and good grades are compatible. Restricted educational plans are associated with more demanding, stressful work. Similarly, ninth-graders who express less intrinsic motivation in school go on to receive higher earnings and perceive more work-related stress in their high school jobs.

However, not all relationships follow this general pattern. The positive relation between psychological engagement in school and learning opportunities at work may reflect a quite generalized positive stance toward learning—whether in school or at work. Perhaps it is not surprising to find that positive perceptions, though corresponding to different domains of action, go together. Moreover, though academic self-esteem is associated with lower actual earnings, the more academically efficacious youth tend to see themselves as well paid. Viewing one's pay as "good" may be more reflective of a positive self-image than of actual remuneration.

The cluster of variables referencing problem behavior and peer orientation exhibit positive correlations with many of the criteria. Whereas prior studies have established a link between problem behavior and hours of work, this analysis suggests that indicators of acting out and peer orientation—problem behaviors in school, alcohol use, smoking, and time spent with friends—predict the quality of work. The jobs involving higher earnings and more social status, as well as the ones that are more stressful, are obtained by the more troublesome, peer-oriented ninth graders. Ninth-grade substance use also predicts higher earnings.

Table 5.4 presents a multivariate analysis, including pertinent controls.[7] Especially striking is the predictive power of gender. As noted in Chapter 3, high school boys perceive more advancement opportunity, receive higher earnings, and think they obtain more status from working in the eyes of their peers. However, boys also perceive greater stressors in their jobs. Girls think they have more learning opportunities at work. Here it is shown that these differences cannot be explained by gender differences in social background, school performance and engagement, or problem behavior. Boys obtain the more extrinsically rewarding and stressful jobs as they move through high school; girls appear to have the more developmentally beneficial kinds of work.

Like the correlational analyses, the multivariate assessment of the precursors of the quality of work support the hypothesized process of selection. Advantage, especially in the form of familial education and early academic performance, precedes more limited extrinsic occupational rewards during high school.

Those who achieve well in school do not appear to find opportunities for learning at work. Instead, it is the less successful academic performers in ninth grade who gravitate toward jobs with greater learning opportunities. Moreover, youth from less advantaged educational backgrounds are more likely to think that their jobs support school performance. Finally, peer orientation is associated with more extrinsically rewarding jobs. The findings suggest an accelerated transition to "adultlike" kinds of work among the less advantaged, less academically motivated and prepared, and more peer-oriented youth.

Work Experiences and Time Use Clusters

We have seen that the more educationally committed ninth graders limit their hours of work, presumably to enable higher academic achievement and eventual academic (and occupational) attainment. By restricting their work investment, low-intensity workers gain more time to devote to their schooling, as well as other activities. As described in Chapter 4, Shanahan and Flaherty (2001) identified two "active" clusters of time use—differentiated only by whether or not the youth was employed at the annual assessment. These clusters entail rather substantial investments of time in all of the activities—relevant to work and nonwork—measured in the YDS. As noted earlier,

Table 5.4. Predictors of adolescent work quality (unstandardized OLS regression coefficients, standard errors)

	Advancement opportunity	Earnings	Work-derived Status	Learning opportunities	Work stressors	Work and school
Socioeconomic factors						
Gender (1 = male)	.21**	32.02***	.40***	−.74**	2.31***	−.24
	(.067)	(6.05)	(.105)	(.244)	(.383)	(.199)
Race (1 = White)	−.06	12.45	.01	−.18	−.47	−.43
	(.090)	(8.21)	(.140)	(.326)	(.513)	(.268)
Nativity (1 = U.S. born)	.05	−32.72*	−.14	.65	.37	−.10
	(.159)	(14.31)	(.247)	(.579)	(.920)	(.465)
Family composition (1 = Intact family)	.02	−5.22	.05	.29	−.93*	.41
	(.075)	(6.74)	(.118)	(.273)	(.431)	(.224)
Parental education	−.05*	−7.63***	−.10**	.00	−.26*	−.15*
	(.022)	(1.99)	(.034)	(.080)	(.126)	(.065)
School performance and engagement						
GPA	−.11*	−16.11**	−.32***	−.59**	−.54	−.16
	(.051)	(4.62)	(.080)	(.186)	(.291)	(.156)
Intrinsic motivation toward school	.04*	−.47	.08**	.24***	−.19	.09
	(.018)	(1.59)	(.028)	(.065)	(.102)	(.053)
Problem behavior and peer orientation						
School problem behavior	−.08*	5.64	.06	−.14	.03	−.07
	(.037)	(3.31)	(.058)	(.135)	(.212)	(.111)
Time spent with friends	.03*	4.27**	.01	.03	.01	.04
	(.014)	(1.29)	(.022)	(.052)	(.082)	(.042)
Constant	2.33***	181.85***	4.42***	10.34***	23.67***	10.36***
	(.307)	(27.86)	(.482)	(1.11)	(1.76)	(.925)
N	629	598	635	625	613	594
R^2	.06	.17	.09	.05	.10	.03

$*p < .05; **p < .01; ***p < .001.$

"active" youth correspond well to the American ideal of well-roundedness.

Low-intensity employment is associated with "active" time use. Not surprisingly, Shanahan and Flaherty find precursors of "active" time use that are quite similar to those that predict low-intensity employment. In their analysis, youth who had high grades and ambitious plans tended to be more active a year later, incorporating a wide range of activities in their weekly schedules, including homework and extracurricular activities. Youth whose ambitions were more restricted were more likely to have time use patterns that did not include extensive involvement in the school. Lower grade-point averages predicted full-time work in the third and fourth years of the study. As was expected, minority status restricted employment: nonwhites were more likely to be in the "active nonworkers" or "low engagement" classes, each characterized by an absence of paid employment.

Clearly, adolescents are active agents, selecting patterns of activities, including paid work, that are consistent with their resources and objectives. Elements of adolescent advantage—in resources, academic interests and performance, and ambition—consistently predict restricted investment in employment. Low-intensity employment patterns enable youth to obtain both immediate and long-term benefits of working, while at the same time allowing time for other, especially educational, activities.

Shanahan and Flaherty report further evidence of the enactment of adolescent agency in the construction of time use patterns. Those youth who earlier placed a high value on helping others tend to have a time use pattern that specialized in the performance of household chores. Call (1996a) showed that YDS youth who spent more time doing family work were also responsive to family need. For example, household size predicted greater time spent in family-related household labor; youth from lower-income families spent more time doing household work and caring for others (mainly siblings). Girls spent more time in all years caring for other family members, and in eleventh and twelfth grades, on household chores.

Since the amount of time spent volunteering did not distinguish the time use clusters, it is not a constituent element in Shanahan and Flaherty's analysis. But since volunteering constitutes a prevalent and potentially formative type of adolescent work activity (see Chapter 4), it deserves mention in this consideration of the precursors of working. Reminiscent of the predictors of low-intensity work patterns, Johnson and her colleagues (1998) found that YDS ninth graders who had higher educational plans, higher educational aspirations, higher grade-point averages, and stronger intrinsic motivation toward school were more likely to volunteer at some time during tenth through twelfth grades. This constitutes evidence that the more academically invested and successful youth, those with higher ambitions, pursue diverse work activities.

Conclusion

From each of the analyses featured in this chapter, there is clear evidence of agency. Youth surely do not spend their time in a random or mostly adventitious way. Distinct differences in work and time use patterns emerge, which are related to backgrounds and orientations measured as early as ninth grade. Adolescents not only seek work that is compatible with their educational goals; their entire pattern of time use is predicted by their prior ambitions.

We find that students of lower socioeconomic background, and those who are less engaged in school, develop a strategy of highly intensive work investment during high school, along with acquisition of more "adultlike" work experiences. Youngsters of higher socioeconomic background, those who are more interested in school, and those with stronger academic performance, tend to limit their hours of work so as to combine paid employment with other activities. Thus two pathways of preparation for adult roles are discerned, one involving intense investment in paid work, the other involving limitation of paid work and balancing of work and other activities.

The analyses of selection to work suggest that youth who have less likelihood of obtaining a college education, because of their family backgrounds, academic performance, or problem behavior, choose to work at higher levels of intensity. In contrast, low-intensity work is selected by youth from higher socioeconomic backgrounds, with stronger academic records and interest. We have inferred from these findings a process of intentional action. Those youth who have the greatest likelihood of succeeding in college strive to obtain balance by limiting their work investment to 20 or fewer hours per week.

Somewhat paradoxically, the analysis of the quality of youthwork does not show that advantage in one context, that of the family or school, fosters advantage in another, the workplace. Instead, the inverse relationships between social position, success, and engagement in family and educational domains, on the one hand, and the quality of work experience, on the other, are consistent with an agentic interpretation of young people's work behavior. Those from more disadvantaged backgrounds obtain jobs that provide higher levels of extrinsic reward. In general, it is the youth who come from less advantaged backgrounds, and whose early school performance indicates less promising academic careers, who steer themselves toward the more rewarding, but also more stressful, "adultlike" jobs. It is the ninth graders with the less promising academic records who move toward jobs with greater learning opportunities, obtaining in the workplace an alternative source of human capital development.

Youth who display high levels of intrinsic motivation toward school seem to indicate a contradictory pattern. Though such involvement in school might be expected to foster attraction to that domain as the major source of learning and engagement, we find instead that youth with this positive orientation toward school later report learning opportunities on the job and a sense of status gained from working. These findings may also express an agentic process: that youth who are strongly oriented toward learning seek out challenge and engagement in multiple domains, including both school and work. If they form friendships with similarly oriented peers, these youth may indeed obtain peer approval for having intrinsically rewarding work.[8]

Early in this chapter, tension was noted between "planful" and "playful" orientations to adolescent life. It is apparent from these analyses that the more advantaged youth, who have higher educational promise and ambition, pursue low-intensity work during high school, whether relatively continuously (at high duration) or not. In doing so, they manage to construct "active" life styles that enable the enactment of "playful" as well as "planful" experiences—spending ample time with peers as well as working and engaging in educational pursuits (homework and the extracurriculum). They are able to construct for themselves patterns of activities that meet the ideal of well-rounded adolescents.

WORKING AND ADOLESCENT DEVELOPMENT

THE MOST PROMINENT ISSUE in the debates surrounding youth employment concerns the long- and short-term consequences of working during adolescence: How does it influence the process of growing up? When interviewers asked YDS participants how their work experience had influenced them, they gave answers like these:

> Taught me how to be quick, cause you really have to get the customers in and out of there and be friendly and it's just interesting and plus it taught more responsibility too because they had a car-wash there and then the food shop plus all the pumps. They had twelve pumps and so you really had to be on your toes because there are . . . shifts that you'd work by yourself and you had to keep everything going.

> It kind of taught me how to deal with people when they're angry or confused or when they want something. I just pretty much know how to respond to them or try to ease them or try to give them what they want or help them. So it helps me.

> I learned how to be a good worker, show up on time, and you learn about breaks and stuff like that. You learn little things like how to break down a cash register, and my math skills improved quite a bit . . . it was actually kind of fun to be able to add or subtract anything immediately. And you learn a little bit more about how business runs. You know, you got to order stuff. You have to stock it. You have to restock it. You have to

watch out for shoplifters. You know, be on time, make sure your uniform is nice. General stuff like that.

As Chapter 4 attests, adolescent work is a multifaceted phenomenon that occurs in many domains. In addition to their paying jobs, teens work in the family, in the neighborhood, at school, and as community volunteers. And paid work itself has multiple dimensions, as documented in Chapter 3. Nonetheless, most prior studies have treated adolescent employment as an unidimensional experience: the amount of time teens spend at work is the sole feature of interest. This preoccupation with hours of work follows from two pervasive assumptions, both of which are challenged by the Youth Development Study. The first is that "youthwork" is a homogeneous phenomenon. The second is that time spent in paid employment drives out more beneficial uses of time.

Controversies about the consequences of teenagers' paid work reflect the contradictory views of adolescence. Adolescence is thought to be a time of exploration and preparation for adult life, a time of planful anticipation and activity. It is also seen as a period of freedom, fun, and active social life, free of the responsibilities of adulthood. The tension lies in the balance: parents and educators want young people to participate in each realm of activity, but in a manner that permits involvement in the other. Youth should achieve in school, but the bookish "nerd" is not to be emulated. Conversely, youth must not become wholly immersed in the peer culture—or in harmful pursuits promoted by undesirable peers, such as delinquency, violence, drug-taking, and alcohol use.

Teenagers who have after-school jobs receive widespread approval, as such employment expresses widely held American values of hard work, individual achievement, and learning by doing. Working in adolescence is thought to contribute to vocational exploration, the development of responsibility, effective management of time and money, and "work readiness," knowing how to behave appropriately at work.

Historical commentaries note the special symbolic meaning of paid work, embodying purposeful preparation and readiness for adulthood. In her historical study of a nineteenth-century mill town, Hareven (1982) documented that boys' initial jobs enabled them to buy their first suits, to begin smoking, to stay out late, and to acquire other privileges. When girls started to work they were allowed to put up their hair, purchase new dresses, and go to dances and movies. Becoming a worker fostered a sense of independence, even for young people who lived with their parents and turned over their paychecks to them. Adolescents in the Depression who contributed to their families through paid work gained confidence and feelings of efficacy from being able to help at a time of crisis (Elder, 1974).

In contrast to these salutary historical images, some contemporary commentaries depict adolescent work as youth culture run amok. Greenberger (1988) describes the typical youthwork setting as age-segregated and dominated by the peer subculture, a place where teenagers playfully enact pranks and games. They delight in impressing one another by "working the system," calling in sick when they are not really ill, giving away food and other goods at the employer's expense, and through it all, reinforcing anti-adult values and behaviors.

Other critics believe that youthwork, instead of fostering vocational preparation, puts young people at risk of "precocious development" (Bachman and Schulenberg, 1993). Working adolescents' job responsibilities and growing economic independence are thought to lead them to think of themselves, prematurely, as adults. This self-conception may encourage withdrawal from what are seen as child-like, dependent activities, such as living with parents and going to school, in favor of residential independence and full-time work. Such an accelerated transition to adulthood deprives young people of opportunities for human capital development through formal education.

Is it possible to reconcile these opposite conceptions of the place of work in the adolescent phase of life? Do part-time jobs foster the development of positive orientations and behaviors that promote later success? Or does paid employment encourage a too strong immersion in the peer culture, a kind of pseudomaturity, and an accelerated movement into adulthood? In view of evidence that environmental forces have their greatest impact when people are entering a new role, adolescents may be particularly sensitive to key dimensions of their work experiences (Van Maanen and Schein, 1979; Mortimer et al., 1988).

It is here that the YDS longitudinal data archive has its greatest utility. From one-time, cross-sectional studies of teenagers it is not possible to discern the direction of presumed "effects," such as whether intensive work produces, or is motivated by, restricted educational achievement. Much of the literature on teenage employment is based on such "snapshots," inferring consequences from contemporaneous associations (Bachman and Schulenberg, 1993; Greenberger and Steinberg, 1986; Steinberg and Dornbusch, 1991). Some longitudinal studies have been plagued by sample-selection problems and low retention rates. Moreover, no other longitudinal studies have monitored the diverse qualities of adolescent work experience.

In this chapter, summarizing more than a decade of research, I examine the consequences of early paid employment for contemporaneous outcomes, measured while the youth were still attending high school. Of central interest are indicators of salutary adolescent adjustment and precursors of successful young adulthood, such as perceived self-efficacy, mood state, and problem behavior. I also consider psychological orientations that are of central importance in occupational decisionmaking.

I follow Bronfenbrenner in his conviction that the effect of any single environmental influence must be understood within the context of the broader life space ecology. According to Bronfenbrenner, a developmentally significant "mesosystem," consisting of the links between the direct spheres of individual involvement (work and family, school and work), must be part of any meaningful developmental analysis. I address the impact of employment on the adequacy of performance and behavioral adjustment in key domains other than work: the family, the peer group, and the school. Given the widely understood significance of achievement in high school for subsequent educational and occupational attainment, adolescents' contemporaneous adjustment and future prospects could be significantly compromised if paid work constituted an impediment to academic progress.

The longitudinal character of the YDS also provides a unique opportunity to examine the longer-term (seven years after high school) consequences of adolescent work. These will be addressed in Chapter 7.

Almost all adolescents expect to be employed after the completion of their schooling, and virtually all teenage girls expect to work after they marry and have children (Johnson and Mortimer, 2000). In fact, YDS girls anticipated that they would attach greater importance to their future careers than did boys. In view of the general similarity of teenage boys' and girls' educational and occupational goals, we might expect to find little gender difference in response to work experiences.

Nonetheless, as they look to the future, adolescent girls also expect family life to be of greater importance to them. Unlike their male counterparts, they usually plan to interrupt their employment to care for their young children. National Monitoring the Future data, collected annually from high school seniors, show that adolescents of both genders think that mothers should be at home when their children are of preschool age. At least while they are still in high school, the majority of young people do not endorse women's dual pursuit of full-time work and parenthood (Schulenberg et al., 1995; Johnson et al., 2001).

Thus there is potential conflict between work and family for both genders, but girls' greater commitment to family life and assumed responsibility for the family make such conflict more salient for them. Interrupting employment while children are young jeopardizes young women's human capital development through work experience, as well as the likelihood of future career advancement. Moreover, girls' and boys' expectation that the mother will withdraw from employment suggests that today's adolescents have not wholly relinquished traditional gender role norms. There appears to be a persistent expectation, on the part of both genders, that men will be the main family breadwinners. If this is the case, then prospects for adult occupational achievement are likely to be a more salient issue for young men. For boys, early success in the workplace may more readily translate into more pronounced contemporaneous outcomes.

Chapter 3 documented that adolescent girls are more likely than boys to be employed throughout high school; when they do work, they report more chances to learn in the job setting and they experience their jobs as less stressful. Still, employment may be perceived as more important for masculine identity. If young men feel they have more at stake in their occupational success, they may be more sensitive to the character of, and their performance in, their early jobs.

Although the primary focus in this chapter is on paid work, I also address the impacts of family work and volunteering. As noted in Chapter 4, unpaid work is sometimes thought to have some of the same benefits, without the drawbacks, of a paid job. For example, household work not only teaches home management skills, it also provides occasion to care for others, a significant developmental experience (Call et al., 1995). Volunteer work in adolescence is widely thought to promote a civic ethic that encourages youth to continue to help others in their communities. What may be lost if adolescents withdraw from such activities in favor of paid employment?

While the YDS draws mainly on the self-reports of young people, the parents' surveys provide an alternative perspective. How do parents think their children have changed as a result of working? The parents can also bring their own experiences to bear in assessing the value of early paid work. In the fourth year of the study we asked them about the benefits and costs of their own early paid jobs. Their retrospective assessments may be illuminating: it is possible that experiences that are problematic at the time have positive aspects that are only appreciated in later years (Shanahan and Mortimer, 1996).

The Parents' Views

As shown in Chapter 1, historical change in the character of youthwork is central to the contemporary critique. Greenberger and Steinberg (1986) note that today's youth are less likely than those in prior generations to have jobs that promote skills that will be useful in future occupations. In their view, adolescent work has declined in both educational value and economic significance, and provides less meaningful exposure to adult contact and guidance.

Most of today's high school students, employed in retail and service jobs in the secondary labor market, have little expectation that their teenage jobs will lead to adult careers. In contrast, prior generations of employed adolescents, at least up to the mid-twentieth century, worked in settings that bore a closer resemblance to their likely adult workplaces. In rural areas they toiled alongside their parents and looked forward to acquiring their own farms. In small towns they were employed in small businesses owned by their families or neighbors. These young workers were likely to be in contact with adults who were either related to or known by their own families. Because higher education was less common than it is today, teenagers who were employed during high school often had entry-level jobs in organizations where they would continue to work after leaving school.

Consistent with this observation, Chapter 3 showed that the teenage jobs held by YDS parents differed from those of their children. The parents represent two historically identifiable cohorts who faced different labor market conditions in adolescence (Aronson et al., 1996): those born before or during World War II (1937–1945), who were adolescents during the 1950s and early 1960s; and the baby boomers born after the war (1946–1955), who were adolescents in the 1960s and early 1970s. As we have seen, the two cohorts tended to have different types of jobs, with the baby boomers being less involved in farming and more in fast-food work.

We asked the parents: "In general, taking into account all your jobs, do you think the work you did as a teenager was beneficial for you?" We also asked whether the work "caused any problems or difficulties for you." Those who responded affirmatively to either question were further queried, "In what ways?" This open-ended question allowed the parent to write in whatever came to mind.

Entirely contrary to the contemporary critique of youth employment, parents expressed tremendous enthusiasm for their early work experiences (see Aronson et al., 1996). To the question about work being beneficial, more than 85 percent of both mothers and fathers responded affirmatively. When given the opportunity to indicate problems or difficulties, there was the same remarkable agreement— that there were none. Thus we found an overwhelming consensus that working during high school was a positive experience. There was virtually no difference in this perception by gender of parent, by the kinds of jobs the parents had as youngsters, or by parental cohort.

The parents gave many illustrations of the advantages of working. They most often mentioned responsibility: "It made me more responsible for getting a better-paying job and not calling in sick whenever I felt like it." "It helped me be more responsible for my actions and learn why my parents couldn't always give me what I wanted."

The psychological growth obtained through working was another prevalent theme—working as teenagers had given them confidence, feelings of self-worth, and faith in their own abilities. They described feeling more independent and self-sufficient as they earned their own money. They also mentioned that working had inculcated disciplined work habits, motivation and commitment to work, dependability, accountability, and an ability to follow through: "I developed a sense of pride in the work I did." "It taught the value of a job well done."

Relatedly, the parents reported that working helped them to identify their own work preferences and job-related skills: "I learned to meet expectations, which kinds of work I enjoyed (hated offices, loved the hospital), and the importance of getting a degree after seeing older people stuck in dead-end jobs." "It taught me I could do anything. It gave me confidence." "It made me a better worker, I put everything I had behind all the jobs I had no matter what it was." "I learned to function well without supervision."

Parents recognized that jobs strengthened their interpersonal skills: "It taught me not to be shy, to speak out and up for what I want." They also mentioned having acquired greater ease in communicating with adults and in dealing with co-workers and customers. One parent acknowledged the benefits of encounters with diverse people in the workplace: "learning all the different types of people and their temperaments." They described having made lasting friendships in the workplace. Interpersonal skills and friendships are key elements in the development of social capital, with consequences for future placement in information-rich social networks.

Parents likewise mentioned other skills they acquired from working, including technical skills as well as those related to time and money management: "I worked many long days and very hard for my pay. I usually spend my money wisely and I'm very conservative." "It made me learn the value of money. I bought all of my own clothes and had a savings account also." Some mentioned having saved part of their earnings for college. Many identified specific skills, such as office operations, bookkeeping, machine use and repair, child care, and cooking. For some, early work experiences enabled them to acquire better adolescent jobs; new skills obtained in each successive job enhanced their attractiveness to subsequent employers. The vast majority of parents believed that working during adolescence yielded competencies that served them well in their adult lives.

Remarkably few parents (13 percent of mothers and 14 percent of fathers) mentioned any problems related to their early jobs. This small minority brought up a range of issues: difficulty finding time for their social lives and extracurricular activities, especially sports;

difficulty finding time for homework; missing school; caring less about school because of work. A few said they had been given too much responsibility at work. But in view of the myriad ways that employment during high school might interfere with teenagers' non-work activities, it is rather remarkable that the parents had so very little to say about its drawbacks.

Though the parents gave quite positive evaluations of their own early experiences as workers, it should be remembered that the kinds of jobs they had differed from those of their children. There is therefore little reason to expect that parents' opinions about their teenage work experiences would coincide with their attitudes about their children's work. But they were overwhelmingly favorable toward their children's employment. Even in Wave 1, when 63 percent of the parents reported that their ninth-grade children had paying jobs (53 percent of the children said they were currently working), the parents voiced nearly unanimous approval (see Phillips and Sandstrom, 1990). When the parents of working ninth graders were asked, "How do you feel about this child's employment?" 42 percent strongly approved, 49 percent approved, and 9 percent said they felt neutral. Remarkably, only 9 parents (of 982) said they either disapproved or strongly disapproved of their children's employment.

Views about the appropriate timing of children's first paid jobs confirm the parental affirmation of the value of early work. When the YDS children were in ninth grade, the parents were asked, "At what age do you think a child should first be allowed to have a paid job outside his or her own home?" Parents specified the ages separately for boys and girls. The modal preferred age to start working was 12 for both genders; the mean was just above 13 (with no significant differences between mothers and fathers). Parents' assessments correspond well to the children's actual initiation of employment— both boys and girls started working when they were about 12½ years old.

Several of the young respondents, when interviewed in their mid-twenties, mentioned the influence of their parents when they were seeking their first jobs:

My parents made me go get a job at fourteen. They did! Yes. They made me and I lied about my age. I said I was fifteen. They thought you should be working, get down there . . . It's to develop a good work ethic. That's why they made me go to work so early.

They thought that having a job would be good for me, and I thought so too. And so you learn how to deal with a schedule and work with managers and stuff like that.

It is conceivable that parents of different socioeconomic levels would have different opinions about when their children should start work. Parents of higher social class, who would want their children to maintain this advantage, might reasonably be expected to have some apprehension about work impinging on time for homework and other beneficial activities. A conception that working necessarily detracts from schoolwork could lead parents who had higher educational aspirations for their children to want them to delay entry into the workforce.

Rather surprisingly, the more advantaged parents (as indicated by higher socioeconomic status, being white, and being native born) wanted their children to start to work earlier, not later (see Phillips and Sandstrom, 1990). The pattern of findings did not differ by gender of the child. Furthermore, both fathers and mothers who had higher educational aspirations for their children wanted them to get paid jobs at earlier ages. In fact, aspirations for the child were found to entirely account for the effect of socioeconomic status on the father's preference for the age at which the child would start work (that is, the effect of socioeconomic status was reduced to insignificance when educational aspiration for the child was incorporated in the model).

This seemingly perplexing finding is illuminated by a consideration of the parents' answers when asked how working had influenced their ninth-grade child. The vast majority—82 percent of the mothers and 79 percent of the fathers—agreed or strongly agreed with the statement "My child has become more independent." Parents also attributed a wide range of other positive consequences to their children's work experiences, including higher self-esteem, greater responsibility, better work habits, and better time-management skills (Phillips and Sandstrom, 1990).

Prior studies have shown that the importance parents place on self-direction in their children increases with socioeconomic status (Kohn, 1969; Alwin, 1988). If employment is perceived as increasing the child's independence (as well as other positive traits that would foster success in school), and if more advantaged parents are more likely to value this set of attributes in their children, these parents' desire to have their children start work at a relatively early age becomes fully comprehensible. This does not mean that the more advantaged parents would endorse high-intensity work, or particular forms of paid work. We saw in Chapter 5 that children whose parents were more highly educated pursued lower-intensity work during high school.[1]

Highly favorable parental attitudes continued to be manifest through their children's high school years. In the children's senior year, most parents agreed that adolescent employment helps youth to mature and to develop good work attitudes. In fact, more than 70 percent of both mothers and fathers agreed or strongly agreed that working had given their children a sense of purpose, taught money management skills, and fostered better use of time. More than 80 percent of the parents saw their children gaining good work habits, self-confidence, the capacity to take responsibility, and the ability to communicate in a mature manner. The parents similarly agreed that working led their children to appreciate the extent of adult responsibilities.

Seventy percent of the parents thought their children's work had no effect on their grades. Approximately 10 percent thought grades had improved as a result of working; less than 20 percent thought grades had gone down. The parents' evaluations of their children's work, as gauged by a series of Likert-type questions incorporated in multi-item indices, bore no discernible relation to parental cohort, to the degree of the parent's own earlier investment in work (the hours the parent worked), or the parent's teenage job type (Aronson et al., 1996).

The Children's Views

The survey questions addressed to parents about their own work experiences and those asked of the teenagers were not the same; parents wrote answers to open-ended questions, while the teenagers' responses were in Likert-type forced-choice format. Because open-ended questions are less likely to elicit comment on any particular issue than forced-choice questions that directly draw attention to it, the percentages of children indicating specific outcomes of work are higher than those for parents. Though direct comparisons are therefore not feasible, some general observations can be made.

Like the parents, when asked directly about the value of working, the youth were exceedingly positive. To illustrate their aggregate assessment of various benefits and costs of employment, I again provide the percentage endorsing the two highest response categories (for example, agree and strongly agree) for key questions about current jobs. Data from workers in Wave 3 (mostly age 16 or 17) are presented because youth at this time were more likely than in earlier years to be employed, and those who were working were predominantly in formal jobs.

Of the employed youth, 90 percent of the girls and 80 percent of the boys agreed that their present jobs had helped them to learn to take responsibility for their work. Two-thirds of the girls and over half of the boys thought they had gained money-management skills. Three-fourths of the youth, irrespective of gender, agreed that their jobs had taught them to be on time, and 88 percent of the girls and 78 percent of the boys thought their jobs had helped them to learn how to get along with others. More than one of four thought their jobs had influenced their career choice.

The teenagers, like their parents, indicated fewer problems in their jobs than benefits. However, a higher percentage of the children indicated problems. From the data at hand we cannot discern whether this is due to the different response formats, to parents' nostalgic perceptions of their youth, or to true differences between the two generations' experiences of working. Almost half the youth reported having less time to spend with their friends because of their jobs. Fatigue (feeling drained of energy after work) was also a problem for about half the eleventh graders. The youth also worried that their jobs interfered with their schoolwork. As in the case of the parents, the youth's job categories (as gauged by the categorical code shown in Chapter 3) bore no relation to these assessments.

Thus, despite intergenerational change in the character of youthwork, parents' recollections of the benefits of their earlier employment and children's contemporaneous reports about the outcomes of their own jobs appear to be quite similar. Both parents and children consider their teenage jobs as more beneficial than problematic. Both generations indicate gains in responsibility and independence, money- and time-management skills, social skills, work skills,

and elements of the work ethic, all of which would presumably facilitate preparation for adult life (Aronson et al., 1996). When they did
report problems, parents' and children's responses were convergent:
both mentioned fatigue, difficulty keeping up academically, and ero-
sion of leisure time.

Moreover, our interviews with young adults echo the very same
themes as the parents' surveys. The enhancement of social skills was a
frequently reported benefit of working. When asked what had been
good about her first job, working in a card shop, an attorney mentioned "people skills":

> I remember being very, very shy when I first started . . . but after
> working you realize that, especially in the context of selling
> something to somebody, everyone is just a person and they have
> the same needs. You know, they go in the card shop. They
> have a mom for Mother's Day. They buy cards for it. They have
> birthdays that they buy for. I guess I was kind of lucky that was
> a job that brought in a lot of different people. I think that was,
> one of the things that I took from it is just kind of developing
> more interpersonal skills, problem-solving skills. Things would
> come up; customers would not be the most well behaved people
> in the world. You just kind of deal with it. Not take things per-
> sonally, so especially at that age, we take everything personally.
> But when you start working you realize that it's not just you.
> Sometimes it's the other people.

Other respondents emphasized the development of responsibility.
For example, a young woman who had worked at a drug store as a
cashier said: "It taught me a lot about responsibility, I mean I had to
be there on time. If there was a shift or a time that I couldn't work, I
was responsible for making sure that got covered." A young woman
who had worked at a pizza parlor told us: "It was fun and it taught
me responsibility . . . to be given the responsibility at 15 to 16 and
that type of independence, that helped a lot. The rewards of doing a
good job and getting paid for how good you do really helped me a
lot." A young man said of his early job as a paperboy: "I learned to
work for what I want in life. I learned some responsibility. I had to be
on time. I had to get it done before I went to school. I had to collect
the money. A little bit of business sense there."

Others recalled learning time-management skills: "I had to stay organized. High school, I think I graduated like fourth in my class, so obviously [working] didn't affect my studies a whole lot. Did it affect my social life? Every now and then, but again you were young and you were willing to go out after work. Who really cared? It taught you how to work hard. Taught you that yes, you can still put in a full day's work, still lead a life, still study and move on."

This evidence may be questioned on the grounds that it is inherently subjective. Still, as argued in Chapter 3, a job's psychological consequences may depend as much (or more) on subjective perceptions of work as on the objective realities. That is, a young worker's sense of responsibility, independence, confidence about job-relevant skills, and good work habits may be generative of occupational commitment and both psychological and behavioral dimensions of engagement in work. We cannot assess behavioral change—whether youth have, in fact, become more independent, more responsible, more careful with money. The parents' and children's own reflections, and the parents' perceptions of their children, are the closest we can come. On the basis of these necessarily subjective reports, we find more evidence for intergenerational continuity than discontinuity in perceptions about the developmental consequences of early employment. Still, consequences of employment may arise about which young people and their parents are subjectively unaware.

Some positive bias could arise from the fact that the surveys of both parents and children sample the views of persons who are, or have been, employed. Parents were asked to reflect on the jobs they had held when they were in high school; those who had not worked during their teenage years had no work experiences to consider. Because of the discretionary character of employment for most adolescents, those who have less positive attitudes about the consequences of employment are probably less likely to have paid jobs at any given time. However, 98 percent of the parents who participated in the Wave 4 survey did tell us about their teenage jobs. And 93 percent of the teenagers were employed at some time during their high school years.

Adolescents' actual work investment patterns provide evidence about the consequences of employment that does not have the disadvantages of subjective reports. Annual reports relevant to young people's mental health, problem behavior, school achievement, work orientations, and related variables enable more systematic assessment of whether greater investment in paid work fosters change in key psychological orientations and behavior.

Working and Mental Health

Much research on adults supports the presumption that the quality of work experience in adolescence is important for development. Adult mental health has repeatedly been shown to be responsive to the conditions of work, especially degree of autonomy on the job, but also role overload, conflict and ambiguity, noxious work conditions, and supervisory relations (Kohn and Schooler, 1983; Kahn, 1981; French et al., 1982; Johansson and Aronsson, 1991). Low levels of extrinsic reward have also been linked to adult distress (McLeod and Kessler, 1990).

But to understand the consequences of adolescent work for mental health, we must place it within the context of this particular life stage. Consolidating orientations toward work and productivity and establishing vocational goals are widely considered major developmental tasks for adolescents, enabling crystallization of an occupational identity (Erikson, 1963; Vondracek et al., 1986). Employment is intricately tied to the successful transition to adulthood, making possible residential and financial independence from parents, key components of "adult" identity in the eyes of young people themselves (Arnett, 1997). Employment also contributes to the adequate performance of adult family roles; traditional gender role norms make this especially the case for men, but many contemporary young women also expect to contribute to their families' income (Johnson and Mortimer, 2000). Young people, as they look forward to adulthood, surely are aware of these links between employment and becoming an adult.

Thus the work role might reasonably be expected to have considerable psychological salience for contemporary adolescents. As observed earlier, the workplace offers opportunities to enact a key component of the desired adultlike "possible self" (Markus et al., 1990). Having a paying job, no matter how menial or part time, provides entry to the world of work, away from the watchful eyes of parents, teachers, and other childhood authorities. It connotes independence and the capacity to function autonomously. The ability to navigate in the work world—to get a job, to perform the tasks and resolve the problems encountered in the work environment, and to manage one's commitments to work, family, school, and peers—may signal to the adolescent a degree of competence with important implications for the future.

Alternatively, it might be argued that while the *adult* work role has high salience for youth as a means of realizing the adult "possible self," the teenager's part-time job has little psychological relevance. Most contemporary adolescents do not expect to continue in the jobs they have in high school. Their emergent work identities may therefore be more closely linked to success in school than to part-time job experiences. Nor do they depend on their jobs, as adults do, to support basic living expenses, to achieve a place in the social community, and to build connections to the wider society. Young people's jobs tend to be more transitory than those of adults, and the very expectation of limited incumbency may lessen their impact.

In seeming support of this point of view, the YDS data provide scant evidence that working itself, or even its intensity at any given time, has demonstrable consequences for key indicators of adolescents' mental health. Work status—whether employed or not—is neither beneficial for nor deleterious to mental health. An array of indicators of mental health have been investigated, including self-esteem, global self-efficacy, depressive affect, self-derogation, and well-being. The number of hours the adolescents spent working each week (at the time of each survey administration) and the pattern of investment in work during high school have been found to bear no consistent relation to these key measures of mental health (Mortimer, Finch, et al., 1996; Mortimer and Johnson, 1998a). Similar mostly null findings are reported in several other studies that have attempted to link adolescent work intensity with indicators of mental health (e.g., Steinberg and Dornbusch, 1991; Bachman et al., 1986).

If there are advantages or disadvantages for mental health associated with moving toward the adultlike possible self by getting a part-time job, they may well be contingent upon what happens at work—whether the youth's experiences foster a sense of competence, or, alternatively, cause distress and undermine positive self-perceptions and optimistic thinking about the future. Does employment provide opportunities for successful, enactive performance accomplishments (Bandura, 1977), or is the young person overwhelmed by time pressure, work overload, and too-difficult tasks? The degree to which employment enables success, or provides occasions for failure, may determine whether the youth develops a sense of forward movement toward the desired possible self.

First let us consider the sense of efficacy, or confidence that one can successfully enact the behaviors necessary to achieve one's goals. Such an orientation is key to Clausen's (1993) notion of planful competence. For if one has little conviction that one is capable of successfully executing a plan, one has little incentive for planning. According to Bandura (1977), a sense of personal efficacy is key to the initiation of coping behavior; it also determines the effort and persistence applied to a problem when initial efforts are unsuccessful. A young man interviewed in the YDS expressed this confidence: "I've come to believe that people often create their own realities and if you decide . . . that you want something, if you decide that you're going to do something, by deciding that you want it, by identifying it as something you want, you find a way to make it happen . . . I made the choices that fit my plan. I directed my life to fit the way I had decided I wanted it to go."

Another young man describes his own life experience: "As I've moved through dealing with the different challenges and obstacles . . . I've learned how to deal with the failures along with the successes and to try and overcome. Perseverance has definitely been a key word that I learned to deal with and learned to not get down about and luckily for me pretty much everything that I've set out to do or wanted to do I've been able to somehow accomplish in some way, shape, or form and that's been a real positive thing for me." But a less sanguine young woman told us: "I don't know that I've got any set interests or goals that I'm working toward . . . I haven't ever had any like set path or set goals that I've been trying to achieve."

Efficacy and related control orientations are important psychological resources at the time of transition to adulthood, when youth are attempting to gain entry to career trajectories that will influence attainments throughout their working lives. A sense of efficacy would also promote the achievement of other goals, unrelated to work. In fact, the more efficacious YDS adolescents were more likely to achieve their senior-year plans for postsecondary educational attainment and residential independence from parents two years beyond high school (Pimentel, 1996). Demonstrating the very long-term significance of early planful orientations, Clausen (1991) found that adolescent boys who exhibited planful competence held occupations of higher prestige when they were observed in middle age. They also had more satisfactory and stable family lives.

Whereas occupational experience, especially occupational self-direction, has been shown to predict efficacy in adulthood (Kohn and Schoenbach, 1983; Miller et al., 1983; Spenner and Otto, 1985; Mortimer and Lorence, 1979b; Mortimer, Lorence, and Kumka, 1986), studies of youth have focused on other determinants of the self-image, such as school grades (Eccles et al., 1996), success in sports (Braddock et al., 1991), or parental support (Gecas and Schwalbe, 1986). Nonetheless, when adolescents are able to do their jobs successfully, they, like adults, are likely to experience what Bandura (1977, 1986) calls "performance accomplishment." Able to observe their own success, they obtain an immediate sense of competence in the work environment. Given the ubiquity of generalization, through which attitudes developed in one setting extend to other settings (Kohn and Schooler, 1983; Miller, 1988), this self-efficacy is likely to generate confidence about work in the future.

Consistent with this line of reasoning, the self-efficacy of employed YDS adolescents, as indicated by the Pearlin Mastery Scale (Pearlin et al., 1981), was observed to increase over a one-year period (from ninth to tenth grade) when they reported conditions in the work environment indicative of success, or success-enabling affordances (Miller, 1988). Youth with high self-efficacy are confident that they can achieve what they set out to do. They tend to agree with statements like "What happens to me in the future mainly depends on me," and to disagree with statements like "Sometimes I feel that I'm being pushed around in life."

Boys' mastery was found to increase when they reported opportunities for advancement in their jobs, when they perceived little conflict between school and work, and when they were free of close supervision (Finch et al., 1991; Call et al., 1995). Girls' efficacy was higher when they reported that they were being paid well. Money has important symbolic meaning and social significance as well as instrumental value (Zelizer, 1985). Feeling adequately paid may constitute a symbolic affirmation of girls' worth and competence as workers in a traditionally masculine domain.[2] Consistent with girls' heightened sensitivity to others (Gilligan, 1982), girls' efficacy also increased when they were able to help people on the job. Girls' self-efficacy di-

Table 6.1. Twelfth-grade global efficacy, depressive affect, and alcohol use regressed on work-quality variables

	12th-grade global efficacy		12th-grade depressive affect		12th-grade alcohol use	
	b	S.E.	b	S.E.	b	S.E.
Parental education	.148**	.053	-.202	.117	-.064	.035
Race	-.276	.216	-.384	.478	.400**	.140
Nativity	.540	.364	-1.61*	.810	.319	.242
Family composition	-.021	.186	.539	.413	-.032	.123
Gender	.353*	.177	-1.26**	.396	.252*	.115
Global efficacy (9th grade)	.346***	.034				
Depressive affect (9th grade)			.266***	.033		
Alcohol use (9th grade)					.267***	.032
Learning opportunities	-.057	.039	.030	.085	-.042	.025
Biweekly earnings	.003**	.001	-.005	.003	.002	.001
Work stressors	-.088***	.023	.167***	.050	.003	.015
Work and school	-.027	.048	-.324**	.105	-.020	.032
Work and grades	.120	.081	-.506**	.176	-.128*	.053
Peer-derived work status	.105	.076	.055	.165	.167***	.049
Wage satisfaction	.366**	.116	-.650**	.253	.010	.075
Autonomy	.000	.063	.166	.137	.113**	.041
Constant	9.55***	1.17	21.70***	2.38	.538	.686
N[a]	828		834		828	
R^2	.196		.158		.155	

*$p < .05$; **$p < .01$; ***$p < .001$.
a. Mean substitution for missing data on work variables was used to increase sample size.

minished when they thought they were being held responsible at work for things that they could not control, and when they did not feel free to express disagreement with their supervisors (Finch et al., 1991; Call et al., 1995).

Chances for advancement, viewing oneself as well paid, and perceiving a lack of conflict between school and work all suggest adequate functioning in the work environment and effective balancing, at least from the teenagers' point of view, of their multiple responsibilities. Finding it difficult to juggle work and school tasks, or feeling overwhelmed by uncontrollable responsibilities at work, appears to produce a general sense of ineffectiveness. Being able to provide valued services to others is further indication of successful performance in the work environment. (These salutary consequences of work experiences were observed controlling background variables, one-year lagged variables, and a selection-to-work hazard.)

Similarly, in calculations using the average indicators of work quality described in Chapter 3, adolescents (both boys and girls) who had higher earnings in their jobs and perceived themselves as being paid well manifested increases in efficacy during the four years of high school (see Table 6.1). Work stressors, in contrast, reduced efficacy.

Little attention has been given to work as a source of depressed mood in adolescents, but this relationship is significant because adolescence is a stage of life in which the manifestation of depression becomes more prevalent (Cicchetti and Toth, 1995; Ebata et al., 1990; Compas and Hammen, 1996). It is also a period of initiation to the workplace, where chronic stressors may be encountered.

Though mood state may appear to be more peripheral than self-efficacy to instrumental action, distress is a likely impediment to successful employment (Mortimer, 1994). Young people who are more distressed prior to labor force entry have been found to have greater difficulty in the job market. Depressive affect and related psychological orientations (life dissatisfaction, a negative outlook, and boredom) predicted subsequent unemployment among Australian school-leavers (Feather and O'Brien, 1986; O'Brien and Feather, 1990; Winefield and Tiggemann, 1985). In a study of adult auto workers, those who were depressed had higher unemployment rates one and two years after the plants had closed (Hamilton et al., 1991).

Analyses of first-year YDS data, gathered when the youth were only 14–15 years old, showed that work stressors and problematic links between school and work were positively associated with depressive affect (measured by items from the Health Insurance Study Mental Health Battery, for example, "Have you felt depressed?" "Have you felt downhearted and blue?"; see Ware et al., 1979; Mortimer et al., 1992). Shanahan and his colleagues (1991; Shanahan, 1992) addressed the consequences of work experiences for adolescent depressed mood longitudinally, through the years of high school. They found that stressors at work heightened boys' depressive affect; acquiring useful skills on the job, in contrast, lessened boys' depressed mood. Both work stressors and job skills are implicated in achievement and thus may be especially salient to adolescent boys.

Girls' depressive affect increased when they encountered circumstances at work in which they were held accountable for things that they could not control. This particular indicator references the reactions of others in the work environment—presumably it would be supervisors or other persons in authority who would hold the girl responsible in such circumstances.

For both genders, evidence of successful coping and success-enabling affordances in the workplace (such as chances to acquire skills on the job) were found to ameliorate adolescents' mood state. In contrast, difficulties and problems, which may connote failure or deficient adaptation to the work environment, heighten distress. Again, extensive controls—for social background, selection to work, and prior depressed mood—bolster the credibility of the conclusions.

An intriguing finding of Shanahan's work, given the pervasive benefits of occupational self-direction for adult mental health, was a positive association between indicators of self-direction at work and boys' depressed mood. Indeed, adolescent boys who had more decisionmaking authority and greater control over their time at work were more depressed than those whose actions on the job were more constrained. Shanahan explains this finding as derived from the novice character of youth workers and from boys' greater sensitivity to achievement-related work experiences. That is, for young men with little work experience, and therefore without adequate knowledge and problem-solving capacities, self-direction may foster uncertainty and heighten the risk of mistakes. At least in the early stages of employment, youth (particularly boys) may need structure and role clarity, rather than autonomy. Moreover, the deleterious effects of work stressors and self-direction on boys' mood state increased when they worked more than 20 hours per week (Shanahan, 1992).

Although the gender differences intriguingly suggest that achievement-related dimensions of work may be more salient to adolescent boys, the general conclusion to be drawn is that the quality of work is consequential for the mental health of both genders. Differences in effect size tend to be small (and sometimes statistically insignificant; see Finch et al., 1991), and they diminish as adolescents grow older and acquire more work experience (gender differences are less pronounced in Shanahan's analyses of depressive affect in twelfth grade than in tenth grade). Furthermore, average indicators of work quality during high school did not significantly interact with gender in influencing Wave 4 depressive affect. We therefore conclude that work stressors increase depressed mood, and that both compatibility between work and school and the perception that one is paid well reduce it, for both genders (see Table 6.1; see also Mortimer, Harley, and Staff, 2002).

Problem Behavior

A central theme in the criticism of youth employment is its association with problem behavior. According to Bachman and Schulenberg (1993), working is part of a syndrome of "precocious development" that includes early involvement in dating (Mihalic and Elliott, 1997) as well as leisure activities that are legitimate, though not thought to be altogether desirable, when engaged in by adults, including drinking, smoking, and drug use. Youth who work may begin to chafe at having to enact dependent, childlike roles, and may become defiant in settings that call for such roles. Trouble in school may ensue. A prominent hypothesis is that the various problem behaviors linked to employment are brought on by insufficient impulse control. According to Gottfredson and Hirschi (1990), working long hours and using alcohol are both expressions of an underlying criminal propensity linked to impulsivity or the inability to delay gratification.

In fact, the association between adolescent employment and problem behavior is highly robust and consistent across a large body of research (Committee, 1998). Intensive work (more than 20 hours per week) is associated with more frequent use of alcohol, cigarettes, and

Table 6.2. Twelfth-grade alcohol use, economic efficacy, and extrinsic work values regressed on background and high school work investment

	12th-grade alcohol use		12th-grade economic efficacy		12th-grade extrinsic work values	
	b	S.E.	b	S.E.	b	S.E.
Parental education	-.037	.031	.132**	.044	-.115	.067
Race	.368**	.128	.201	.183	-.130	.276
Nativity	.325	.222	-.429	.312	-.642	.468
Family composition	-.085	.110	-.060	.157	-.274	.234
Gender	.324***	.099	-.055	.144	-.462*	.214
Alcohol use (9th grade)	.299***	.035				
Economic efficacy (10th grade)			.489***	.031		
Extrinsic values (9th grade)					.303***	.031
Steady[a]	-.183	.139	-.149	.199	-.600*	.297
Occasional	-.519***	.141	-.588**	.202	-.579[b]	.300
Sporadic	.103	.151	-.279	.217	-.399	.324
No work	-.614**	.216	-.942**	.311	-1.352**	.466
Constant	.982***	.265	6.508***	.514	14.5***	.915
N	795		827		810	
R²	.166		.262		.138	

*p < .05; **p < .01; ***p < .001.
a. Reference category is the "most invested" pattern.
b. p = .054.

illegal drugs (Bachman and Schulenberg, 1993; Greenberger and Steinberg, 1986; Mihalic and Elliot, 1997; Resnick et al., 1997; Schulenberg and Bachman, 1993; Steinberg, Fegley, and Dornbusch, 1993). Employed students engage in more deviance and school misconduct than students who do not work (Greenberger and Steinberg, 1986; Steinberg and Dornbusch, 1991; Tanner and Krahn, 1991; Wright et al., 1997).

Long hours of work have also been linked to theft, trouble with the police (especially for boys) and, if working more than 30 hours, aggressive behavior (Bachman and Schulenberg, 1993). According to the National Youth Survey, minor delinquency is more prevalent among full-time than among part-time adolescent workers, and more prevalent among part-time workers than among nonworkers (Wofford, 1988). Still, the nonworking adolescents were found to engage in more serious offenses than the workers (such as aggravated assault or theft of items worth more than $50).

There is evidence that highly intensive work may be more conducive to delinquency among youth who already have problems in their families and at school. Analyzing data from the 1988 National Survey of Family and Households, Wright and colleagues (1997) found that long hours of work increased delinquent behavior only for boys who were already considered at high risk for delinquency (those with criminal parents, parental rejection, low school commitment, and so on); it had no direct effect for girls or low-risk boys.

In the domain of problem behavior, subjective perception and objective evidence clearly do not mesh. The YDS parents did not mention problem behavior, deviance, or association with "undesirable peers" as drawbacks of employment, when describing either their own experiences or those of their children. But the more objectively measured intensity of work during high school was positively associated with the YDS adolescents' alcohol use, controlling for past alcohol use (measured one year previously), family background variables, and gender (Mortimer, Finch, et al., 1996). Adolescents who worked more intensively also reported more problem behavior in school, but only in tenth grade. Furthermore, "occasional" workers and nonworkers drank less frequently in Wave 4 than the most invested adolescent workers; sporadic and steady workers did not differ from the latter reference category (see Table 6.2).

Links between the quality of work and adolescent problem behavior have been subjected to little empirical scrutiny. However, Schulenberg and Bachman (1993) found heightened substance use among youth working in low-quality jobs—jobs that made little use of their talents, were unconnected to anticipated future jobs, and were being performed only for the money. We found that adolescent workers drink more when they think work gives them status in the eyes of their friends and when their jobs are more autonomous (see Table 6.1). However, drinking diminishes when they perceive little conflict between work and getting good grades.[3] These analyses, based on average reports of work experiences during the teenage years, suggest that excessive responsibility and perceived conflict between employment and academic performance may increase the use of alcohol as a stress-reducer.

Alternatively, these work experiences—status from working, autonomy, and not perceiving conflicts between school performance and work—could also be interpreted as indicators of adultlike status. It is not possible with the data at hand to adjudicate between these alternative interpretations. The empirical findings do, however, indicate that work quality is implicated in adolescent alcohol use.

All available evidence points to the conclusion that intensive work in adolescence is linked to problem behavior. But how worrisome are these trends? First, it is important to consider the strength of this influence. Osgood (1999: 177) suggests that the effects of employment, though consistent and robust across studies, are of relatively small magnitude:

> Indeed, research on crime and drug use indicates that the modest increases in these behaviors that appear to result from employment may not be so foreboding. The increases in problem behavior associated with teen employment pale in comparison to correlates such as sex, age, and success at school. Also, Hagan (1991) and Newcomb and Bentler (1988) find that middle-class adolescents who engage in a limited amount of minor problem behavior are at least as likely to be successful in early adulthood as middle-class students who do not.

Second, is the heightened problem behavior that is linked to adolescent employment persistent into adulthood? If these consequences were only short-term, they would presumably be less worrisome. Because of the absence of long-term studies, little is known about the continuity of problem behavior among adolescents who are more invested in work.[4] However, four years after high school, the work investment types no longer predicted drinking behavior: the other young people's alcohol use had caught up to that of the high-intensity workers, erasing earlier differences (Mortimer and Johnson, 1998a; see McMorris and Uggen, 2000).

Vocational Development

Because work-related attitudes and values tend to become more stable as people move through their work careers (Mortimer et al., 1988; Lorence and Mortimer, 1985; Mortimer and Lorence, 1979a), a focus on adolescence is particularly strategic for the study of vocational development. Adolescence may be thought of as a critical period in which orientations toward work and achievement-related habits of behavior begin to crystallize.

As we have seen, the YDS parents expressed enthusiastic approbation of their children's, as well as their own, prior employment as preparation for adult work. And even the most prominent critics of youthwork note links between adolescent employment and positive work attitudes, such as punctuality, dependability, and personal responsibility (Greenberger, 1984; Steinberg, Greenberger, Garduque, and McAuliffe, 1982), and girls' self-reliance (Greenberger, 1984).

Working during adolescence presents opportunities to think about the self in relation to occupational goals—to consider the kinds of job tasks one most likes and dislikes, the rewards and problems typically encountered by persons in various fields, the credentials needed to obtain attractive positions, and the strategies that might optimize future work conditions. These are the very kinds of thought processes that Clausen (1993) called "planful competence." As argued in Chapter 5, the particular choices embodied in such planfulness may differ, depending on the adolescent's resources and educational promise.

Working also brings with it certain generic behavioral capacities, inducing "work readiness"—knowledge about how to present oneself at a job interview, assurance that one can get to work on time, meet employers' expectations, and accept responsibility. The experience of successfully combining school and work could promote a self-image as one who is able to meet the challenges of working as well as other adult roles.

As the parents and young adults recognized in reflecting on their own experience, employed youth learn how to relate to other people in the work setting. Working can thereby enhance interpersonal skills, especially in dealing with types of people the teen would not ordinarily encounter in the neighborhood, in school, or among friends. According to the Panel on Youth (1974: 4), "experience with persons differing in social class, subculture, and in age" is a necessary ingredient for becoming a well-functioning adult in contemporary society. Such experience is likely to be helpful in adult (as well as adolescent) employment contexts.

The crystallization of work values—preferences for occupational experiences and rewards—is prerequisite to deliberate occupational choice. That is, adolescents who have prioritized the rewards that are potentially obtainable through work can assess the potential of certain jobs to fulfill their preferences and set their occupational goals accordingly. Though deliberate choice among a range of alternatives is probably more common for middle- and upper-middle-class youth, who have a wider range of opportunities than their less advantaged peers, such preferences come into play, at least minimally, in most job-search situations. In the absence of dire necessity, even when there is only one job alternative or offer presented, the youth could have the option of continuing the search. Selection of work on the basis of one's value priorities, interests, and abilities enhances the degree of "person-environment fit." Young people's occupational values, in fact, are significantly predictive of subsequent job experiences (Mortimer and Lorence, 1979a; Mortimer, Pimentel, et al., 1996).

Each year during high school, the YDS youth were asked how important various features of work would be to them when seeking a full-time job after completing their schooling. The list of features included extrinsic considerations, such as money, social status, advancement, and security, as well as intrinsic features, such as autonomy, compatibility with one's own interests and abilities, and chances to work with people and to be helpful to others.

Consistent with the null findings regarding work intensity and mental health, yearly analyses of YDS data yield no evidence that hours of work influenced intrinsic work values. However, the "most invested" workers in high school had stronger extrinsic values than the "steady" workers and the "nonworkers," net of preexisting, ninth-grade differences (see Table 6.2). Employed adolescents, both boys and girls, who had opportunities to learn skills on the job became more interested in intrinsic and people-oriented, as well as extrinsic, occupational values (Mortimer, Pimentel, et al., 1996). Increased engagement in the task, resulting from the learning process itself, could heighten awareness of the diverse experiences and rewards that work has to offer. Moreover, successful mastery of work tasks as a result of such opportunities would be likely to foster confidence in one's capacity to achieve in the work sphere, making occupational rewards feel more within reach.

A further psychological dimension, of relevance to vocational development, is the sense of economic efficacy. While most attention has been directed to global efficacy, the general sense that one can accomplish what one sets out to do, there is evidence that efficacy may not be the same across all domains of life experience. A person might feel highly efficacious in the school domain but not in relations with peers. The YDS assessed efficacy in the economic realm by asking the adolescents to rate (on a 5-point scale from "very low" to "very high") the chances that they would have a job that paid well, be able to own their own home, and have work they enjoyed doing.

We assumed that if youth think they are capable of achieving in the world of work, that is, if they express a high degree of economic efficacy, they will be more likely to be actively engaged in planning and preparing for their futures, and they will also have higher achievement-related goals. In fact, there was much support for these suppositions (Grabowski et al., 2001). Economic efficacy, measured in eleventh grade, was found to have a positive influence on educational plans measured during the senior year. Furthermore, youth who felt more efficacious in the economic realm were more likely to have talked to counselors, taken college entrance exams, and requested or submitted college applications. They were thus more engaged in actions that would help them to achieve their educational goals.

Following the youth beyond high school enabled us to observe longer-term consequences of economic efficacy. Two years after high school, the more efficacious youth had higher post-secondary educational attainment, both because of these concrete actions and because economic efficacy promoted higher education directly (Grabowski

et al., 2001). While global and economic efficacy are positively related, economic efficacy appeared to be far more important for educational attainment.

It therefore is important to know whether work experiences during high school can enhance this domain-specific sense of competency. Even with key background variables (gender, race, nativity,
family composition, and parental education) and economic efficacy
four years earlier controlled, occasional workers and nonworkers exhibited less confidence in being able to achieve their economic goals
in the future than the most invested workers; sporadic and steady
workers manifested levels of efficacy similar to those of the most invested (see Table 6.2). Assessment of tenth- and eleventh-grade work
experiences (averaged, if the youth worked both years) showed that
the perception that one is paid well raised eleventh-grade economic
efficacy for both genders (Grabowski et al., 2001). This evidence of
effective functioning in work heightens the expectation that one will
continue to be successful in the economic sphere in the future.

The Ecology of Work

WORK AND THE FAMILY
Unlike prior generations of youth, who worked alongside their parents on family farms, in the skilled trades, and in small businesses,
contemporary American youth work in restaurants, retail stores, gas
stations, movie theaters, and other locales away from parents and
other relatives. Whereas employment in the previous situation might
be thought of as supporting family cohesion, as the youth contributed
to the family's economic well-being, contemporary youthwork is
more likely to be seen as drawing the adolescent away from the family and disrupting its collective activities.

When adolescents are employed, they spend less time in contact with other family members (Greenberger and Steinberg, 1986;
Greenberger et al., 1980; Steinberg and Dornbusch, 1991). About
half of the teenagers in Greenberger and Steinberg's sample said they
helped around the house less often after they became employed. The
more hours adolescents worked, the less often they had dinner with
their families (Greenberger et al., 1980). There is also evidence that
when children are employed, disagreement with parents becomes
more frequent (Manning, 1990). Bachman and Schulenberg (1993),

using the national Monitoring the Future surveys of high school seniors, found that nonworkers had the fewest arguments with their parents, and that arguments became more frequent with hours of work (up to 20 hours).

There is some indication that the consequences of employment may be more deleterious for girls' family relationships than for those of boys. Steinberg and colleagues found that both employment and hours of work were associated with declines in the closeness of family relationships for girls who entered the labor force for the first time between tenth and eleventh grades. In contrast, the quality of relations between parents and adolescent sons improved with both working and hours of work (Steinberg, Greenberger, Garduque, Ruggiero, and Vaux 1982).

To assess the quality of the parent-child relationship, we asked the YDS youth a series of questions: how much they wanted to be like their parents when they became adults, how close they felt to their parents, how often they did things that they enjoyed with their parents, how often they talked to parents about personal concerns and decisions, how often the parents talked to them about the same things, and how often the parents listened to their side of an argument (Mortimer and Shanahan, 1994). Though these items could indicate different relationship dimensions, such as support, identification, communication, and family democracy, they are all key to good parenting (Steinberg, 1990); they were also positively related to one another.

We found no consistent evidence that work status or hours of work influence the quality of parent-adolescent relations. It is not surprising that YDS teenagers spend less time with their families when they work more hours, given that adolescence is a time of separation and individuation from parents. Youth who work achieve a degree of social, economic, and emotional (Shanahan et al., 1991) independence from parents. But to what extent should the reduced time with parents be interpreted as a negative trend? The critics warn that parents will not monitor employed youth sufficiently, promoting deviance. McMorris and Uggen (2000) further suggest that weakened bonds to the family (and the school) are promotive of deviance.

In the YDS, the parents saw their children's greater independence, linked to working, as a positive step toward adulthood (Phillips and Sandstrom, 1990; Aronson et al., 1996). However, McMorris and

Uggen (1998), using growth curve analytic techniques, found that youth who report that work gives them greater independence from their families are more likely to increase their drinking during high school. This indicator of independence from parents partially mediated the effect of work intensity on alcohol use. Still, as we have seen, the more frequent alcohol use by the more intensive workers during high school did not persist in young adulthood. What is more important than the impact on time together, arguments, or even independence is that there is no firm evidence that adolescent employment diminishes the closeness and supportive quality of the parent-teenager relationship.

In fact, in some circumstances, just the opposite may be closer to the truth. Boys, but not girls, appear to gain a sense of independence from the family by working, and become closer to their fathers as they acquire skills on the job (Mortimer and Shanahan, 1994). These findings suggest that parents may approve of boys' employment more than that of girls, despite boys' and girls' convergent aspirations and achievement orientations.

Furthermore, positive experiences at work can sometimes buffer, or reduce the ill effects of, problems in the family. Call (1996b; Call and Mortimer, 2001) shows that a supportive relationship with a supervisor reduces the negative consequences of strain in the parent-child relationship for both boys and girls. That is, a lack of closeness and communication in the parent-child relationship diminished the adolescent's sense of well-being, self-esteem, and efficacy only when supervisory support was absent. When a supportive supervisor was present, there were no significant relationships between family distress and these indicators of psychological health (see Table 6.3).

This pattern of findings confirms Bronfenbrenner's claim that the mesosystem structure of interrelations needs to be considered if we are to understand the developmental implications of any single domain of experience. Youth who are having difficulties in the family may have greater need for positive experiences and relationships elsewhere in their lives. Work can be one such source of comfort and support.

Additional evidence attesting to the import of the surrounding context derives from Shanahan and colleagues' (1996) comparison of the effects of adolescents' work on parent-child relationships in urban St. Paul and rural Iowa settings. While hours of work reduced adolescents' time with their families in the YDS panel, rural Iowa youth who worked more than 10 hours per week spent more time with their families than those who worked fewer hours. Moreover, in rural Iowa, adolescents' earnings fostered more sharing of advice between parent and adolescent and stronger emotional ties. In contrast, in the YDS panel earnings did not have these positive outcomes.

The authors' interpretation of these findings highlights differences in the meaning of work for the family in rural and urban contexts. Earnings can be used to support the adolescent's individualistic pursuits or the collective well-being of the family. In both urban and rural settings, the more communal uses of earnings enhanced relationships between parents and children. But the rural youth were more likely than their urban counterparts to give money to their parents, to pay for school fees, or to save at least part of their earnings for college.

WORK AND PEER RELATIONS

Like relationships in the family, peer friendships are sometimes thought to be compromised by youthwork (Greenberger, 1988). Though teenagers are often surrounded by peer co-workers, the typical youth workplace—with required tasks to be accomplished and high turnover—is not a likely context for the development of strong friendships. We asked YDS adolescents, "When things get rough, do you have a friend (or friends) you can really talk to, someone you can turn to for support and understanding?" Contrary to Greenberger's hypothesis, there were no differences between working and nonworking teens in perceived support from friends. Moreover, hours of work, measured in the annual surveys, had no discernible consequence for this indicator of support (Mortimer and Shanahan, 1991). Assessment of the association between this relational indicator and the work-investment pattern likewise yielded null findings.

To the contrary, the pattern of work investment over time, or the quality of work experience, might possibly enhance peer relationships. We saw in Chapter 3 that the adolescents who are most invested in work feel that working gives them status among their peers. Moreover, youth with the more learning-enhancing jobs become closer to their peers over time (Mortimer and Shanahan, 1994).

While adolescent employment does not seem to undermine the capacity to develop supportive friendships, it might influence peer rela-

Table 6.3. Moderating effects of work comfort on the relationship between family discomfort and 10th-grade adolescent adjustment

Well-being	No supervisor support		Supervisor support	
	b	beta	b	beta
Family discomfort	-1.384	-.221**	.195	.032
Socioeconomic status	-.149	-.072	.034	.020
Race	.256	.034	.797	.114
Nativity	1.136	.088	-.929	-.094
Gender	.926	.151*	-.295	-.052
Well-being (9th grade)	.370	.364***	.258	.280***
N	199		105	
R^2	.251***		.093	

Self-esteem	No supervisor support		Supervisor support	
	b	beta	b	beta
Family discomfort	-1.084	-.199**	.161	.031
Socioeconomic status	-.001	-.005	.032	.022
Race	-.116	-.018	-.870	-.146
Nativity	1.054	.100	1.311	.002
Gender	.266	.050	-.404	-.084
Self-esteem (9th grade)	.507	.444***	.517	.465***
N	199		105	
R^2	.321***		.211***	

	No supervisor support		Supervisor support	
Global efficacy	b	beta	b	beta
Family discomfort	−1.145	−.212**	.403	.068
Socioeconomic status	.049	.027	.126	.080
Race	−.575	−.089	.397	.059
Nativity	.698	.068	−.568	−.059
Gender	.226	.042	.204	.038
Efficacy (9th grade)	.513	.449***	.440	.401***
N	196		101	
R^2	.279***		.170**	

*$p < .05$; **$p < .01$; ***$p < .001$.
Source: Adapted from Call and Mortimer (2001: 111).

tions and activities in other inauspicious ways. Osgood (1999) observes that unstructured socializing with peers, away from authority figures, encourages teens' and young adults' delinquency and substance use. If working reduces the availability of such unstructured time, it may diminish youthful deviance. However, Osgood shows, using Monitoring the Future data from high school seniors, that teenagers who work more hours also have more active social lives, spending more time in activities like "cruising," shopping, and going to parties and bars. If teenagers simply hang out with their work friends before or after work, this unstructured time may be a breeding ground for delinquent acts.

Links between working, trouble-making friends, and problem behavior are therefore of considerable interest. In the YDS, having older peers at work did not mediate the effects of employment on alcohol use (Mortimer, Finch, et al., 1996); nor did time spent with work friends (McMorris and Uggen, 2000). Using data from the National Youth Survey, Ploeger (1997) finds employment to be positively related to delinquent behavior, especially that involving alcohol and drug use. In that study, workers also reported more delinquent friends than nonworkers. Importantly, exposure to delinquent peers fully accounted for the employment effect. But this is an aggregate trend; it remains possible that employment could have different implications for delinquent behavior, as well as for more prosocial activities, depending on the particular peers with whom the adolescent comes in contact at work.

WORK AND SCHOOL ACHIEVEMENT

Historically, the tradeoff between working and school attendance prompted legal restrictions on child labor to promote universal secondary schooling. In a 1923 study (cited by Zelizer, 1985) based on the school records of children in rural North Dakota, 59 percent of those aged 10–14 had been kept home to work in defiance of child labor regulations. Today, concern about the compatibility of schooling and work addresses a different set of issues. Critics fear that employment will erode teenagers' involvement in school, diminishing their capacity to perform well there and, especially, to get good grades.

Indeed, the association between working and school achievement is one of the most frequently studied topics among researchers of youth employment; it is also the area of greatest controversy and inconsistency in empirical findings. This issue is quite salient to adolescents themselves. They know that college admissions officers attach great importance to high school grades. If working interferes with teenagers' educational performance, subsequent attainments may be jeopardized. Educational attainment is becoming ever more important as the income gap between college graduates and high school graduates widens (Mischel et al., 1999).

Nonetheless, the YDS parents did not seem to be very concerned about this issue. As we have seen, the vast majority thought that their children's jobs had no effects on their grades. Moreover, in response to the open-ended questions asked when the panel members were in ninth grade, some parents mentioned that jobs provided incentives to do well in school. In the short run, some parents required their children to meet certain standards of academic achievement before they would be permitted to work, or to work many hours. Some parents suggested that through employment their children had come to appreciate the value of education, having learned that the kinds of jobs available to them would be restricted if they were to curtail their schooling. Parents also recognized improved time-management skills resulting from employment. Many noted that their children were saving their earnings for college. Some pointed out that the self-confidence gained from working spilled over to school, enhancing their children's academic performance. Very few of the parents of ninth graders suggested that work caused a psychological withdrawal from school or increased fatigue that interfered with schoolwork (Phillips and Sandstrom, 1990).

When we asked the parents a similar series of questions four years later, when most of their children were seniors in high school, the pattern of responses was similar, indicating a generally positive assessment of the consequences of work in the educational domain. As noted earlier, 82 percent of both mothers and fathers said their children's grades had either stayed the same or improved as a result of working. Only 6 percent of the fathers and 8 percent of the mothers reported that they often had disagreements with their employed teenagers about neglecting their schoolwork.

The youth themselves, at least by eleventh grade, were not as sanguine. Almost half of working youth said working gave them less time to do their homework. Although a majority believed their grades did not suffer as a result of their jobs, about a fourth reported that their grades had gone down (Aronson et al., 1996).

One interviewee recalled having missed out on extracurricular activities because of her work: "Sometimes I feel it was a bad thing. I should have stayed in school 'cause I could have gotten on like the paper at school, but that was after school, and I was working. I probably started working when I was 16 . . . I'd get out of school early and go to work, and that was, 30, 35 hours a week" (Aronson, 1998). A male respondent who worked "10–15 hours a week maximum" found it easier to balance school and work: "I don't think it cut much in to my study time because I set time when I'd study . . . I'd study after school . . . before work . . . and I only work three days a week, so I mean, that's four nights a week without anything."

Lack of consensus about the impact of employment on education also appears in a large body of systematic research on the link between adolescent employment and academic performance. Some researchers have reported negative associations between employment, or hours spent working, and grades (Lewin-Epstein, 1981; Greenberger and Steinberg, 1986; McNeil, 1984; Ruscoe et al., 1996; Finch and Mortimer, 1985; Steinberg and Dornbusch, 1991; Steinberg et al., 1993; Mortimer and Finch, 1986; Marsh, 1991), but others question whether this association is causal or spurious.

Some circumstances appear to foster positive relations between work and academic achievement. Marsh (1991) and Ruscoe and colleagues (1996) found positive effects of employment on grades, but only when the worker was saving earnings for college. This connection of employment to a valued future possible self, as college student, is likely to transform its meaning. Consistently, D'Amico's (1994) analysis of the National Longitudinal Survey youth data showed that employment of low intensity (20 hours per week or fewer) lessened high school dropout rates.

Often, however, investigations of the relation between adolescent work and grades, as well as other indicators of school performance and engagement, yield null findings. Employment and hours spent working have been found to have no significant independent effects on grades in several methodologically sound studies (see Mihalic and Elliot, 1997; Schoenhals et al., 1998; Warren et al., 2000).

As shown in Chapter 5, early academic engagement and performance are significant sources of selection to work; it is therefore necessary to take prior differences in academic performance into account
in determining whether employment has any independent influence.
In the YDS panel, hours spent working had no demonstrable effects
on grades, in analyses of data from tenth and eleventh grades
(Mortimer, Finch, et al., 1996). However, YDS seniors who worked
20 or fewer hours per week had significantly higher grades than students who did not work at all (Schill et al., 1985, and Lillydahl,
1990, also show curvilinear patterns). Still, grade-point average
proved to be unrelated to the pattern of investment in work (defined
by duration and intensity) during the last three years of high school
(Mortimer and Johnson, 1998b). Assessment of grade-point average
and indicators of work quality also yielded no significant relations.

Given the predominant zero-sum assumptions about working and
studying, the diversity of results obtained from these investigations,
many of which are longitudinal and incorporate numerous relevant
controls, may seem rather surprising. With some exceptions (a
babysitter may study while children are napping; youth who work as
parking attendants, night watchmen, and receptionists may be permitted to do homework during "slow" periods), working and studying surely preclude each other. Still, as we saw in Chapter 4, most
youth who work have quite diversified patterns of time use—and
working does not appear to detract from time spent in homework or
any other single activity (Shanahan and Flaherty, 2001).

In the YDS, work investment bore no demonstrable relation to
time spent doing homework (Mortimer, Finch, et al., 1996; Mortimer
and Johnson, 1998b). Schoenhals and colleagues (1998), using National Educational Longitudinal Study data, also report that time
spent working had no significant effect on homework time or on discretionary reading. It is sometimes alleged that teenagers select less
demanding courses and tracks so as to accommodate their work
schedules. We find, however, that an indicator of this strategy is not
consistently associated with the work pattern. In tenth, eleventh, and
twelfth grades, we asked, "Have you avoided taking any difficult
courses this year because of the time needed for studying?" The response (yes or no) was associated ($p < .05$) with work investment
only in tenth grade, when nonworkers (18 percent) and steady work-

ers (22 percent) were less likely to answer yes than were occasional (33 percent), sporadic (32 percent), and most invested (32 percent) workers. Taken together, the empirical evidence does not support the contention that working in adolescence detracts from educational engagement, number of hours spent doing homework, or academic achievement in high school (Mortimer et al., 1993; Mortimer, Finch, et al., 1996; Mortimer and Johnson, 1998b). The empirical evidence surely calls into question the assertion that if youth spend less time working they will increase their academic engagement.

These null patterns are consistent with parents' report that teenagers become better time managers when they are employed. Being an effective time manager implies being able to prioritize activities and allocate one's time according to their importance. One young woman who had worked at a drug store during high school, interviewed in her 20s, pointed out this benefit of working: "I think one good thing about work and that job was that it really forces you to prioritize. I mean, if you have to be at work on Saturday, from 9 to 3, then you know that you either have to get up and study before you go to work or in the afternoons when you get home, if you want to go out and hang out with friends, you have to get that work done sometime."

In the National Educational Longitudinal Survey, hours worked per week had a strong negative effect on time spent watching television in the tenth grade. Osgood (1999), using Monitoring the Future data for high school seniors, also found that hours of work bore a strong negative association with television viewing. This is a mode of time use that would have difficulty competing with more attractive alternatives like sports and other extracurricular activities or time with friends. If it is television watching, a passive activity with little educational benefit (Smith, 1992; Csikszentmihalyi, 1990), that is sacrificed when hours of work increase, it is not surprising that homework and grades are not affected. If, in fact, the key tradeoff is between time spent working and time spent in front of the tube, might this yield a somewhat more favorable perspective on working and educational achievement?

Furthermore, because the national average for high school students' investment in homework is so low (less than 4 hours per week), work hours must by necessity be drawn from other, more time-consuming activities. As Osgood (1999: 181–182) puts it,

WORKING AND ADOLESCENT DEVELOPMENT

"Even when working 30 hours a week, it shouldn't be hard to find four hours for studying."[5]

Unpaid Work

Fears that paid jobs encroach upon other potentially valuable forms of work—in the family, at school, or in the community—might be relieved by the findings presented in Chapter 4. Most employed adolescents appear to be able to perform these various kinds of work in tandem. Still, it is pertinent to consider the relevance of unpaid work, especially doing household chores and volunteer work, to the process of growing up.

It may reasonably be contended that paid work has the stronger potential to make the teenager feel like an adult. As we have seen, at least after the first year of high school, adolescent employment tends to occur in formal workplaces, where adults are likely to be found, rather than in private homes, which are the most frequent venues of more childlike, informal work. Like adults, adolescents in the workplace are paid for their labors. As they continue to work, parents may increasingly expect them to pay many of their own expenses, decreasing their economic dependency.

Unpaid work, particularly in the home, may be seen as more childlike than paid work. When doing chores around the house, the teenager is subject to parental supervision and evaluation. As Call and colleagues (1995) have shown, when housework is carried out under childlike conditions—for example, when parents order youth to do chores rather than asking or suggesting—it depresses adolescents' sense of mastery.

Unlike both housework and paid work, school attendance is compulsory for children and early teens, and student is a traditionally pre-adult role (though growing numbers of adults are returning to school for skill upgrading, recertification, or advanced degrees). These characteristics reduce the capacity of schoolwork to confer an adultlike sense of responsibility and autonomy. Moreover, adolescents are typically not paid for their educational efforts (though some parents offer monetary incentives for good grades).

But ironically, given these pre-adult features, schoolwork is much more pertinent to eventual occupational attainment than these other forms of adolescent work. Schoolwork has immediate benefits as well as long-term consequences for chances in life. This is increasingly the case as opportunities expand for highly educated, technically skilled workers, and as work contracts for those who do not have post-secondary education. Many youth (and their parents) are well aware of the declining economic prospects of those who do not go to college (Schneider and Stevenson, 1999). Academic achievement, as indicated by school grades, has pervasive psychological consequences, especially for self-esteem and efficacy (Eccles et al., 1996).

Volunteerism constitutes a further arena for learning about work. Volunteer work draws the adolescent away from familiar family and school domains, providing exposure to new situations, different types of people, and challenging problems. It also appears to restrain egoistic tendencies, encouraging adolescents to look beyond themselves, to find value and fulfillment in helping others, being useful to society, and participating in the broader community. However, if volunteer work is organized by the school, or worse, required, intrinsic motivation and autonomy may be compromised. Even when volunteering is not officially required, many youth may feel it is necessary to impress college admissions officers. Although the benefits of volunteering are often proclaimed, few longitudinal studies have examined its impacts on development. We found that volunteering enhances service values: teenagers who volunteered their labor during high school became more committed to being good citizens in their communities; volunteering also fostered the more altruistic, people-oriented, and intrinsic work values (Johnson et al., 1998).

Thus the YDS demonstrates that unpaid work has important implications for growing up. Chores, performed at home, enable the youth to contribute to the family, and the manner in which chores are allocated has significant consequences for adolescents' sense of competence. Too much such work can drive the young person away from home (Cooney and Mortimer, 1999). The YDS also demonstrates important socializing influences of volunteer work, effects on young people's occupational and civic values.

With the exception of rather extreme exploitative situations, the value of unpaid work in family and volunteer settings is generally not contested. The fact that most adolescents who do paid work are able to participate in these activities is reassuring, given the manifold benefits of unpaid work.

Conclusion

As we have seen, the pattern and quality of adolescent work are most important for adolescent development and achievement. Neither employment status nor hours of work significantly influenced the high school students' mental health, educational achievement, vocational development, or family and peer relationships.

The acquisition of adultlike problem behaviors—drinking and smoking—during high school, fostered by intensive adolescent work experience, represents what Jessor and colleagues (1991) would consider a premature claim to adult status. Of considerable importance is whether these early problem behaviors are precursors to continued difficulties as youth move into adulthood. This possibility is the subject of continued interest and analysis. At least with respect to alcohol use, the effect of intensive work during high school does not appear to persist beyond these early years (McMorris and Uggen, 2000).

During high school, the quality of work experience appears to matter far more than hours of work for the psychosocial outcomes under scrutiny. That is, youth who have more successful experiences in the workplace become more competent, in terms of both a general, global sense of efficacy and efficacy in the economic domain. There is also evidence that high-quality work experiences involving learning opportunities help adolescents acquire occupational values. Opportunities for learning and advancement on the job, the perception that one is being paid well, and limited stressors at work all appear to have significant psychosocial benefits. Though there is reason to expect boys to be more psychologically responsive to early work than girls, the Youth Development Study provides little support for this expectation. The YDS findings with respect to educational achievement have considerable significance, given the widespread fear that paid work during high school will necessarily undermine young people's educational performance. This fear, fostered by the pervasive assumption that the allocation of time between work and school is a zero-sum game, is not borne out by our data. Youth who had different levels of investment in paid work during high school did not differ in their grades.

THE TRANSITION TO ADULTHOOD

THE SAME CONTROVERSIES and contradictions that surround paid work during adolescence arise in debates about later consequences of teenage employment—consequences that are only manifest after high school. When viewed in terms of preparation for adult work, early employment is often considered beneficial, reducing the likelihood of problematic early career trajectories (Hansen et al., 2001). To the extent that teenage employment engenders planfulness, youth who have had meaningful work experience during high school may be less likely to "flounder" after high school—to move in and out of school, shift college majors or other sequences of study, or drift from one temporary, part-time, or otherwise unstable job to another in the secondary labor market. Young people whose vocational interests and capacities crystallize early on, as a result of employment during high school, may identify their occupational goals more rapidly and move more straightforwardly through postsecondary educational programs that enable them to realize those goals.

Early employment may also enhance understanding of the labor market, including the economic rewards of training and work experience. There is evidence that young people obtain a sense of their own economic value through paid work. In a Canadian study, high school graduates who had worked during high school were found to be less willing to accept menial jobs than their peers who had not (Lowe and Krahn, 1992). Employment was likewise associated with higher scores on a test of economic literacy (covering diminishing returns, opportunity costs, and demand theory).

Analyses of data from the Youth Development Study have already documented that work of high quality (for example, presenting opportunities for learning) encourages positive work values and other personal resources (such as general and economic efficacy) that are likely to be beneficial in the job market (Mortimer, Harley, and Aronson, 1999). These psychological assets, when combined with more accurate understanding of the labor market and more fully crystallized occupational values, augur well for a successful transition to adult work.

Most parents and educators, welcoming the prospect of vocationally successful, economically self-sufficient young adults, would consider this positive scenario quite attractive. Acquisition and successful maintenance of the work role are widely understood markers of the transition to adulthood. Failure to obtain stable, full-time employment jeopardizes a young person's standard of living, impedes successful family transitions (to marriage and parenthood), and increases susceptibility to deviant, even criminal behavior. Indeed, as noted in the Introduction, much of the concern about unemployment among minority youth arises from the assumption that the absence of opportunities for teenage work leads to weak adult attachment to the labor force. Furthermore, the acquisition of adult work is recognized as a crucial turning point with respect to whether adolescent delinquency will continue into adulthood (Sampson and Laub, 1993).

But might youth enter too quickly into full-time jobs and career trajectories that divert them from the postsecondary education that would foster adult socioeconomic attainment? Given the importance of higher education for success in the contemporary labor market, any such premature diversion is to be avoided. This possibility brings forth fears of "accelerated" transition to adulthood.

Aquilino (1999) posits that technological changes increasing the need for higher education make a lengthening period of dependency, a "post-adolescent" stage (at ages 18–24) an increasingly adaptive strategy for future work roles. According to his analysis, youth who postpone marriage and parenthood have greater chances for marital success because they have more time to acquire emotional maturity and the capacity for intimate, caring relations. He argues that this new stage "involves preparation for work and family roles through education, vocational training, entry-level jobs, trial relationships, and periods of living with parents or in semiautonomous living arrangements" (170). Arnett (2000) extends the argument further, heralding a new life stage of "emerging adulthood," which continues the youthful moratorium through the late twenties and beyond, enabling young people to explore their interests and potentials while putting off the economic and familial responsibilities of adulthood.

Thus the contradiction: work experience during high school may provide a valuable foundation for the acquisition of human, social, and financial capital. But more ominously, it may channel youth too soon into full-time work and family formation, shortening the youthful exploratory period, restricting educational and occupational attainment, and impeding a successful transition to adult work and family roles.

The Youth Development Study data make it possible to examine achievement-related behaviors in the years after high school that could be harbingers of future attainment—postsecondary education, full-time work, and earnings—as well as more subjective perceptions of being on a career "track." It also lets us look at family-related indicators of transition to adulthood: marriage and parenthood. These analyses draw on data collected up to seven years after high school.

Providing some support for the critics' concerns, in an earlier cohort of participants in the National Longitudinal Survey of Youth (NLSY), who were between the ages of 16 and 19 in 1979, greater temporal investment in work during high school predicted a small decrement in educational attainment by 1991 (Carr et al., 1996). But this study also demonstrated vocational benefits to those youth who had substantial prior involvement in work during adolescence. Youth who had cumulated more hours of work during high school also had the more continuous employment and higher income up to a decade following high school. With educational attainment controlled, employment in high school had positive effects on employment and wages ten years later.

Ruhm (1997), utilizing data from the same source, confirmed these advantages, showing that six to nine years following high school, students who had worked during their senior year had higher earnings, wages, occupational status, and fringe benefits (though less postsecondary schooling) than those who had not. Moreover, Ruhm showed that students who had invested more hours in work had greater economic gains (controlling family background, family environment, and the young person's ability and motivation toward school). The maximum economic advantages occurred for students who had worked 21–24 hours per week. Numerous other studies likewise report that paid employment during high school is associated with successful labor market attainment, as measured by employment, duration of employment (or unemployment), and income attainment (Freeman and Wise, 1979; Marsh, 1991; Meyer and Wise, 1982: Milhalic and Elliott, 1997; Mortimer and Finch, 1986; Ruhm, 1995; Steel, 1991).

However, controversy still surrounds the causal impact of employment on these outcomes. It could be argued that those who choose to work during high school, or those who work more hours, have higher energy, stronger work motivation (what economists call "taste for work"), or other unmeasured qualities that would predict both employment propensity during high school and labor market success in early adulthood. Such qualities may not be adequately captured by commonly included controls, such as family socioeconomic background, academic achievement, and educational motivation. Econometric modeling of NLSY data, taking into account such unobserved heterogeneity, showed that working during high school did not affect wages at age 27 (Hotz et al., forthcoming).

This corpus of literature is predicated on a fundamental assumption: that what matters is whether the youth is employed or not, and, in most studies, how extensive that employment is. Thus analysts focus on the number of hours worked per week, or a measure of cumulative investment in work. This approach has two drawbacks. First, it does not take into account the patterning of labor force experience. We saw in Chapter 3 that panel members accrued almost identical total hours of work during three years of high school in two different ways: through a pattern of long duration with low intensity (less than 20 hours per week) employment; and through a pattern of short duration with high intensity. Accumulating work hours through nearly continuous, moderate work gives a youth substantial employment experience while at the same time allowing participation in extracurricular activities, homework, and social activities with peers. Highly intensive work, in relatively short bursts, can make for the same cumulative investment, but may be considerably less compatible with these other developmentally beneficial activities.

Second, this literature does not address the experiences that youth have in their early jobs. In one exceptional study, the quality of early work was found to be associated with early occupational attainment:

skill utilization in adolescent work predicted success in the job market during the first three years after high school (Stern and Nakata, 1989).

As we shall see, the YDS provides considerable evidence that the experience of paid work in adolescence, including its temporal patterning and its quality, is integral to early socioeconomic attainment. Recall that we have defined five employment patterns: "occasional" (low duration, low intensity), "sporadic" (low duration, high intensity), "steady" (high duration, low intensity), "most invested" (high duration, high intensity), and nonworking. By Wave 10, YDS participants were seven years beyond high school, mostly 24–25 years old. These data allow assessment of the longer-term implications of both the pattern and the quality of employment during high school.

Educational Attainment

The educational attainment of the panel seven years after high school was somewhat higher than that of recent national cohorts of youth. A fourth had received B.A. degrees, another fourth had some college, and 27.1 percent had ended their education with a high school degree or G.E.D. Smaller proportions had received technical training (13.3 percent), associate-level degrees (7.4 percent), or higher-level degrees (Master's or Ph.D.'s, 1.1 percent).

Data from the monthly life history calendar enable assessment of the number of months the youth were attending school each year following high school. It should be noted that young people were counted as being "in school" if they spent any time at all during a given month in educational pursuits. As a result, figures for total duration of postsecondary education may be somewhat exaggerated. Consistent with earlier analyses (Mortimer and Johnson, 1998a), significant variation between the work pattern groups are observed.

By seven years after high school, youth of both genders who had worked at high intensity (regardless of duration) in high school had achieved fewer months of postsecondary education than the low-intensity workers or the nonworkers. Among women, those who had pursued the two low-intensity patterns ("occasional" and "steady") and those who had not worked during high school showed similar investment in education, averaging 35 months from 1992 to 1998. Young women who had been in the "most invested" and "sporadic" categories had attended school for only 26 and 22 months respectively.

Male low-intensity workers averaged close to 40 months of schooling during this seven-year period, while the male high-intensity workers accumulated only 21 and 23 months for the sporadic and most invested workers, respectively. Unlike the women, young men who had not worked during high school did not quite match their peers who had worked at low intensity in educational investment after high school (they averaged 34 months of schooling). It is thus clear that there is a substantial association between investment in paid work during high school and postsecondary schooling, and that the major divide occurs between those who worked previously at high and low intensity.

A somewhat different pattern emerged with respect to receipt of a bachelor's degree or higher. Consistent with their lower temporal investment in postsecondary schooling, youth who worked at high intensity during high school were less likely to have achieved bachelor's degrees: for young men, only 11 percent had done so. Similarly, for young women, only 11 percent of the "sporadic" workers and 15 percent of the "most invested" had achieved bachelor's degrees seven years after high school. As for young men who had worked at lower intensity during high school, fully 45 percent of the "steady" workers had achieved bachelor's degrees. This is consistent with their higher levels of school attendance in the first four years after high school (Mortimer and Johnson, 1998a). A third of the young men who had followed the "occasional" pattern in high school had received the B.A. degree, as had 29 percent of the nonworkers.

Like the men, the women who had worked at high intensity during high school were notably unlikely to obtain college degrees. However, among women it was the nonworkers during high school who had the highest educational attainment, with 42 percent receiving B.A. degrees. Those who had pursued the "steady" work pattern came next, with 38 percent, while only 29 percent of the women who had been "occasional" workers had achieved four-year college degrees seven years after high school.

These findings suggest that the "steady" work pattern fosters a more effective translation of months of postsecondary educational attendance into college degrees. Though the female "steady" and "occasional" workers achieved almost identical numbers of months in school (about 35), the former "steady" workers were almost a third more likely than the "occasional" workers to achieve B.A. degrees (despite their much greater cumulative temporal investment in paid work in adolescence).

While the men in the two low-intensity work groups also accumulated equivalent numbers of months of postsecondary educational attendance (39–40), again we find a strong educational premium for the "steady" pattern. It could be that this work pattern, involving nearly continuous employment at low intensity, fosters adaptation to a similar combination of school and work after high school, conducive to higher academic performance and attainment. (No data on college grade-point average were obtained in the YDS.)

It is especially interesting that the women who had not worked in high school were so much more educationally successful than their male counterparts: although they had accrued nearly identical amounts of schooling (35 months for women and 34 for men), 42 percent of the women but only 29 percent of the men had obtained B.A. degrees. Nonworking women did not differ from nonworking men in social background, including parental education, race, nativity, and family composition, or in indicators of educational promise upon entry to high school.

To determine whether differential educational attainment linked to the work patterns is spurious, attributable to prior differences between the work pattern groups (described in Chapter 5), a multivariate logistic regression analysis was conducted, with receipt of the B.A. degree (or higher) as the outcome. The analysis includes controls for parental education, family income, nativity (whether born in the U.S. or not) and race (white or minority). Gender is also included, because of its association with work patterns during high school and educational achievement.

Because psychological resources might also influence the patterns of work during high school, controls are introduced for economic self-efficacy in tenth grade (found to be more predictive of early educational achievement than global efficacy, Grabowski et al., 2001), and for educational promise. The educational promise index is a composite derived from grade-point average in ninth grade, intrinsic motivation toward schoolwork (described earlier; see Table 4.1), academic self-esteem (the perception of self as intelligent, a good reader, and high in school ability), and educational plans. "High promise" youth are likely to have much greater eventual educational success; upon entry to high school they had scores that were above the median on at least three of the four indicators; "low promise" youth scored below the median on two or more.

To represent the work patterns, four dummy variables are included, with the reference category consisting of the "most invested" workers. Because it is commonly thought that work during high school pulls young people away from school and limits educational attainment (and socioeconomic attainment generally), youth who were most invested in paid employment represent the most pertinent base of comparison. If investment in work is the phenomenon that matters most for educational attainment, we would expect this subgroup to have the least educational success. If this were the case, the coefficients for all of the other groups would be positive (since they reflect the difference in B.A. receipt, net of other predictors, between members of each work category and the "most invested" workers).

To assess whether the effects of work investment differed by gender, a series of preliminary analyses included conditional terms, the interaction of gender with each work pattern. None of these terms was statistically significant; thus, net of the background and psychological variables, there are no differences between men and women in the effects of the work patterns on educational attainment. The findings to be reported therefore include both genders (see Table 7.1).

Not surprisingly, young people whose parents were more highly educated are more likely to achieve the B.A. degree. Youth who were born outside the United States are more likely to achieve the B.A. than their native-born counterparts. Members of the "high promise" group, who at entry to high school exhibited the most engagement in education, are almost five and one-half times more likely to receive the B.A. than those who manifested less promise. Students who had greater economic efficacy in tenth grade are also more likely to achieve B.A. degrees. With the background and psychological variables taken into account, there are no significant differences in B.A. receipt by gender or by family income.

Net of the socioeconomic and psychological resources, there are no differences in B.A. receipt between the "most invested" workers

Table 7.1. B.A. receipt by 1998, regressed on background and early work
             patterns

	b	S.E.	Exp (b)
Parental education	.513***	.076	1.67
Family income	.002	.057	1.00
Race	.418	.347	1.52
Nativity	−1.220*	.490	.30
Family composition	.435	.297	1.55
Gender	−.174	.226	.84
Promise	1.696***	.272	5.45
Economic efficacy	.160**	.056	1.17
Steady[a]	1.126***	.320	3.08
Occasional	.514	.341	1.67
Sporadic	−.054	.437	.95
No work	1.073*	.506	2.92
Constant	−6.013	.928	
N	669		

*$p < .05$; **$p < .01$; ***$p < .001$.
a. Reference category is the "most invested" pattern.

and two of the other work patterns, "occasional" and "sporadic."
The "steady" workers, however, are shown to be three times as likely
to achieve B.A.'s than the "most invested" workers. It may be concluded that the "steady" work pattern during high school has a
significant positive effect on attainment of the B.A. degree even after
background variables, prior educational promise, and economic
efficacy are controlled. In this analysis, nonworkers are almost three
times as likely to achieve the B.A. as youth who were the most at-
tached to the labor force during adolescence.

We have seen that the "steady" workers invested a relatively large
number of months in postsecondary education, but not more than the
other low-intensity workers. When months of schooling are added to
the equation as an additional predictor, the pattern of findings
changes little. Clearly, the amount of time spent in school does matter, as it has a significant positive effect on B.A. receipt ($p < .001$).
Still, the coefficient for the "steady" work pattern hardly changes at
all with this additional control—from 1.126 to 1.316 ($p < .01$).
Youth who pursued a "steady" work pattern during high school are
still 3.7 times more likely than the "most invested" workers to receive
a B.A. degree. The advantage of the nonworking group is reduced to

insignificance with this additional control, indicating that nonworking youth are more likely to achieve the B.A. precisely because they invest more time in postsecondary education.

Note, however, that knowing the number of months of schooling provides no information about the type of postsecondary school attended. Those who had been high-intensity workers during high school were more likely to be attending vocational schools and community colleges during the following years; the formerly steady workers had a greater propensity to attend four-year colleges. The advantage of the "steady" group finally disappeared when a final set of controls was introduced reflecting the kind of education received after high school (dummy variables indicating whether the respondent attended a vocational school, a community college, or a governmental job training program; or attended a four year college). Thus adolescents who pursue the "steady" work pattern during high school are more likely to receive B.A. degrees because they gravitate toward the types of educational institutions that confer them.

Balancing school and work during high school is thus shown to foster human capital development through educational attainment.[1] Those youth who work nearly continuously but limit their employment to 20 hours per week or less are able to participate in sports and other extracurricular offerings. These activities foster connection to the school, both socially and psychologically. Early labor force involvement of high duration that averages more than 20 hours per week is associated with lower levels of B.A. receipt. It is especially noteworthy that the "occasional" workers do not differ from the "most invested" workers in this key indicator of attainment.

Shanahan and Flaherty (2000) find a clear distinction between the postsecondary educational trajectories of those who pursued more focused and more multifaceted uses of time during high school. Consistent with the trend reported here, youth who engaged in many activities while in high school, whether employed or not, had more months of postsecondary education than those who concentrated on a single use of time, such as friends, work, or other activities. All indications point to the conclusion that early employment is not an impediment to higher educational attainment, as long as it occurs in balanced combination with other activities—which, as Shanahan and Flaherty show, is the typical pattern for adolescents who are employed during high school.

Socioeconomic Attainment

Whereas some youth may be thought to be "floundering" seven years after high school, still holding jobs with little career potential, others are pursuing work that they think will lead to lifelong careers. Does early investment in paid work, or the experience of different kinds of work during high school, increase young adults' capacity to obtain jobs that are linked to their career goals? The job held at the time of the 1998 survey was classified in one of three categories: the youth's chosen career (coded 2), which applied to 32 percent of the panel; a job that would prepare for that career by providing pertinent knowledge and skills (coded 1), which applied to 39 percent; or a job unrelated to the career (coded 0; "don't knows" were also placed in this category), which applied to 28 percent. Again, after showing that gender did not condition the effects of the work variables on this indicator, a model was estimated which included, as predictors, the same variables considered in the educational attainment analysis: four work-investment categories (with the "most invested" group constituting the reference category), the five socioeconomic background variables, gender, educational promise in ninth grade, and economic efficacy in tenth grade.

Also included were two variables representing the experience of work: the learning potential of the job, and earnings, as indicated by a learning potential index and by the average wage rates of jobs held at the time of the survey administrations in tenth, eleventh, and twelfth grades. Youth who scored high on the learning potential index described their jobs as challenging, as giving them a chance to learn a lot of new things, and as using their skills and abilities. They also thought that what they were learning in their jobs would be useful to them in later life. As discussed earlier, jobs that enable adolescents to learn new things contribute to human capital growth and vocational development. Opportunities to acquire skills in early jobs enhanced both intrinsic and extrinsic work values over time (Mortimer, Pimental, et al., 1996).

Earnings in high school jobs may be especially indicative of the capacity to achieve in the work domain in the future. Earnings constitute a tangible indicator of worth to the employer. Youth who have higher earnings, by virtue of that very fact, have the more "adult-like" jobs.

What is especially interesting is how few of the earlier variables influence the career relevance of the 1998 job, held seven years after high school (see Table 7.2). With only one exception, neither the background variables, gender, nor the early psychological resources (represented by educational promise and economic efficacy) influence whether the respondent will occupy a job that is perceived as pertinent to the career. The notable exception is race: whites are more likely to have career-relevant jobs seven years after high school than the members of minority groups.

While the work-investment patterns also yield mainly null findings, those who did not work during high school had less career-relevant jobs in 1998 than the "most invested" workers, who again constitute the reference category (beta = $-.099$, $p < .05$). The findings suggest that those who are employed during high school may have an advantage in identifying, and securing, career-relevant work.[2] One young woman reflected on the subsequent benefits of her high school jobs:

> I think all of them helped me get where I am now, 'cause I know a lot of people who have a hard time finding jobs and a hard time getting their career started because they don't have the experiences that I've had, and it could probably be what you can take from your experience because like when I go into an interview . . . I can talk about my skills with specifics. I can say, if someone says, "Okay, describe a situation," or "Do you work well under pressure?" Well, instead of saying, yes, which everyone will say, I can say, "Well, here are examples." . . . I started working at a card shop, but that experience helped me get the next thing and that experience helped me get the next thing. So, I think you advance up and it just kind of assimilates.

Consistently, those young people who reported more general learning opportunities in their high school jobs (see Chapter 5) are more apt to perceive their jobs seven years after high school as career-related (beta = $.101$, $p < .05$). As shown earlier, youth who had greater difficulty in school—those with lower grade-point averages— were more likely to report that their jobs during high school had learning potential. The present findings constitute evidence that a strategy of seeking learning opportunities in high school jobs has subsequent vocational benefit. As we have seen, the opportunity to learn

Table 7.2. Career relevance and earnings, 1997, regressed on background and early work variables

	Career relevance		Earnings	
	b	S.E.	b	S.E.
Parental education	−.016	.023	−191	304
Family income	.011	.017	193	231
Race	.215*	.093	3701**	1271
Nativity	.037	.161	−769	2012
Family composition	.036	.083	374	1104
Gender	.080	.067	4771***	897
Promise	.132	.073	775	976
Economic efficacy	.007	.015	625**	207
Steady[a]	.010	.093	52	1264
Occasional	−.077	.095	−198	1304
Sporadic	−.123	.103	−12	1416
No work	−.365*	.161	−5629**	1966
Learning potential in high school[b]	.029*	.012	262	160
Average earnings in high school	.001	.001	12	8
Constant	1.158	.296	1930	4038
N	594		597	
	$R^2 = .053$; F = 2.319**		$R^2 = .119$; F = 5.62***	

*p < .05; **p < .01; ***p < .001.
a. Reference category is the "most invested" pattern.
b. Mean substitution for missing data on work variables was used to increase sample size.

in early jobs enhances vocational development by crystallizing occupational values, possibly increasing the likelihood that youth will be able to find jobs that are linked to their career interests, or at least jobs that enable them to prepare for future careers.

Since both the information about high school work experience and that about career relevance in 1998 are based on self-report, their association must be viewed with caution. Even over this long span of time, their association may be a function of an enduring psychological outlook rather than an effect of early work experience.

Earlier analyses (Mortimer and Johnson, 1998a), based on survey data collected four years after high school, showed that the young men who had been high-intensity workers during adolescence had higher 1994 earnings than their peers who had worked at lower levels of intensity. The latter, who were more likely to be in school, were sacrificing immediate earnings for more long-term economic success.

We also examined the implications of early work for income attainment seven years after high school. The panel reported average earnings of $19,064 for 1997 (in 1995 and 1998 they reported their pretax earnings for the previous year). Men reported 29 percent higher earnings than women ($21,850 vs. $16,983). Figure 7.1 shows average incomes in 1994 and 1997 by gender. Six years after high school, men who had been high-intensity workers in adolescence had somewhat higher incomes than those who had worked steadily, but the steady workers were not far behind. Those who had been occasional workers and nonworkers in high school had lower 1997 incomes. The 1994 and 1997 earnings differences between work-investment groups were less pronounced among women, but women who had not worked during high school had particularly low earnings at both times. These trends are clearly linked to the propensity to be attending school.

In the multivariate findings (Table 7.2), the strongest predictor is gender—even with the numerous controls, men still report, on the average, $4,771 more in earnings than women $p < .001$.[3] Whites have higher earnings than minorities ($b = 3701$, $p < .01$). The fact that greater economic efficacy measured during the second year of high school predicts higher earnings eight years later, net of all the background and other predictors, is testimony to the importance of early attitudes for attainment ($b = 625$, $p < .01$).

Most interesting from the perspective of this book are the work-

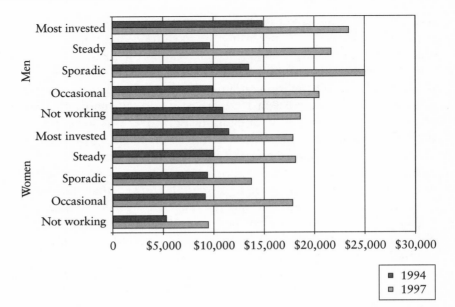

Figure 7.1. Average income, 1994 and 1997, by gender and high school work
investment.

investment coefficients. Apparently there are now no significant differences in earnings, dependent on the pattern of work investment,
among those who were employed during high school. The early advantage of the high-intensity workers has disappeared. What does
matter is whether the adolescent worked at all. Those who did not
work have substantially lower earnings than their peers who were
most invested in work during high school (b = −5629, p < .01). (Assessment of logged earnings yielded a similar pattern, though race no
longer had a significant effect.) Further analysis showed that the earnings disadvantage for those who did not work during high school is
only partially attributable to their greater likelihood of being in
school during the previous year (44 percent of the nonworkers and
30 percent of those with other work patterns reported that they had
attended school for at least one month during the prior year). (When
this variable is added to the equation with 1 = attended, 0 = not, the
coefficient changes from −5629 to −4919, only a 13 percent decrease.)

Family Formation

Does high school work pattern, or the content of early work, influence marriage and cohabitation? According to the "precocious maturity" argument, young people who are employed during high school, and especially those who work in high-intensity, adultlike jobs, will come to see themselves as adult and want to move quickly into adult family roles. An earlier investigation of this thesis showed that the patterns of work investment during high school had no bearing on family formation—success in establishing residential independence, marriage/cohabitation, or parenthood—four years after high school, when the panelists were 21–22 (Mortimer and Johnson, 1998a). On the basis of that analysis, we concluded that work investment during high school had no significant implications for accelerated family transitions.

By 1998, seven years after high school, when youth are mostly 24–25 years old, those who cohabit, marry, or have children may no longer be considered "precocious," since this is a much more normative age for family formation. By this time, substantial minorities of the youth were cohabiting (25 percent), were married (26 percent), or had become parents (38 percent), and 64 percent lived independently of their parents. We investigated whether early work experience during high school had any effect on indicators of family formation seven years after high school.

We found that those who had been the "most invested" workers in adolescence were more likely to be married or cohabiting in 1998 than those with other early work patterns (see Figure 7.2). Youth who had pursued the "steady" work pattern among the men, and the "nonworking" pattern among the women (who were the most likely to obtain four-year college degrees), were the least likely to be cohabiting at this time.

In the multivariate analyses (estimated with logistic regression), again, initial investigation showed that the work variables did not interact with gender or with promise in predicting these relational outcomes (respondents were coded 1 if married or cohabiting). As shown in Table 7.3, even when background and psychological variables were controlled, men were considerably less likely than women to be married or cohabiting in 1998.

The pattern of work investment during high school does appear to

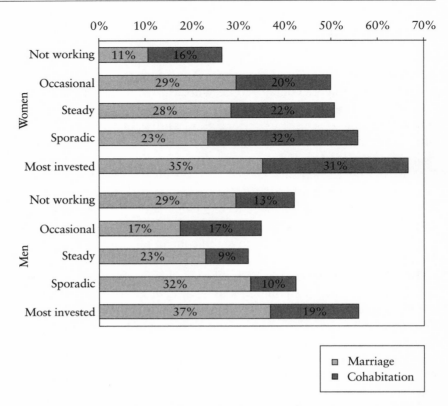

Figure 7.2.   Marriage and cohabitation, 1998 (age 24–25) by gender and high
school work investment.

matter, affecting the likelihood of marriage and cohabitation for both
genders seven years after high school. The "most invested" workers,
the reference category, were more likely to be married or cohabiting
than the "steady" workers, the "occasional" workers, or the nonworkers. (They did not differ significantly from those in the "sporadic" work category.) Similarly, those who had earned more during
high school, net of the work patterns, were more likely to be married
or cohabiting. It is especially interesting that these work experiences
are more important than the socioeconomic background variables
and educational promise in fostering these now more normatively
timed markers of transition to adulthood.

With respect to parenthood, a similar pattern is apparent (see

Table 7.3. Marriage/cohabitation and parenthood at age 24–25, regressed on background and early work variables

	Marriage/cohabitation			Parenthood		
	b	S.E.	Exp (b)	b	S.E.	Exp (b)
Parental education	-.080	.059	.923	-.119	.069	.888
Family income	-.062	.044	.940	-.146**	.050	.864
Race	.175	.233	1.191	-.595	.248	.552
Nativity	-.196	.391	.822	1.179*	.512	3.250
Family composition	-.100	.207	.905	.126	.222	1.135
Gender	-.582***	.171	.559	-.769***	.193	.464
Promise	-.156	.181	.856	-.429*	.196	.651
Economic efficacy	.018	.033	1.018	-.051	.038	.950
Steady[a]	-.483*	.238	.617	-.527*	.257	.590
Occasional	-.471[b]	.242	.624	-.511	.264	.600
Sporadic	-.399	.260	.671	-.069	.271	.933
No work	-1.078**	.395	.340	-.828	.457	.437
Learning potential in high school	.015	.030	1.015	-.075*	.034	.928
Average earnings in high school	.003*	.001	1.003	.001	.002	1.001
Constant	.558	.734		1.927	.861	
N	671			673		
	$R^2 = .053$; F = 2.319**			$R^2 = .119$; F = 5.62***		

*p < .05; **p < .01; ***p < .001.
a. Reference category is the "most invested" pattern.
b. p = .052

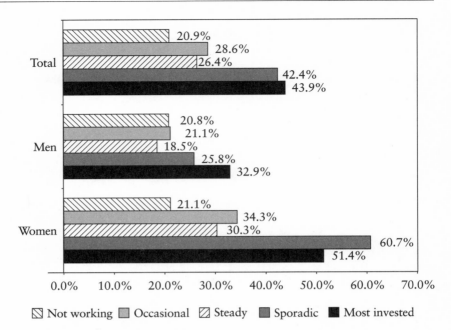

Figure 7.3. Parenthood, 1998, by gender and high school work investment.

Figure 7.3). The high-intensity teenage workers are more likely to be parents, seven years beyond high school, than the other work-investment groups. When the background and early psychological dimensions are controlled, youth who pursued the "steady" work pattern are still less likely to be parents than those who invested most in paid employment. Having learning potential in high school jobs also lessens the likelihood of parenthood. Girls are more likely to be parents than boys and native-born youth are more likely to be parents than immigrants. Higher family income reduces the likelihood of parenthood (see Table 7.3).

When combined with the earlier findings that marriage/cohabitation and parenthood were not more typical of high-intensity workers four years after high school (Mortimer and Johnson, 1998a), the 1998 findings point to the conclusion that adolescent investment in work fosters normatively timed, not precocious, transition to family roles.

Educational Promise

In Chapter 5 we saw the processes of selection through which ninth graders with limited family resources, educational engagement, and ambition acquired high-intensity work during high school. It was suggested that their investment in work might be a rational strategy: that adolescents who had little reason to expect to be successful in college would attempt to attain human, social, and financial capital through work experience. Limited educational promise also predicted more rewarding, but also more stressful, work experiences. For example, teenagers who had lower grade-point averages upon entry to high school described their subsequent jobs as having greater learning opportunities. However, these youth also reported more stressors in their high school jobs. In short, these youth appeared to have the more adultlike jobs, which might be more relevant to future occupational attainments.

These patterns of selection suggest that the consequences of adolescent work experience may be dependent on educational promise. That is, we must consider the nature of both the person and the context to understand the process of development (Vondracek et al., 1986). Work experiences are likely to have different outcomes depending on their relevance to the adultlike "possible self." Consider a teenager whose job is merely a way to earn spending money, or a source of savings for college. This teenager may seek chances for learning, advancement opportunities, or a source of competence in school rather than at work. A second young person, who does not plan to go to college and has little anticipation of success in school, may seek these experiences in the work setting. Teenagers like this one may see little connection between their schoolwork and the tasks they will be called upon to perform in occupational or other adult roles. They may invest in work, rather than school, as a way to prepare for future occupational success.

Given these patterns, we assessed whether, seven years after high school, educational promise conditioned, or moderated, the effects of the work-investment patterns on measures of success. For the most part, this investigation yielded null findings. For example, educational promise did not condition the effects of the work pattern on income. Moreover, educational promise did not moderate the effects of

Table 7.4. Logistic regression predicting B.A. receipt by 1998, by educational promise

	High promise			Low promise		
	b	S.E.	Exp (b)	b	S.E.	Exp (b)
Parental education	.415***	.083	1.52	.904***	.199	2.47
Family income	.025	.063	1.03	-.108	.139	.90
Race	.416	.378	1.52	.428	.910	1.53
Nativity	-1.102*	.540	.33	-1.710	1.21	.18
Family composition	.160	.332	1.17	1.758*	.839	5.80
Gender	-.009	.244	.99	-1.013	.710	.36
Economic efficacy	.138*	.065	1.15	.259[b]	.136	1.30
Steady[a]	.792*	.353	2.21	2.476**	.877	11.89
Occasional	.466	.370	1.59	.655	1.107	1.93
Sporadic	-.059	.492	.94	.653	1.130	1.92
No work	1.30*	.600	3.65	.636	1.467	1.89
Constant	-3.648	1.095		-9.048	2.356	
N	350			319		

*p < .05; **p < .01; ***p < .001.
a. Reference category is the "most invested" pattern.
b. p = .057.

the employment pattern, or those of two dimensions of work experience (earnings and learning potential), on the perception that the job held seven years after high school is related to the chosen career.

There is one noteworthy exception to this general pattern of null findings. The "steady" work pattern appears to be especially predictive of educational attainment for youth who had little earlier educational promise. Ironically, given that youth who have low promise tend to veer away from "steady" work activity (as shown in Chapter 5), when they do follow this pattern it has educational benefits for them, as indicated by receipt of a bachelor's degree. Among youth of low educational promise who worked at high duration and low intensity ($N = 70$), 23 percent earned bachelor's degrees. Among the remainder of the youth of low promise ($N = 273$), less than 3 percent did so. (Among youth of high promise, the "steady" workers were more likely than all the other working groups to achieve B.A.'s, but the differences were less pronounced; those who had not worked in high school were even more likely to obtain B.A.'s, but there were only 22 individuals in this category.) Indicating the robust character of this finding, an interaction term, representing the interaction between promise and the balanced work pattern, was statistically significant ($p < .01$) when included in the model predicting B.A. receipt. No other interactions between promise and work pattern were statistically significant. Nor did promise condition the effects of the high school work experiences (earnings and learning opportunities) on the objective and subjective attainments.

The conditioning effect of promise in influencing educational attainment is shown in Table 7.4. Indeed, while the "steady" pattern is beneficial for both high- and low-promise groups, its effect on the educational attainment of the low-promise youth is considerably greater: all else equal, low-promise youth who pursued the "steady" employment pattern were almost twelve times more likely to receive B.A.'s than their counterparts who had been "most invested" in work during high school. The likelihood of achieving the B.A. among high-promise youth who pursued the "steady" employment pattern was about double that of like teenagers who were "most invested" workers during high school.

A guiding hypothesis of this investigation was that boys' development and attainment would be more strongly influenced by high school work experience than that of girls. Extensive testing of such conditioning by gender yielded mainly null findings. That is, work-investment pattern, learning potential, and earnings tended to have quite similar effects on boys' and girls' educational attainment, acquisition of career-relevant jobs, and earnings. These null findings point to the ubiquitous character of the effects of early work experience.

Conclusion

The parent of a ninth grader reflected about what the daughter had gained from working: "She has learned a good deal about how to manage her money, including saving for college and, as a female, how to be financially independent and secure . . . Working and studying hard are their own rewards, but learning that she can have control over her own life in important aspects like taking care of herself, is one of the great lessons of young adulthood."

The YDS data show that young people who pursue moderate employment during high school accrue important benefits as they make the transition to adulthood. Most important, those who were "steady" workers during high school, employed almost all months of observation but working less than 20 hours per week, had pronounced educational success, especially with respect to four-year college degrees. The fact that the advantage of those who pursued the "steady" pattern persisted, even when the duration of postsecondary schooling was controlled, suggests that continuous, low-intensity employment in adolescence enables youth to move more efficiently toward B.A. degrees.

As for the acceleration thesis, teen employment of more than 20 hours per week appeared to enhance the transition to full-time work four years after high school (Mortimer and Johnson, 1998a, 1999) and to foster higher earnings at this time. By seven years after high school, patterns of high school work investment or experience no longer predict advantages with respect to the acquisition of full-time work. Still, those who were *not* employed during high school are found to be less likely to perceive their current jobs as career-relevant. Those who were nonworkers in high school also report less income seven years thereafter, indicating delay in achieving a major objective indicator of vocational success. This does not appear to be attributable to their greater propensity to be attending school at this time.

We found little evidence that working in adolescence encourages precocious cohabitation, marriage, or parenthood; instead, we found that highly intensive work during high school fosters normatively timed transitions to family roles.

Should young people work during high school? The evidence from the Youth Development Study indicates that paid work can have marked advantages for adolescents, particularly when it is pursued steadily, and characterized by learning opportunities. Steady employment fosters postsecondary educational attainment, and this effect appears to be particularly strong for adolescents who have relatively low educational promise upon entry to high school. Adolescents who reported learning opportunities in their high school jobs were further along in their career trajectories seven years after high school than those whose early jobs provided fewer challenges and chances to use their skills and abilities. All told, teenage work, especially if pursued consistently and moderately, appears to confer advantages in the early socioeconomic career.

WORKING AND BECOMING ADULT

EACH OLDER GENERATION debates the proper ways to prepare young people for adulthood. The preeminent objective, most would agree, is to help youth to become well-functioning adults, able to take responsibility for themselves as well as for others and to find some degree of personal fulfillment in doing so. How are youth to be prepared for their futures? We have considered two general answers to this question.

On the one hand, it is argued that the young must be protected and removed from the social worlds of adulthood. Following G. Stanley Hall, developmental psychologists have long emphasized that optimal development necessitates a lengthy moratorium on the cares and responsibilities of adult roles. Youth must be allowed to entertain new interests and identities in a tentative fashion, without enduring commitment or serious consequence. To actualize their manifold potentials—social, moral, intellectual, and vocational—they should be encouraged to enact well-rounded, multifaceted life styles within youthful enclaves, free from exploitation by adults and protected from the dangers of "precocious maturity."

On the other hand, it is contended that to be able to find their proper niche in the adult world, the young must first be exposed to, and meaningfully incorporated into, adult institutions. Only by interacting with adults in real-world contexts can youth develop the values, interests, and perspectives that will equip them to make critical choices as they navigate their pathways to adulthood. Through such experiences they will acquire a mature perspective on life and a knowledge of the world beyond their own families, schools, and neighborhoods. More pragmatically, they will acquire the habits of mind and behavior, the information, and the skills they will need for adequate performance of adult roles in the future.

This debate takes on special meaning in contemporary America. During the past half-century the transition to adulthood has become prolonged; in more recent decades, the timing and sequencing of transition markers have become more variable and unpredictable as well (Shanahan, 2000a). As structural imperatives weaken and normative guidelines about the early life course become less clear, young people are enabled, even required, to construct individualized life paths. Indeed, it is contended that "pre-adulthood" should no longer be conceptualized as simply an extension of adolescence; some commentators suggest that a new life phase has arisen, extending well into the third decade of life (Aquilino, 1999; Keniston, 1968; Klein, 1990; Shanahan, 2000b), variously called "post-adolescence," "youth," "young adulthood," and "emerging adulthood" (Arnett, 2000).

This transitional phase of life, characterized by growing, but not complete autonomy and continued exploration, becomes increasingly extended as more and more high school graduates, up to two-thirds in recent cohorts, attend colleges or other postsecondary educational institutions. They are responding to a labor market that places an ever greater premium on higher education. Most highly rewarded are the well-educated (preferably with four-year college degrees) "generalists," flexible workers who can adapt to new marketplace conditions, who know how to learn and relearn as the need arises. Hence the assumption of key markers of adulthood—full-time work, marriage, and parenthood—usually rather incompatible with the student role (Mortimer, Oesterle, and Krüger, forthcoming), tends to be postponed.

At the same time, the early life course has become more "disorderly" (Rindfuss et al., 1987), with young people moving in and out of more or less "adultlike" roles. Rather than pursuing a stable progression toward adulthood, they often follow trajectories characterized by shifts in direction, reversals, and new starts. In growing numbers, American youth establish independent residences and subsequently return to the parental home; cohabit in relationships that are more tentative and unstable than marriage; and become parents before marriage (Spain and Bianchi, 1996). Also, many young entrants to the full-time labor force soon return to school to enhance their general educational credentials or to obtain vocationally specific training (Arum and Hout, 1998).

In some quarters, these changes in the process of becoming adult are cause for celebration (see Arnett, 2000). The postponement of key life decisions allows young people to make more informed choices when the time eventually comes (Aquilino, 1999). Greater maturity enables them to cope more effectively with the relational, vocational, and other demands of adulthood. A longer pre-adult period allows additional years—for many youth up to a decade or more following high school—for pursuit of relationships with intimate partners as well as for experimentation with various occupational roles. This life experience, so the argument goes, makes for more stable and fulfilling work and family commitments.

During this period, some youth participate in community service, political activism, religious activities, or other involvements that can be more intensive in the absence of economic dependents and career pressures. These transitional activities can foster the crystallization of life-long values and civic engagement (McAdam, 1988). Seen in its most salutary light, this prolonged period of exploration is beneficial for youth, good for the social institutions in which they will find their place as adults, and eminently affordable in an affluent society.

Moreover, in an era of increasing biological longevity, "post-adolescents" in their late teens and early twenties may be perceived, relatively speaking, as "younger" than prior cohorts of the same biological age. Given rapid social and economic change, it may be considered unrealistic, even counterproductive, to assume that they are ready to make serious choices in vocational, familial, or other realms and to enter these spheres as fully functioning adults.

What then is the place of "youthwork," paid jobs during adolescence, in this modern context? One common answer to this question is that paid work has little, if any, legitimacy in this early phase of life because it is incompatible with educational attainment (Greenberger and Steinberg, 1986; Steinberg et al., 1993). Critics of youthwork allege that the menial jobs available to high school students provide little opportunity for reading, writing, or for the practice of other skills learned in school, nor do these jobs encourage problem-solving or creative thinking. Whatever minimal skills and behavioral "work readiness" such jobs may offer can be learned quickly, during the summer or at vacation times, when they do not disrupt the educational process. If students become overburdened with jobs during the school year, they will have little time to take part in extracurricular activities that allow them to explore their interests and contribute to the civic life of the high school.

Critics are also troubled because teenagers' jobs provide them with relatively large amounts of spending money. Working propels many adolescents into a state of "premature affluence" and extravagant consumerism (Bachman, 1983). The critics worry that taking adult-like responsibility in the workplace will encourage adolescents to feel entitled to other adult prerogatives, such as the use of alcohol, and to chafe under adult authority. These elements of precocious maturity, so the argument goes, by making the dependent role of student dissatisfying, will discourage youth from long-term educational investment and will foster premature entry to adult roles, especially full-time work and family formation.

Given our rapidly changing and complex society, it is plausible to argue that the early acquisition of diverse forms of human and social capital—planful competence, maturity, and a multitude of life skills —has become increasingly important. Some of these resources are most readily cultivated in the protected educational setting; however, a degree of integration into the adult world may also be necessary for optimal development.

Writing in the mid-1970s, Coleman (Panel, 1974) argued that confining teenagers' extrafamilial experience to school deprives them of experience with real-world problems and contacts with adults in a variety of roles. He contended that schools fostered distinctively youthful subcultures that were, paradoxically, anti-intellectual and educationally counterproductive. Interest in having fun superseded serious orientation to achievement. The dangers of immersion in the peer subculture, particularly outside the school context, have been further elaborated by contemporary criminologists. For example, Osgood (1999) notes that spending large amounts of time in unsupervised activities with peers is associated with troublemaking and problems with the law.

Coleman contended that youth must be exposed to the adult world of work to appreciate the practical value of their educational experiences. The Presidential Task Force he led advocated more opportunities for teenagers to work while attending school, preferably in programs linked to their coursework.

Supporting this view, Glen Elder's pathbreaking research provided evidence that work experience in adolescence constitutes valuable preparation for adulthood. Drawing on historical archives on youth during the Depression as well as in contemporary hard-pressed rural communities, Elder and his colleagues have demonstrated that adolescent work instills a sense of competence and responsibility with lifelong benefits (Elder, 1974; Elder and Conger, 2000). Still, critics of youthwork point out that circumstances during the Great Depression and in present-day rural communities are quite different from the social worlds of most contemporary adolescents. The typical American adolescent, of middle-class origin and living in a city or a suburb, has little experience with economic hardship.

Nonetheless, fundamental concerns have emerged about the schools' near monopoly on preparing adolescents for their futures, especially for their occupational roles. Schneider and Stevenson (1999) marshal much evidence that parents, teachers, and adolescents themselves are so focused on college that future vocations are given scant attention. High school seniors overwhelmingly plan to go to college, to obtain four-year or postgraduate degrees, and to obtain professional and managerial work. However, many lack a clear understanding of the fields of study or credentials needed to enter particular lines of work.

Rather than being concerned about their teenagers' lack of vocational interest, many parents worry that vocational courses or participation in school-to-work programs might deflect their children from obtaining college degrees. Moreover, in view of the ever changing character of the labor force, specific forms of vocational preparation may seem irrelevant for their children's futures.

Contemporary adolescents' lack of engagement with occupational choice goes hand in hand with American secondary schools' nearly exclusive focus on higher education. Given the educational system's porous character, allowing easy reentry, youth who choose a vocational direction relatively late are still able to enhance their educational credentials. In the absence of the need to make firm occupational choices at any particular time, serious occupational considerations can be postponed seemingly indefinitely (Heckhausen,

1999). The acceptance of "late bloomers" is much in accord with the American ideology of open opportunity.

Schneider and Stevenson's (1999) national study highlights the costs of adolescents' (and their parents') single-minded focus on educational attainment. Without a sense of direction to help them choose particular courses of study, youth become less engaged with higher education. After leaving high school, many drift, moving from one major or college to another, becoming discouraged, stopping out or dropping out of college, while in the meantime accruing substantial financial debt. In fact, only about one-fourth of recent cohorts of young people have attained the B.A. degree (Kerckhoff, 2002). Occupational opportunities narrow as youth get tired of going to school, obtaining little fulfillment from educational pursuits that are not clearly linked to their futures. One-fourth of those aged 25–29 are "college dropouts."

Establishment in full-time work is a central marker of adulthood, as it enables economic independence from parents and assures a legitimate place in the community. This is increasingly the case for girls as it has always been for boys. In the present era of dual-worker families and high divorce rates, teenage girls cannot realistically expect that future husbands will provide for them and their children. Given later marriage, family instability, and decline in remarriage (Spain and Bianchi, 1996), adolescents, both male and female, can look forward to longer periods of life outside of traditional family roles—the 2000 U.S. Census reports that less than one-quarter of American households are nuclear families of husband, wife, and children. Consistent with these trends, adolescent girls overwhelmingly plan to have work careers in addition to being spouses and parents.

Despite the importance of establishment in work, American youth receive little institutional support in this process. Unlike their counterparts elsewhere in the world (Mortimer and Krüger, 2000; Rosenbaum et al., 1990), most American young people must find jobs on their own. This is especially the case for the vast majority of youth who do not graduate from college.

The generalized credentials of the American educational system (high school diplomas, B.A. degrees) offer little in the way of specific vocational certification and provide few signals to employers, or to youth themselves, about an individual's capacity to perform particular jobs (Kerckhoff, 2002). Upon the completion of education, many young people move from job to job trying to find an appropriate occupational niche. While this exploration may be productive for some youth, yielding ever closer job "fits" with personal interests and capacities, Hamilton (1990) worries that "floundering" from job to job diminishes the acquisition of human capital during this formative time of life, reducing later economic productivity and attainment.

When the economy is growing and the demand for labor is strong, most youth are readily absorbed into the labor force even if they lack occupational direction or vocational training. But in a context of economic restructuring, heightening global competition, and the increasing prevalence of part-time, temporary, or other forms of nonstandard employment (Kalleberg et al., 2000), occupational establishment may become increasingly precarious. In fact, attaining "good jobs"—full-time work with health and other benefits as well as advancement opportunities—is becoming increasingly difficult for youth (Fussell, 2002).

What place does, and should, work have in adolescents' preparation for their futures? Given its longitudinal scope and comprehensive measurement of teenage work investment, its attention to the quality of work experience, and its monitoring of adolescent involvement in diverse activities, the Youth Development Study is uniquely suited to address the debate over whether adolescents should be "protected" from or "incorporated" into the world of work.

The Character of Youthwork

Young people's paid work changes as they move through high school. Initial jobs, in the early teens, are informal—babysitting and yardwork. As they grow older, adolescents move into more formal employment, first in the fast-food industry and subsequently in a wider range of settings. They move from simple jobs to more complex ones requiring further training and involving greater supervisory responsibility.

Paid jobs during high school are nearly universal: 93 percent of the YDS participants were employed for at least some time while school was in session. But youthwork is far from homogeneous. As in the adult workforce, there are distinct, gender-linked patterns of working. Adolescent girls are more likely than boys to hold paid jobs during each year of high school, but boys work longer hours than girls.

A key finding is that a focus on work status (employed or not), hours of work at a particular time, or even cumulative hours over a longer period, obscures fundamental variability in adolescent work. In fact, adolescents who worked sporadically at high intensity accumulated almost identical numbers of hours as those who worked rather continuously at low intensity, but these two patterns were associated with markedly different precursors and consequences. Low-intensity work allows adolescents to participate in an array of other activities, including unpaid work in more "protected" settings (housework, homework, volunteering). More intensive work, of more than 20 hours per week, is part of more focused and concentrated, less well-rounded lifestyles.

The desirable qualities of productive activities other than paid employment are widely recognized. Being unpaid, they are not motivated by and do not foster materialistic values. Household work is an outgrowth of family membership (Miller and Yung, 1990) as well as a contributor to family cohesion. While ninth-grade boys and girls do similar amounts of housework, boys' contributions to family labor decline markedly during the ensuing four years. Girls' housework likewise declines initially, but levels off after ninth grade at a much higher level than that of boys. Thus the sex-typing of family work increases during high school. This pattern may prepare young women for later juggling of work and family roles, given women's substantial responsibility for the "second shift" of family work (Hochschild, 1989).

Volunteer work gives youth experiences outside their usual surroundings, and, in some circumstances, encourages a broad civic identity and empathy with the less fortunate (Youniss et al., 1997). Volunteer work fosters intrinsic and altruistic work motivations—desires for work that involves helping others and community service, as well as the capacity to express one's interests. Although they differed in regard to paid work and housework, boys and girls in the YDS had similar patterns of participation in volunteering.

Most significantly, the YDS shows that there is no empirically discernible tradeoff between paid work and these other valuable youth activities; in fact, most youth who are employed during high school participate simultaneously in a broad range of other settings. Shanahan and Flaherty's (2001) cluster analysis of YDS data, and their tracking of movements between time use clusters through the years of high school, show that workers and nonworkers are highly similar with respect to their other uses of time. Employed youth in the multifaceted "active" time-use cluster differed hardly at all from those whose similarly active, multifocused pattern did not involve paid work. Despite averaging close to 20 hours per week on the job, "active" employed youth spent as much time as their nonworking counterparts doing homework, engaged in extracurricular pursuits, helping their families with housework, and spending time with friends. Tellingly, the background and attitudinal precursors of these two active patterns were much the same, and youth readily moved between the two patterns from one year to the next.

Juxtaposing the senior-year time-use clusters and the cumulative work-investment patterns showed that adolescents who pursued low-intensity work were more likely to have multifaceted patterns of time use. It can be concluded that most working youth, especially when they limit their hours of work, do not sacrifice involvement in distinctly "adolescent" activities. Low-intensity workers may be "protected," given their high levels of participation in school, in extracurricular activities, and in their families, yet still "incorporated," albeit to a limited degree, in the world of work.

Given its apparent benefits, it is important to know what enables teenagers to pursue low-intensity employment. In Chapter 5 we saw clear patterns of selection to the pattern of investment in work and to work of varying quality. High-intensity work is more prevalent among boys and among the less advantaged teenagers. Minority youth, those whose parents had less formal education, and those from non-intact families had relatively little propensity for the "steady" (high duration, low intensity) pattern of work.

The "most invested" workers during high school, who worked at both high duration and high intensity, exhibited relatively little interest in their schoolwork in ninth grade (in comparison with those who were to pursue the "steady" work pattern), relatively low academic performance, and high orientation toward peers. "Sporadic" employment, high in intensity but low in duration, was also more prevalent among youth who, as ninth graders, had lower levels of academic performance, lower educational aspirations, more frequent problem behavior, and strong peer orientation.

The findings clearly suggest an agentic interpretation of adolescent activities during high school. Consistently, those ninth graders who were to pursue the "steady" pattern of employment had relatively high educational aspirations early on. During high school they were especially likely to seek early jobs to save money for their future educations. Those with the "most invested" pattern of employment were distinguished by their interest in acquiring skills.

In general, youth who pursued lower-intensity patterns of employment were different from the start in their motivations for working, their positive attitudes toward school, and their educational ambitions. They had stronger resources of various kinds—attitudinal and familial—to realize their educational goals and to support their successful movement toward adulthood. Apparently they neither sought nor found high levels of extrinsic rewards in their high school employment: they thought they obtained less status from their friends from their jobs; they had fewer advancement opportunities and lower earnings.

Thus the more advantaged youngsters, whose parents have more education and who themselves have greater intellectual interest, higher academic performance, and stronger ambitions, limit their hours of work so as to allow paid employment as well as other activities. As shown in Chapter 5, more advantaged and ambitious youth constructed multifaceted patterns of time use enabling the enactment of playful and planful life styles.

In contrast, ninth graders who had lower grades either selected themselves or were selected by employers for jobs that may be more conducive to the acquisition of human capital through work. In general, teenagers from lower socioeconomic backgrounds, those who were less engaged in school, and those whose early school performance indicated less promising academic careers followed a strategy of intensive investment in work—work that involved more chances for advancement, more learning opportunities, and higher earnings, but also more demands. They steered themselves toward the more rewarding but also more stressful "adultlike" jobs.

The YDS thus demonstrates two pathways of preparation for adulthood, one involving limitation of paid work and balancing of employment and other activities; the second involving more intensive investment in paid work, more adultlike jobs, and more focused time-use patterns in general. The distinction between protection and incorporation thus appears to be overdrawn. The well-rounded, active teenagers, the majority of youth in the YDS panel, are those who par-

ticipate in the distinctively youthful arenas of school and extracurricular activities as well as in the family. However, these active teenagers
are also likely to be incorporated into the adult world of employment, holding time-limited jobs. The active, well-rounded adolescent
lifestyle entails flexible movement in and out of the labor force,
needed to accommodate diverse obligations and activities.

Psycho-Social Consequences

Because of its presumed "opportunity costs," paid work is thought to
pose a threat to academic engagement, school performance, and
eventual educational attainment. If paid work were to challenge adolescents' capacity to juggle their multifaceted roles, and pose undue
stress, it could threaten teenagers' mental health. And if it hastened
the transition to adulthood, it could reduce educational and occupational attainment, lead to the premature establishment of family
roles, and in the process, jeopardize many facets of well-being.

According to a more positive scenario, working during adolescence, by allowing adolescents to move toward desired adult "possible selves," could have positive consequences for both mental health
and socioeconomic attainment. Successful performance in high
school jobs could demonstrate to parents and peers, as well as to the
youth themselves, that young people are capable of functioning
within the crucially important occupational sphere.

Work in adolescence may have both contemporaneous and longer-
term outcomes; given the highly formative character of this time of
life, it is reasonable to suppose that any contemporaneous influences
of youthwork on mental health, values, self-concepts, and identities
will have lasting consequences in subsequent developmental phases
(Alwin et al., 1991). Does employment during high school make
youth's movement through the increasingly protracted phase of
"emerging adulthood" easier or more difficult? How does it influence
educational attainment and establishment in work? Does its influence
vary depending on the degree of investment in employment or on its
quality?

CONTEMPORANEOUS OUTCOMES

YDS participants who worked longer hours exhibited more problem
behavior during high school and drank more alcohol; these may be

considered defiant and "adultlike" behaviors in accord with the "precocious maturity" thesis (Mortimer, Finch, et al., 1996). The pattern is consistent with Greenberger and Steinberg's (1986) contention that there is a causal link between these problems and adolescent work. However, it is also in accord with Bachman and Schulenberg's (1993) alternative conceptualization—that paid work is part of a syndrome of more rapid movement toward adulthood. According to their view, paid work, problem behaviors, and adultlike ways of spending leisure time (including drinking and other substance use) reinforce one another over time.

Despite the clear link between work hours and problem behaviors, the quality of work appears to matter far more than its quantity for adolescent mental health and development. Whereas the YDS teenagers generally perceived their work experiences as positive and reported high levels of job satisfaction, their descriptions were not wholly favorable. Girls described their jobs in more desirable terms than boys—as involving more opportunities for learning and service to others, as well as fewer noxious and stressful work conditions. Boys engaged in more supervision of other workers and had higher earnings and more frequent opportunities for advancement. Boys also thought their work gave them more status in the eyes of their peers.

In general, youth whose jobs signify successful movement toward adulthood express more confidence, have more strongly crystallized work values, and show less depressive affect. Those who perceive their work as stressful manifest more depressed mood than other employed youth (Shanahan et al., 1991; Mortimer et al., 2002). Depressive affect is also linked to perceptions of incompatibility between work and school. Rather ominously, in light of the prevalent critique of youthwork, many adolescents report strain in balancing their part-time jobs with the demands of schoolwork.

What is especially important is the developmental specificity of the association between work and mental health. While numerous studies have pointed to self-direction as the key feature of work as it affects adult mental health (Kohn and Schooler, 1983; Mortimer and Lorence, 1995), our analyses suggest that the freedom to make one's own decisions at work is not conducive to young people's mental health. In fact, adolescents reported more depressed mood as their degree of control in the workplace increased. Adolescents, relative newcomers on the job scene, do not appear to react well to autonomy.

Youth who feel they are well-rewarded at work and have advancement opportunities gain a sense of competence or efficacy over time (Finch et al., 1991). Positive work experiences also foster a dimension of efficacy that is specific to the work environment (Grabowski et al., 2001). Thus youth whose experiences in the workplace are positive come to think of themselves as more likely to be successful adult workers—to obtain work that brings them satisfaction, is well paid, and allows them to live in the locations they prefer. Confidence about work is especially conducive to educationally successful behavior—getting good grades, actively seeking information about college, consulting with counselors, taking admittance tests, and achieving postsecondary educational attainment.

Youth whose jobs provided learning opportunities developed more strongly crystallized work values of both an intrinsic and extrinsic character (Mortimer, Pimentel, et al., 1996). Being able to learn new skills in the work environment may convey the message that they will be able to succeed, and to obtain diverse occupational rewards in the future.

Though adolescents' values are not the only bases of their occupational decisions, prominent theories of occupational choice and career development posit that individuals choose occupations largely on the basis of their valuation of the rewards they perceive those occupations to offer (Super et al., 1963; Ginzberg et al., 1951; Mortimer and Lorence, 1995). Moreover, occupational values are predictive of both college majors and eventual occupational destinations (Davis, 1964, 1965; Mortimer and Lorence, 1979a; Mortimer and Kumka, 1982; Ryu and Mortimer, 1996). Those youth who have more well-formed notions about what they want in their adult work are likely to have a stronger sense of direction and be better equipped to choose educational programs and further work and nonwork experiences that will enable them to realize their goals.

Values surely change over time, as individuals encounter new work experiences and learn about various desirable and undesirable aspects of employment (Mortimer and Lorence, 1979a). Still, it is reasonable to expect that young people who are more engaged in thinking about vocational issues—what they are looking for in adult work, what kinds of work might bring greater satisfaction and support desired lifestyles—will be able to make better choices as they move into full-time adult work and eventual careers.

It bears repeating that despite change in the character of youthwork in recent history, the quite sanguine patterns observed in the adolescent YDS panel members are corroborated by their parents. Responsibility, independence, "character"—these are the adjectives that repeatedly came up when parents were asked to describe the benefits and costs of their ninth graders' paid jobs (Phillips and Sandstrom, 1990). When queried again in their children's senior year of high school, the parents were overwhelmingly positive about their own work experiences, emphasizing, above all, that they had helped them to become responsible adults.

INFLUENCE ON OTHER DEVELOPMENTAL CONTEXTS

Adolescents have diverse arenas of comfort and challenge in their lives; optimal development depends on finding the appropriate balance (Call and Mortimer, 2001). They are called upon to achieve in school, perform effectively at work, and make decisions that will have lasting consequences for their futures. At the same time, they must find comfort and acceptance to soothe them at times of stress and bolster their confidence in the face of setback and failure.

Despite grave warnings that adolescents' most intimate ties and sources of social support are threatened by paid work (Greenberger, 1988), we found no evidence that this is the case. While working adolescents spent less time with their families, there was little indication that the quality of their relations with their parents suffered as a result of increasing investment in work. In fact, positive experiences at work appeared to draw adolescent boys and their fathers closer together (Mortimer and Shanahan, 1994). Similarly, there was no evidence that working disrupts supportive bonds between peers.

With respect to the relationship between paid work and academic achievement, we found no evidence that working either promotes or interferes with school performance (Mortimer, Finch, et al., 1996; Mortimer and Johnson, 1998b). As detailed in Chapter 6, some prior studies show negative effects of work hours on grades, and others, like the YDS, no significant effects. In the parents' minds, working during high school does not threaten their children's educational and occupational attainments. Most parents, when asked directly, reported that their children's jobs had no effects on their grades; those who did think there was some influence were split about whether that influence was positive or negative. Furthermore, parents emphasized that their children (and they themselves) had become better time managers as a result of working, better able to set priorities and get the important tasks done.

In regard to balancing the demands of work with those of school, there appears to be a gap between perception and reality. Many teenagers reported that balancing work and school was difficult. Although few parents mentioned any "costs" of work, those who did also highlighted this difficulty. But at the same time, the accumulated objective evidence does not show that employment jeopardizes students' grades.

Some contend that this pattern is due to the exceedingly low educational demands placed on American high school students. Others argue that the time spent at work must lessen the time devoted to other activities: if youth are working, as many do, as much as 20 hours per week, and if they average less than five hours per week on homework, the time must be made up somewhere else (Osgood, 1999). If paid jobs cut into time for television (Schoenhals et al., 1998) or other unproductive pursuits (such as computer games and surfing the Internet), then it is wholly reasonable to find that adolescents' grades are relatively unaffected by their jobs.

However, the evidence about young people's use of time shows that a "zero-sum" way of thinking is fundamentally faulty. Most adolescents, whether employed or not, engage in many activities. Their well-rounded patterns of time use indicate that they make time for the diverse activities that are valued by them, by their parents, by their teachers, and more generally in our culture. Having paid jobs does not prevent them from doing so, or from maintaining their grade-point averages.

THE TRANSITION TO ADULTHOOD

Some commentators, including the critics of youthwork, maintain that the transition to adulthood often occurs too rapidly, with problems arising from the absence of a lengthy "moratorium" on adultlike responsibilities. Others warn that the transition takes too long—as youth move between school and work, change educational programs and schools, and explore various occupational niches. For

Hamilton (1990) and Schneider and Stevenson (1999), contemporary adolescence is increasingly, and unnecessarily, prolonged.

The effects of youthwork on this transition cannot be fully assessed here, since many YDS panel members, as gauged by standard "markers of adulthood," had not yet completed this process by 1998. Seven years after most graduated from high school, about one of four had still been attending school for at least part of the prior year. Only 27 percent had married; close to a third had become parents. As might be expected, most had left school before having children: only one in five had become parents while still attending school.

With this caveat in mind, let us address some central concerns of the critics of youthwork. What influence does early work have on educational attainment during the seven years after high school? Is there any evidence from the YDS that young people who invest more time in employment during high school have a precocious transition to adulthood?

The "steady" pattern of work appears especially conducive to postsecondary educational attainment: youth who pursued this pattern of nearly continuous employment completed the most months of postsecondary education during the four years following high school (Mortimer and Johnson, 1998b). While for the girls this pattern could be attributable to prior characteristics—family social background and earlier academic propensity—for the boys, differences between the work-investment groups persisted even after application of numerous controls.

It might be argued that months of education is a poor proxy for educational attainment because the type of educational program is not taken into account. That is, equal weight is given to a month of college and a month of instruction in auto mechanics. A more definitive measure of educational attainment is receipt of a B.A. (or B.S.) degree. We saw in Chapter 7 that the "steady" pattern of work investment is more conducive to higher educational attainment, as measured by this consequential achievement, than more intensive labor force involvement. Despite their extensive duration of employment, the steady workers were not disadvantaged relative to those youth who worked little during high school (the "occasional" workers). In fact, there were no differences among occasional, sporadic, and most invested workers on this criterion.

What is particularly interesting is the strong influence of the "steady" pattern among youth with little educational promise. We saw in Chapter 5 that ninth-grade intrinsic motivation toward school, higher grade-point average, and high educational aspirations were significantly predictive of the work investment patterns. Those with little promise were decidedly unlikely to pursue the "steady" work pattern. However, those who somehow managed to maintain this pattern were much more likely to achieve the B.A., even after a wide range of background and achievement-related precursors were controlled.

Several prior studies have documented that youth who work during high school, and those who devote more hours to work, are more vocationally successful after leaving school—achieving more months of employment after high school, fewer months of unemployment, higher earnings, and more benefits (see Committee, 1998). Consistent with these studies, YDS youth who pursued the more intensive teenage work patterns had higher earnings immediately following high school. By 1997, however, six years after high school, the earnings profiles were very similar across the work-investment groups. Still, teenage nonworkers were at a distinct disadvantage. It is expected that those who pursued low-intensity work during high school and subsequently invested more time in postsecondary education will eventually surpass their less-educated peers in earnings.

In addition to early school-leaving and entry into full-time work, childbearing is a central component of the "precocious maturity" syndrome. More youth in the high-intensity work categories had married and had children by seven years after high school (see Chapter 7). However, few of the births to those who pursued high-intensity work occurred at a time that would be considered "precocious." Young people who worked more intensively during high school moved toward marriage and parenthood faster than other youth, but at an age that may still be considered "normative," in their early to mid-twenties. Meanwhile, the youth who pursued the "steady" work pattern and those who did little or no work during high school appear to be delaying family formation past the averages for their age group.

Whereas the YDS research team is continuing to investigate the longer-term consequences of adolescent investment in work and of work quality, the analyses thus far suggest that negative behavioral consequences of employment are not lasting. For example, four years after high school, we find no differences in alcohol use among adolescents who manifested varying levels of investment in high school work (Mortimer and Johnson, 1998a; McMorris and Uggen, 2000). Moreover, recent assessment of the effects of the quality of youthwork on depressive affect four years after high school revealed few long-term effects (Mortimer et al., 2002).

Taken together, analyses of both selection to work and the consequences of work point to the same general conclusion: young people are agentic actors who adapt to their educational and work opportunities in resourceful ways. More advantaged youth seek low-intensity work that does not interfere with the many other activities that constitute the well-rounded adolescent lifestyle. These youth express concern about conflicts between school and work, signifying their interest in balancing work and school so as not to jeopardize their academic performance. As a result of their less intensive employment, they do not have to sacrifice extracurricular activities, household chores, or relationships with parents and friends to obtain the benefits of paid work. As they begin the transition to adulthood, they continue to invest in education, readying themselves for entry to advantageous occupational and earnings trajectories.

Here again, it is not a matter of "protection" or "incorporation." Young people who have greater initial advantages, in the form of family resources or their own educational ambitions, come to have "active" lifestyles—with or without paid work—that predict higher educational attainment (Shanahan and Flaherty, 2000). Young people with less educational ambition and fewer family resources tend to pursue more intensive employment during high school, work that is both more demanding and more stressful. However, they also describe their jobs as giving them more opportunities for learning and advancement, and choose their early jobs for their learning potential. These youth may also be considered purposeful—taking advantage of an alternative source of human capital formation, work experience. They reap the benefits of this strategy in higher earnings immediately after high school. However, this is not the optimal strategy with respect to lifetime earnings attainment, since they will soon be surpassed by their more highly educated former schoolmates.

Implications for Future Studies

Lacking national scope, the YDS has obvious limitations. It cannot address regional variations in youth employment, particularly rural-urban differences (Shanahan et al., 1996; Elder and Conger, 2001) and the circumstances in the poorest urban enclaves (Newman, 1999). As it focuses on a single midwestern city, it is unlikely to be exactly replicated elsewhere in America. Still, the YDS panel members' labor force participation rates and types of employment are quite similar to national profiles (Committee, 1998). The findings replicate some relationships noted in prior studies (such as associations between hours of employment and problem behavior).

Future studies should address the longer-term consequences of early paid jobs, as young people complete the transition to adulthood. This is particularly important given the prolonged character of this transition. Our analyses indicate that steady work during adolescence does not lead to any disadvantage in higher educational attainment, as measured seven years beyond high school, in comparison to young people who had more limited or no investment in paid work. Given lengthening periods of higher education, it is possible that youth who pursued more intensive work as teenagers will eventually catch up to the steady workers, as they continue taking courses, going to night school, and attaining further degrees. Young people who restricted their labor force participation during high school might eventually surpass the steady workers in educational attainment. As noted at the beginning of this chapter, the extended period of exploration allows some youth to pursue higher education sporadically. The longer-term benefits or disadvantages of slower vs. faster completion of education, in the present context, are not known.

Still, it is possible that some consequences of early work may not be fully observable until the young people become established in enduring, career-type jobs. For example, during high school, jobs that were stressful and demanding, and required more decisionmaking and control, contributed to depressive affect. Further analyses of data from the 1995 survey showed that work conditions experienced during high school had few longer-term effects on depressive affect or well-being (Mortimer et al., 2002).

Moreover, the consequences of early work may become fully apparent only under certain conditions. For example, some work activities, though experienced as stressful and difficult, may challenge youth to develop new and more effective coping responses, heightening their thresholds of reactivity to subsequently experienced stressors (Shanahan and Mortimer, 1996). In the presence of similar stresses in more adultlike jobs, they may respond more competently than if they had had less experience with these problems in the past. We will address this phenomenon, elsewhere termed "eustress," as more waves of YDS data become available.

Research should also be undertaken over more extended periods of time to more fully comprehend the consequences of youth employment. As both the economy and youth labor markets change, it is important to continue to examine both investment and quality of work in diverse settings, their effects on adolescents, and their implications for successful passage to adulthood.

Implications for Policy

Adolescence and the transition to adulthood are highly formative phases of the life course; the values, self-concepts and identities, and behavioral patterns that develop at this time have lasting consequences. As one young woman commented: "I feel like you sort of become sort of the person you are, while you're a teenager. Not that everything is set in stone from that point, but . . . I feel like the core of who I am is pretty much the same . . . since high school." Choices and commitments are made at this time that launch youth onto more or less rewarding, beneficial, and health-promoting trajectories—in higher education, family life, and work. How can adults help youth to make this momentous transition?

In considering the application of the YDS findings, it is useful to broaden our perspective. Modell aptly entitled his comprehensive historical study *Into One's Own* (1989) highlighting youth's increasingly independent and individualized processes of initiation of intimate relationships, courtship, and family formation. Arguably, the extension of the pre-adulthood phase has also put young people increasingly "on their own" with respect to the transition to work.

As the transition to adulthood is elongated, the need for serious consideration of future work is effectively postponed. For most high school students, work is a distant prospect. When we asked an attorney in her twenties whether she had ever thought about working after high school, she replied: "No, for me it was just automatic college. So, no matter what we did or no matter what I wanted to do, college was just like an extension of high school. It wasn't like a choice at all." Similarly, an accountant reported: "In high school, I guess I did think about things, but I didn't think real far out. It was more like, geez, what do you want to major in in college?" Expectations and institutional supports for continuing education (scholarships and loans, night classes, employer-paid certification or degree programs) foster more lengthy postsecondary schooling. Many youth prolong their college experience beyond the traditional four years. But the concern is not about youth who do eventually achieve their college degrees. When they finally finish college, these highly educated labor market entrants bring strong credentials to potential employers and have the benefit of college placement offices to help them find suitable work.

However, the vast majority of American young people who enter the labor force do not have such impressive educational credentials—including the small portion who drop out of high school, high school graduates, and the large numbers who drop out of college. Like prior generations of young people, they must make their way to "careerlike" jobs on their own; however, they do this at older ages when their connections to "protective" institutions are more tenuous.

Many young people do not begin thinking about their longer-term vocational objectives during high school, as their focus is preparing for, and getting into, college (Schneider and Stevenson, 1999). In the absence of information and practical guidance, goals may be vague. A YDS clerical worker in her mid-twenties, who was planning to return to school, described her earlier way of thinking right after high school: "I had a dreamy mind. I used to think that I'd run away and find somebody famous and they would teach me the ropes and I'd be a famous movie star or singer or something. I mean, I had all these things going through my head, but basically what I did was work."

Some of our young adult interviewees indicated that they were less motivated when they got to college because of the lack of clear connection between their education and future work prospects. For example, a young woman who had dropped out of college and then returned told us:

I went to school two and a half years and then I stopped going to school because I knew I didn't want to do accounting, but did not know what I wanted to do, so I basically had all of my generals and all of my electives done and didn't want a degree in something that I didn't want to do . . . I didn't do so well in school. And part of that was because I didn't know what I wanted to do, so therefore I didn't really feel like certain classes I was in were worth my time.

Even in their mid-twenties, many young people have not yet settled on an area of work that might constitute a career. As one young woman who had completed high school and was attending "night school" put it,

I feel as if everything interests me. I start taking a class and it interests me and I'm like, well, maybe I'll do that . . . For example, my first class was Intro to Psychology, which I took because I enjoyed psychology classes in high school, so I thought, well, maybe I'll do something in that field, maybe being a counselor, maybe not being an actual psychiatrist, because that would require me going to school for the rest of my life . . . Then I took an English Comp class because I always enjoyed English, and I was like, well, maybe I'll do something in the English field, or in writing, or something like that. So I feel in a way as if I'm still in high school because I don't know really what I want to do when I grow up.

Another, who had a B.A. but at the time of the interview was pursuing two additional B.A.'s in other subjects, said: "Everything looks good. It's like the kid in a candy store type attitude. I have never been particularly focused on one thing . . . I've never been very good at picking one thing out and following it. So afraid of not liking what I pick and then getting stuck."

A young man who worked as a customer service representative was thinking of returning to school but was unclear about what to study:

RESPONDENT: It's just I haven't found that right spot yet. I don't know what it is. That's why . . . I'm thinking about school again, 'cause it may push me into actually staying somewhere I want to be and doing what I want to do.

INTERVIEWER: When you think about possibly going back to school, what do you think you'd want to look into or study?

RESPONDENT: I guess I'm unsure because I have to . . . I'm not sure what's really available. It's been so long since I've been back. There's so many courses out there that are available. I'd have to do a little research on that and find out what I'm interested in. It'd be something with art, I know that. Whether it was for architectural drafting or . . . I'd like to do that, but that takes a long time. That's one of my concerns there.

INTERVIEWER: Of getting an architecture degree. Have you ever had the opportunity to talk to anybody who's gone into that field?

RESPONDENT: No. I don't even know anybody in that field.

INTERVIEWER: Have you ever read up about it? About what possibly you'd be doing?

RESPONDENT: No. The last time I was actually really, really interested in it was when I was coming out of high school. I always wanted to take that class and I never took it. Just never took it, but I've always wanted to do it . . .

Even with a B.A. in hand, there may be difficulty establishing oneself in careerlike employment without a clear occupational direction. When asked "What did you think you'd do once you left college?" a female graduate student replied:

I don't think I had a concrete idea of—I mean I knew I would work, I knew I would live on my own and support myself, but I didn't have—I didn't have an idea of what—what that was going to be. And then when I graduated, I couldn't find a full-time job, so I worked several part-time jobs for the first year, year and a half . . . it was a really hard time for me because I was really looking for full-time employment, and even though I had my undergraduate degree, it took me a college year, year and a half, to find a full-time job.

Only 8 percent of the YDS panel retained the same vocational goal from high school graduation to seven years beyond high school (Mortimer, Zimmer-Gembeck, et al., 2002; see Rindfuss et al., 1999, for national evidence of change in occupational direction to the mid-twenties). As the voices of the youth themselves suggest, some did not become seriously engaged with issues of vocational choice until they were well beyond high school. By this time, young people are less likely to be ensconced in educational institutions whose purpose is to protect, shelter, and guide them to adulthood. They make career decisions in increasingly independent and "unprotected" environments. The clerical worker who described her earlier thinking as "dreamy" came to rely on chance contacts when, in her mid-twenties, she began to think about business marketing. When asked how she had been finding out about that, she replied:

> Just asking people. Talking to different people . . . that are in marketing . . . I just thought I'd ask people that I see in the building, that worked in sales, and ask them their background and if they knew anybody. I even talked to my friend's first-grade schoolteacher, whose husband was [in marketing].

Clearly, there are benefits, as well as drawbacks, of part-time teenage work. But are there ways in which this experience can be made more beneficial, so as to foster young people's exercise of agency in the pursuit of their goals? Our analyses suggest that adolescent efficacy is, in fact, responsive to high-quality work experiences. Occupational values, central to the formation of work goals, are also linked to employment experiences. How can educators and others encourage youth to be more planful and strategic as they move toward their adult futures?

A central conclusion from the YDS is that more limited investment in work during high school has more beneficial educational consequences. Those who guide teenagers—teachers, counselors, parents—should be aware of the benefits of multifaceted patterns of time use and lifestyles. The well-rounded adolescent has been found to achieve the highest educational credentials and to postpone full-time work and parenthood.

Furthermore, we should give greater attention to the quality of work for all youth (Hamilton, 1999). Our findings with respect to the crystallization of occupational values are especially pertinent. Youth should be able to learn new things from their jobs. As we have seen, this new learning need not be technical or complex. YDS teenagers gained "work readiness" from their jobs as they adapted to workplace rules and routines, and as they learned to get along with their supervisors, customers, and clients, to carry out instructions, and to handle money.

Of course, most teenagers who work are employed in the labor market, not in school-supervised programs, such as internships, job shadowing, or other "school-to-work" initiatives. Not surprisingly, research has demonstrated that school-supervised work is of higher quality than other work (Stone et al., 1990). Schools' encouragement of higher-quality teenage work can take many forms. Employment may occur in the school itself—vocational programs sometimes permit youth to run entrepreneurial establishments from their high schools. Alternatively, youth may be placed as interns in organizations linked to their vocational objectives, "shadowing" adult workers as they perform their jobs. Many innovative programs that connect schooling and work were developed in response to the School-to-Work Opportunities Act of 1994 (Borman, 1991; Stone and Mortimer, 1998).

One young man told us about a program during high school that had helped him to choose and enter a career:

> When I was like in ninth grade we did a survey, I think it was for the Boy Scouts of America, and they have a division called the exploring division. It's part of the Boy Scouts of America, but it's more career focused and, like the police department, has an exploring post. Most police departments do, fire departments, they're pretty much in every career field now, and it's basically so you can learn about that job if you're interested before you actually spend all the money to go to school and become that. So we did this career interest survey, and the police department sent me a letter. So when I was 15, I joined St. Paul's exploring program, which is a volunteer position, and I did that for seven years and then when I was 21 I got hired as a parking enforcement officer for St. Paul and then when I was 23 I got hired as a police officer.

A young woman who was in college lamented the absence of such programs in high school:

> "Parents taking their kids to work day" is so that they can see what it's like to work and that's great, but let's take it a little further and let's get them out in other things. It's kind of like field trips . . . let's put them in some other environments when they're in high school to kind of get an idea. I don't think we do that,

and I'm truly amazed at people who know what they want to do at 18 and do it. My mom is one of them. She wanted to be a nurse. You know, thirty years later, she still loves being a nurse, and that's what she did straight out of high school at 18, went to college for that, and it's like, how did you know that? There are a lot of people that went to school at 18, they knew what they wanted to do, but I think we need to have some more options for people who don't [know] what they want to do. Like me.

A young man spent two years in a pre-engineering program, only to discover that the field he had chosen, environmental engineering, was not what he had anticipated:

I knew I liked trees and I was trying to go into environmental engineering and I thought that would be kind of a great job, but it turned out environmental engineering was building waste treatment plants, which I really didn't know what it really was. It sounded like in engineering you could pick anything, civil or electrical and there was this one called environmental. "Oh, I'll take that. I like the environment." Then when I was talking about transferring [from a two-year to a four-year program], I think that's when I realized that I didn't want to build a waste treatment plant or a dump or something like that and that's what environmental engineering turned out to be, so it was a revolutionary moment for me.

This young man subsequently discovered a college program in forestry, which was much more to his liking.

The Cornell Youth and Work Program (Hamilton and Hamilton, 1997) provides an exemplary model of the kinds of experiences that facilitate young people's learning about and adaptation to the adult workforce. While this demonstration project applied principles from the German apprenticeship system (Hamilton and Lempert, 1996) and emphasized preparation for work in particular contexts (health care, administrative and office technology, and manufacturing and engineering technology), it offers lessons applicable to diverse work settings and student circumstances. The program emphasized breadth of experiences offered the participating high school students: employers were encouraged to expose the youth to a variety of jobs and work settings, include them in all-firm events and communications, and promote their involvement in projects that transcended particular units and circumstances. This enabled the youth to master a variety of skills and learn about the organization and the industry as a whole. In addition, the work experience was designed to build technical competence, personal and social competence, and vocational development. The best workplace supervisors presented clear expectations and provided feedback about the students' progress in meeting them. They promoted learning by teaching work skills and by encouraging high academic achievement. This high-quality work-based learning, along with complementary instruction, counseling, and encouragement by teachers in the schools, helped the teenagers to formulate their career goals and to learn more about the kinds of jobs that would mesh with their emerging interests and abilities.

Employers should be encouraged to join schools in such cooperative programs. Hamilton and Hamilton recommend field trips and job-shadowing programs for younger youth, enabling them to visit diverse workplaces. Such early encounters in the workplace pave the way for more intensive service learning and unpaid internships and for cooperative learning programs and paid internships. Through these experiences, young people move from tentative and short-term involvements to greater investment and commitment; from initial exploration, to gaining personal and social competence as they perform routine tasks, to greater technical competence as they learn to plan, perform, and evaluate more complex job tasks. After high school, some youth move on to college with a greater sense of career direction thanks to their work-based learning. Others continue work-based learning in the form of longer-term apprenticeships leading to certification.

Because programs such as these require considerable commitment of staff and time on the part of both schools and employers, they are difficult to initiate and sustain. Most young people participate in the naturally occurring labor market, without such institutional connections between school and work. Nonetheless, some of the principles enunciated by the Hamiltons can be applied to these circumstances as well. We saw in Chapter 3 that teenagers' jobs involve greater responsibility, authority, and complexity as they grow older. As their work evolves, they gain some of the same breadth of experience that other young people gain from a planned workplace "curriculum."

Teachers, counselors, and parents should be aware of the benefits of holding different kinds of jobs, and of moving from those involving simple tasks and limited experiences to those involving more learning-rich environments and possibilities for career exploration. They should help young people to formulate more specific visions of their occupational futures. It is important that these programs not be construed as deflecting youth from college or as constraining their opportunities, but instead as expanding their options. Otherwise they will be firmly resisted, as illustrated in the following exchange with a young woman who had become a schoolteacher:

INTERVIEWER: Did you ever think about work you might do once you left high school?

RESPONDENT: Not really. No.

INTERVIEWER: Did anybody talk to you about it while you were in high school?

RESPONDENT: Yeah. The school had a couple people come around and what not. Then I found out my mom didn't want me to go anywhere but college. I started talking about trade, da-da-da, and it's like, no. She called my friend's mom and was kind of frantic, "What's wrong with Carol? How come she doesn't want to go to college?"

Educators may not be taking full advantage of the fact that most students do participate in the labor market at least some time during high school. This provides an opportunity to demonstrate the relevance of schooling to "real life." We asked the seniors, "In class discussions at school, do the students ever talk about their jobs or get ideas about how to do their jobs better?" Only half responded affirmatively. Only 17 percent agreed that "I contribute more to class discussions because of what I learn at work." Still, 54 percent agreed that "My job has taught me the importance of getting a good education." Employed students recognize the connections between school and work, and they may therefore be responsive to teachers' efforts to better integrate these aspects of their lives.

Youth should be encouraged to talk about their work experiences in class or write about them in term papers and other assignments. Teachers can then help them to become aware of the kinds of opportunities, problems, and constraints in their jobs that are generalizable to other workplace settings, and encourage them to think about the kind of employment they would like to have in the future and the credentials they would need to obtain it. As Youniss and colleagues (1997) have pointed out with respect to volunteer work, the lessons to be learned from work experience are not always transparent. But through class discussions, reflection, and writing, youth can learn about the broader moral, social, and even political implications of their observations and volunteer experiences. It is these reflections and messages that have the strongest impact on their development.

Similarly, experiences in babysitting, yardwork, and fast-food jobs, as well as in clerical employment and manual labor, may have lessons to teach that are not immediately evident to teenage workers. Encouraging youth to exchange information about their jobs in school could also increase their awareness of new opportunities in the labor market, fostering productive exploration of vocational goals.

It has been suggested that parents, teachers, and employers might examine the places of employment for teenagers in their own communities, establish criteria for their evaluation, and certify them as appropriate or inappropriate for youth (Committee, 1998). Such criteria, at a minimum, would include compliance with federal and state hours regulations and the avoidance of hazardous work conditions. Through their ratings, adults could also encourage employers to offer flexible work schedules, enabling teenagers to shift their total hours and times of work to allow for special school projects and extracurricular activities.

At the least, educators, parents, and others entrusted with the care of youth are urged to be more sensitive to teenagers' work experiences—the amount of time they work, their learning opportunities, their exposure to stress, and the compatibility of their work with other activities constructed for the purpose of educating youth and guiding them to adulthood. The YDS reveals that most employed adolescents find combining work and school to be stressful. Greater awareness of such stress could lead to changes, in both paid work and school settings, to foster greater compatibility between them.

Surely the goal is not to encourage young people to make firm and lasting occupational commitments while they are still in high school. Still, teenage work can have lasting consequences. Three YDS interviewees noted explicit connections between their adolescent and early adult jobs. A young man who was working as a care manager for adults with disabilities said: "In high school, when I was just a lifeguard, I would lifeguard for a . . . program for adults with disabilities, so I started working with people with disabilities in tenth grade and I've done that ever since." A photographer recalled her high school job in a photo shop: "It helped me learn a lot more about photography and printing on a basic level. I learned about overexposure and underexposure. I learned what the different film speeds did. I learned a lot more about customer service. I learned how to work the printing machine. I learned what was up in the film developing machine and stuff like that, so I learned a little bit more of the technical stuff." A police officer told us:

> When I was seventeen in high school, I went on a ride-along . . . and I liked it, liked what I saw, good exposure to different types of things, and it was pretty much the day that I decided that this was what I wanted to do and carried on from there . . . I became a community service officer here in this department . . . I applied for it as a part-time position . . . work on the streets also to help out the cops and more of your minor calls, your animal complaints, your parking complaints, to help out on accidents, that kind of a thing, so I did that for three years while I was going to school and that gave the good final exposure that I needed to really determine if this is what I wanted to do.

More typically, employment during high school helps to indicate congenial, or uncongenial, vocational directions, thus promoting exploration. A young woman looked back on her high school jobs in retail sales and fast food: "I realized then that I really liked to be around people. I think that was probably the first thing, is that I would not be happy working at a desk job where I'm not ever around anybody else." An accountant commented on his early job in a fast-food outlet: "It gave me my first real experience with how a business works, paperwork, inventory, accounting-wise . . . It kind of helped me have an idea, when I was trying to decide later, what I wanted to do, types of careers. When I saw the paperwork that the store had to do in the accounting, just the minimal stuff that had to be done in there, it was one of the things that gave me an inclination toward doing what I do now."

Clausen (1991) demonstrated that the more planful adolescents of a prior generation, born before the Great Depression, were those who subsequently made more informed and better decisions with respect to both work and family. Even though the transition to adulthood now takes a different form, it is likely that today's young people would also benefit from more serious early engagement with their occupational futures. For occupational choice is not a one-time decision but rather a process of exploration and discovery. As a social worker told us:

> Probably all of my jobs that I've had have really pushed me toward social work, even in a round-about way. I mean even working at the drug store really involved me in working with people . . . trying to help someone find what they want in a drug store, which is, even as dull as that sounds, sort of helping people, sort of moves in the direction of helping people get what they need, which is what I think . . . social work is about.

The recommendations set forth here are built on the premise that this exploratory process is likely to be more successful if it begins at a time when young people are still under the auspices of "protected" institutions, and when the best opportunity to pursue higher education—before the onset of parental and other adultlike responsibilities—still lies before, not behind, them.

Working has clearly become an integral part of growing up in America. The large service sector of our economy benefits much from the flexibility in young people's hours of work. Parents are enthusiastic about their children's employment and about their own early jobs, and teenagers want paid work that enables them to try out future "possible selves." Thus it is unlikely that employment of adolescents will be restricted in the future, either by law or because of employers', parents', or teenagers' preferences. Given that youthwork is probably here to stay, let us build on its potentials and help parents, educators, and teenagers themselves to identify, and thereby avoid, the more deleterious patterns and conditions of paid work. Doing so will enable adolescents to be more effectively incorporated, as well as protected, as they make their initial forays into the adult world.

APPENDIX, NOTES, REFERENCES, & INDEX

Panel Selection

Recruitment of the panel of ninth graders utilized "active consent," now the standard practice in most studies of families and school-age children (Weinberger et al., 1990). Following procedures set forth by the University of Minnesota's Institutional Review Board, an invitation was sent to each designated student and to a parent or guardian, along with the letter of endorsement from the research director of the St. Paul Schools. Both letters indicated the purpose of the study in general terms.

The procedures of the research were also described. Each year the students were to be released from one class period to fill out a questionnaire. Those who were not present on survey days would be sent questionnaires by mail. Surveys of parents during the first and fourth years of the study would be administered by mail.

The letters also indicated the broad content of the surveys, provided assurance of confidentiality, and described the incentives to participate. In addition to the opportunity to contribute to the research, the students were offered payment of $10 for completing each survey.

Besides the three letters, the packet sent to each targeted household contained two consent forms, one for the parent or guardian and one for the child, along with an addressed stamped envelope to be returned to the principal investigator. Two signatures—that of the student participant and that of one parent or guardian—were required. When the consent forms were returned, the principal investigator cosigned them and returned them to the consenting household.

Clearly, this rather extensive invitation packet and consent procedure necessitated quite active involvement on the part of the parent and the student, unlike more passive consent procedures commonly employed in research on adolescents. When there is "passive consent," students are typically told that a study is going to take place on a given day and are asked to take home a written notice for their parents. Parents who do not wish to have their children participate must inform the school of their preference. If the parents do not take any action, consent is assumed. Such passive consent procedures typically yield about 95 percent consent (Weinberger et al., 1990; Steinberg and Avenevoli, 1998). In our study, perhaps as a result of the active consent procedure, just about two-thirds of those invited agreed to participate—1,139 of 1,779 randomly drawn cases. This rate is typical for studies utilizing active consent with schoolchildren; when both parent and child participation is requested, as in the YDS, "it is common to have two-thirds of the invited families decline" (Weinberger et al., 1990: 1374).

In light of the active character of the consent process, it could plausibly be argued that those who agreed to participate in the Youth Development Study are different from those who did not. Consenting parents might have more education and greater appreciation of the importance of scientific research. They might be more trusting of the investigators' promises of confidentiality. Such parents might also be more interested in the topic of work, either in their own lives or with respect to their children. And their children might be better adjusted: parents of less well adjusted children might possibly try to protect them by refusing to participate in a study of this kind.

Since no data could be obtained directly from the families who chose not to participate, we could not explore these various possibilities. But we could investigate the demographic aspects of panel representation. Of the 1,139 students who consented to be in the study, 1,105 actually filled out surveys at the first wave (or survey year). In some ways their families looked very similar to the community as a whole. For example, according to the 1980 Census, 23 percent of families with children under 18 in St. Paul were headed by women without a husband present; 23 percent of the YDS respondents likewise lived in single-parent female-headed households in the spring of 1988. Moreover, the racial and ethnic composition of the first-wave participants was quite similar to that of the St. Paul School District as a whole.

However, the findings presented in this book exclude one ethnic group: Hmong refugee families from Southeast Asia, who arrived in the Minneapolis–St. Paul area close to the time the study began. The Hmong constituted 9 percent of the ninth-grade student body as a whole and 9 percent of the first-wave study participants. Because the Hmong are a very recent immigrant group with limited knowledge of English, studying them required procedures quite different from those utilized for the rest of the sample, and the data obtained from Hmong and non-Hmong participants were not comparable.

Although we could not comprehensively compare families who did and did not consent to be part of the study, access to the home addresses of both groups allowed us to compare the socioeconomic characteristics of the census tracts in which they resided. Tract-level data from the 1980 Census (U.S. Bureau of the Census, 1982a), were used to characterize the neighborhood of each eligible non-Hmong family. Socioeconomic characteristics for the tract of residence included household income, occupation, ethnic composition (percentage white), and single-parent status, as well as the prevalence of public assistance, high school completion, college completion, female employment, male employment, and extended unemployment (15 or more weeks). This information was supplemented by the child's school, age, and gender (provided by the St. Paul School District).

A probit analysis (reported in Finch et al., 1991) showed that none of these socioeconomic contextual or individual-level variables were significant predictors of the decision to participate. In fact, there were very few statistically significant predictors. One high school had a higher likelihood of participation, and students enrolled in educational programs for those with special problems were less likely to join the study. Students who were older than their fellow ninth graders were less likely to be involved; 94 percent of ninth-grade participants were 14 or 15 years old; 6 percent were 16 or 17. As in other research (Weinberger et al., 1990), girls were more likely than boys to agree to participate: 524 girls and 476 boys completed first-wave questionnaires.

We concluded that, insofar as could be determined with the available data, the initial panel, consisting of those who completed first-wave surveys, was representative of the total population of St. Paul ninth graders who attended public school.

NOTES

CHAPTER 1 SHOULD ADOLESCENTS WORK?

1. This system was perpetuated in America in the early nineteenth century in foster care; foster parents obtained child houseworkers in return for food and board, while sometimes offering training in the skills of farming or a trade (Zelizer, 1985: 173).

2. Buchmann (1989) argues that the "destandardized" and "individualized" postmodern life course renders particular decisions made during adolescence, such as those concerning education and work, less important for future attainment. This claim may be questionable (Pimentel, 1996), and it does not imply that the need for multiple competencies and forms of capital would diminish.

CHAPTER 2 THE YOUTH DEVELOPMENT STUDY

1. Demographic data from U.S. Bureau of the Census (1995, July 7), "St. Paul City: Persons, Total," Census of Population and Housing, 1990 <venus.census.gov/cdrom/lookup/914948161> (1998, Dec. 29); and U.S. Bureau of the Census (1995, July 7), "Minneapolis—St. Paul, MN—WI MSA: Persons, Total," Census of Population and Housing, 1990 <venus.census.gov/cdrom/lookup/915413939> (1999, Jan. 3).

2. The 1993 General Social Survey asked a national sample of 1,606 respondents how important it was for them to have a fulfilling job. Excluding those who were students, retired, or "keeping house," they were also asked, "If you were to get enough money to live as comfortably as you would like for the rest of your life, would you continue to work or would you stop working?" On neither of these questions did persons from the Midwest, South, East, and South significantly differ.

3. If attempts are not made to estimate prevalence, the loss of subjects at the lower ends of variable distributions is not so problematic; however, restriction of variance would be likely to attenuate relations between the predictors and the outcomes.

CHAPTER 3   TIME ALLOCATION AND QUALITY OF WORK

1. In fact, a small number of respondents each year gave responses to this question that clearly referred to household chores (paid or unpaid). These responses were coded as "work at home." If the respondent worked in a family business, this was considered to be a paid job. If the respondent was employed for pay in a family business that was located in the home, this was likewise considered to be employment.

2. These figures include the respondents who participated in the study each year, whether or not they were attending school at the time. We do not separate or exclude those not attending school because of the difficulty of determining dropout status from attendance at a particular survey date. Some young people move in and out of school; if not attending at one time, they may return subsequently. Starting in Wave 3 (1990), when most respondents were 16–17 and in their junior year, we asked about their course of study (college preparatory, vocational, etc.) and provided the option "I am not in school." In 1990, 5.9 percent of the total responding to this question so indicated; in 1991, 10.4 percent did so.

3. Youth under 16 can work 8 hours per day and 40 hours per week, but they are prohibited from working from 9 P.M. to 7 A.M. Youth aged 16 and 17 do not have cumulative hours restrictions. They cannot work between 11 P.M. and 5 A.M. before a school day, but with written parental permission they can finish work a half-hour later and start a half-hour earlier.

4. Gender differences were gauged here by mean scores on a job skills index, an additive composite of five items: How much has your job helped you to . . . follow directions? To get along with people? To be on time? To take responsibility for your work? To manage your money? (1 = not at all; 4 = a great deal).

5. Job commitment was measured by an index of responses to five questions: "How often are you interested enough on your job to do more work than your job requires?" "How often do you feel that your work is meaningful and important?" "Most of my interests are centered around my job." "I am very much involved personally in my job." "The most important things that happen to me involve my job."

6. To form indices, unweighted items were summed.

7. Psychological engagement was measured by the indicators of commitment (see note 5) and the following questions: "How often do you feel bored at work, or that time is dragging?" "How satisfied are you with your job as a whole?" Respondents also indicated how "true" the following statement was: "My job gives me a chance to be helpful of others."

8. Work and school compatibility is registered by five questions, which respondents rated from 1 = strongly disagree to 4 = strongly agree: "What I have learned in school helps me do better on my job." "My job provides information about things I am studying in school." "I contribute more to class discussions because of what I learn at work." "My job has taught me the importance of getting a good education." "My job has made me recognize the subjects I really like and don't like."

CHAPTER 4   THE ECOLOGY OF YOUTHWORK

1. The findings related to time with parents should be viewed with caution, because the questions on this topic asked the adolescent to evaluate the amount of time spent with the parent. They read, "Does (your parent) spend enough time with you or do you wish (he or she) spent more time with you?" The response options ranged from "spends enough time" to "wish (he or she) spent a lot more time with me."

2. Other, variable-based analyses of YDS data (see Chapter 6) show that work intensity is unrelated to amount of time spent doing homework (Mortimer, Finch, et al., 1996; see also Schoenhals et al., 1998).

CHAPTER 5   PRECURSORS OF INVESTMENT IN WORK

1. All significant differences are in favor of girls—who are more likely, in at least one year, to have sought employment to buy things, to save for future education, to have the experience of working, to learn new skills, and to get out of the house.

2. To simplify Figure 5.2, gender differences are not shown. By Wave 4, 80 percent of girls and 60 percent of boys use their earnings to buy clothes (p < .001); 52 percent of girls and 36 percent of boys use them for school expenses (p < .001). However, 62 percent of boys and 39 percent of girls use them for cars (p < .001), and 45 percent of boys and 36 percent of girls use them to buy food (p < .05).

3. The YDS also asked about why youth had sought their first jobs, but these jobs may have been obtained some years before high school.

4. These items were subject to a confirmatory factor analysis (using

LISREL VII, Jöreskog and Sörbom, 1989); unstandardized lambda co-efficients (item weights) were used to form weighted additive indices.

5. Whereas logistic regression is used to assess the effects of predictors on a dichotomous outcome, multinomial logistic regression predicts differences in the likelihood of membership across a set of mutually exclusive, nominal categories. The regression coefficients represent the effect of each predictor on placement in a category, relative to a reference category, while controlling the other independent variables. Exponentiated, the coefficient indicates the likelihood or "risk" of being in a category, relative to the reference category.

6. In estimating the equations, the variables were initially entered in an ordered sequence. The first set represents social location (including family income); the second, educational performance and engagement (including homework time, educational plans, and academic self-esteem); the third, problem behavior and peer orientation (including frequency of alcohol use and smoking). The models were estimated using LIMDEP (Limited Dependent Variables, Version 7.0, Greene, 1995). In a second step, several predictors were deleted to simplify the models and to increase sample size. Family income, homework time, educational plans, and academic self-esteem had no significant effects in the multivariate analysis. Ninth-grade alcohol use and smoking were also dropped, given their low explanatory power (smoking affected only the likelihood of being in the small nonworker category; as smoking increased, youth were less likely to be without employment).

7. Paralleling the prior analysis of selection to temporal investment patterns, the work-quality variables were regressed on the entire set of predictors (using ordinary least squares regression). Again, variables were dropped to obtain a more parsimonious representation of the key influences on youth work quality and to increase sample size. The variable representing interference between work and grades is not included, given the absence of significant predictors.

8. Interestingly, however, we do not find that youth with greater or lesser intrinsic motivation toward school, split at the median, come to have different types of jobs. For example, by Wave 4 they are equally likely to be doing restaurant/food work, and are similarly distributed across other job types.

CHAPTER 6   WORKING AND ADOLESCENT DEVELOPMENT

1. Parents of the ninth graders were also asked about changes they would like to make in their children's jobs. Approximately two-thirds indicated none. Those who did suggest changes tended to endorse stronger engagement in work. For example, more parents wanted their children to work more hours than fewer hours. Some said that given their children's high level

of responsibility at work, they should be paid more (Phillips and Sandstrom, 1990).

2. Though pay evaluation had no statistically significant effect for boys, corresponding coefficients for boys and girls were not significantly different.

3. In one of few statistically significant interactions between gender and work quality, we found that perceived compatibility of employment and school performance reduced alcohol use for boys, but not for girls, while learning opportunities at work reduced it for girls, but not for boys.

4. Mihalic and Elliott (1997), analyzing data from the National Youth Survey, find links between the duration of early work (ages 12–16), measured in years, and alcohol use (for both genders) and marijuana use (for males only) at ages 27–28.

5. Osgood (1999: 182) also observes, "Perhaps the 'zero-sum' logic does apply in this case: the total combined hours that American teens spend in work and watching television may approach a limit where it is difficult for one to increase without the other decreasing."

CHAPTER 7 THE TRANSITION TO ADULTHOOD

1. Shifting the dependent variable to an ordinal measure of educational attainment also demonstrated the advantage of the "steady" workers.

2. Although 30 percent of the panel had spent at least some time in school during the previous year, the relative lack of career relevance in their current jobs is not attributable to the greater propensity to be in school. In fact, the coefficient representing the effect of not working changed hardly at all when this control (whether attending school during the previous year or not) was added (from $-.365$ to $-.359$, $p < .05$ for both). Moreover, whether youth were attending school or not in 1998 had no significant influence, net of the other variables in the model, on career relevance.

3. Analyses of gender/work variable interactions in the determination of earnings again yielded mainly null findings. There was some indication that wage rates during high school had a stronger positive effect on 1998 earnings for men than for women. However, when analyzed separately by gender, earnings had no significant influence in either group.

REFERENCES

Alwin, Duane F. 1988. "From Obedience to Authority: Changes in Traits Desired in Children, 1924–1978." *Public Opinion Quarterly* 52: 33–52.

Alwin, Duane F., Ronald L. Cohen, and Theodore M. Newcomb. 1991. *Political Attitudes over the Life Span: The Bennington Women after Fifty Years*. Madison: University of Wisconsin Press.

Aquilino, William S. 1999. "Rethinking the Young Adult Stage: Prolonged Dependency as an Adaptive Strategy." Pp. 168–175 in Booth, Crouter, and Shanahan, eds., 1999.

Ariès, Philippe. 1962. *Centuries of Childhood: A Social History of Family Life*. Trans. Robert Baldick. New York: Knopf.

Arnett, Jeffrey J. 1997. "Young People's Conceptions of the Transition to Adulthood." *Youth and Society* 29: 1–23.

——— 2000. "Emerging Adulthood: A Theory of Development from the Late Teens through the Twenties." *American Psychologist* 55: 469–480.

Aronson, Pamela J. 1996. "Divergent Pathways in Young Women's Transition to Adulthood." Presented at the Annual Meeting of the American Sociological Association, New York.

——— 1998. "Coming of Age in the 1990s: Women's Identities, Life Paths, and Attitudes towards Feminism." PhD diss., University of Minnesota.

Aronson, Pamela J., Jeylan T. Mortimer, Carol Zierman, and Michael Hacker. 1996. "Generational Differences in Early Work Experiences and Evaluations." Pp. 25–62 in Mortimer and Finch, eds., 1996.

Arum, R., and M. Hout. 1998. "The Early Returns: The Transition from School to Work in the United States." Pp. 471–510 in Y. Shavit and W. Muller, eds., *From School to Work: A Comparative Study of Educational Qualifications and Occupational Destinations*. Oxford: Clarendon Press.

Bachman, Jerald G., Dawn E. Bare, and Eric I. Frankie. 1986. "Correlates of Employment among High School Seniors." Monitoring the Future Occasional Paper 20. Ann Arbor: Institute for Social Research, University of Michigan.

Bachman, Jerald G., and John Schulenberg. 1992. "Part-Time Work by High School Seniors: Sorting Out Correlates and Possible Consequences." Monitoring the Future Occasional Paper 32. Ann Arbor: Institute for Social Research, University of Michigan.

—— 1993. "How Part-Time Work Intensity Relates to Drug Use, Problem Behavior, Time Use, and Satisfaction among High School Seniors: Are These Consequences or Merely Correlates?" *Developmental Psychology* 29: 220–235.

Bandura, Albert. 1977. "Self-efficacy: Toward a Unifying Theory of Behavioral Change." *Psychological Review* 84: 191–215.

—— 1986. *Social Foundations of Thought and Action: A Social Cognitive Theory.* Englewood Cliffs, N.J.: Prentice-Hall.

Becker, Gary S. 1993. *Human Capital: A Theoretical and Empirical Analysis, with Special Reference to Education.* 3rd ed. Chicago: University of Chicago Press.

Bidwell, Charles, Barbara Schneider, and Kathryn Borman. 1998. "Working: Perceptions and Experiences of American Teenagers." Pp. 160–182 in Kathryn Borman and Barbara Schneider, eds., *The Adolescent Years: Social Influences and Educational Challenges.* Ninety-seventh Yearbook of the National Society for the Study of Education. Part I. Chicago: University of Chicago Press.

Bills, D. B., L. B. Helms, and M. Ozcan. 1995. "The Impact of Student Employment on Teachers' Attitudes and Behaviors toward Working Students." *Youth and Society* 27: 169–193.

Blau, F. D., and M. A. Ferber. 1985. "Women in the Labor Market: The Last Twenty Years." Pp. 19–49 in L. Larwood, A. H. Stromberg, and B. A. Gutek, eds., *Women and Work: An Annual Review,* vol. 1. Beverly Hills: Sage.

Booth, Alan, Ann C. Crouter, and Michael J. Shanahan, eds. 1999. *Transitions to Adulthood in a Changing Economy: No Work, No Family, No Future?* Westport, Conn.: Praeger.

Borman, Kathryn M. 1991. *The First "Real" Job: A Study of Young Workers.* Albany: State University of New York Press.

Boulding, Elise. 1980. "The Labor of U.S. Farm Women: A Knowledge Gap." *Sociology of Work and Occupations* 7: 261–290.

Bourdieu, Pierre. 1977. "Cultural Reproduction and Social Reproduction." In J. Karabel and A. H. Halsey, eds., *Power and Ideology in Education.* New York: Oxford University Press.

Braddock, Jomills H., D. A. Royster, L. F. Winfield, and R. Hawkins. 1991. "Bouncing Back: Sports and Academic Resilience among African-American Males." *Education and Urban Society* 24: 113–131.

Bronfenbrenner, Urie. 1979. *The Ecology of Human Development.* Cambridge, Mass.: Harvard University Press.

——— 1986. "Recent Advances in Research on the Ecology of Human Development." Pp. 287–309 in Rainer K. Silbereisen, K. Eyferth, and G. Rudinger, eds., *Development as Action in Context: Problem Behavior and Normal Youth Development.* New York: Springer-Verlag.

Bronfenbrenner, Urie, Peter McClelland, Elaine Wethington, Phyllis Moen, and Stephen J. Ceci. 1996. *The State of Americans: This Generation and the Next.* New York: Free Press.

Brown, Benson Bradford, and Wendy Theobald. 1998. "Learning Contexts beyond the Classroom: Extracurricular Activities, Community Organizations, and Peer Groups." Pp. 109–141 in Kathryn Borman and Barbara Schneider, eds., *The Adolescent Years: Social Influences and Educational Challenges.* Ninety-seventh Yearbook of the National Society for the Study of Education. Part I. Chicago: University of Chicago Press.

Buchmann, M. 1989. *The Script of Life in Modern Society.* Chicago: University of Chicago Press.

Call, Kathleen T. 1996a. "The Implications of Helpfulness for Possible Selves." Pp. 63–96 in Mortimer and Finch, eds., 1996.

——— 1996b. "Adolescent Work as an 'Arena of Comfort' under Conditions of Family Discomfort." Pp. 129–166 in Mortimer and Finch, eds., 1996.

Call, Kathleen T., and Miles McNall. 1992. "Poverty, Ethnicity, Youth Adjustment: A Comparison of Poor Hmong and Non-Hmong Adolescents." Pp. 373–392 in Wim Meeus, Martin de Goede, Willem Kox, and Klaus Hurrelmann, eds., *Adolescence, Careers, and Cultures.* New York: De Gruyter.

Call, Kathleen T., and Jeylan T. Mortimer. 2001. *Arenas of Comfort in Adolescence: A Study of Adjustment in Context.* Mahwah, N.J.: Lawrence Erlbaum.

Call, Kathleen T., Jeylan T. Mortimer, and Michael Shanahan. 1995. "Helpfulness and the Development of Competence in Adolescence." *Child Development* 66: 129–138.

Carr, Rhoda V., James D. Wright, and Charles J. Brody. 1996. "Effects of High School Work Experience a Decade Later: Evidence from the National Longitudinal Survey." *Sociology of Education* 69: 66–81.

Chaplin, Duncan, and Jane Hannaway. 1996. "High School Employment: Meaningful Connections for At-Risk Youth." Presented at the Annual Meeting of the American Educational Research Association, New York.

Cicchetti, D., and S. L. Toth. 1995. "Developmental Psychopathology and Disorder of Affect." Pp. 369–420 in D. Cicchetti and D. J. Cohen, eds., *Developmental Psychopathology*, vol. 2: *Risk, Disorder, and Adaptation*. New York: Wiley.

Clausen, John S. 1991. "Adolescent Competence and the Shaping of the Life Course." *American Journal of Sociology* 96: 805–842.

———— 1993. *American Lives: Looking Back at the Children of the Great Depression*. New York: Free Press.

Coleman, James S. 1961. *The Adolescent Society: The Social Life of the Teenager and Its Impact on Education*. New York: Free Press.

———— 1990. *Foundations of Social Theory*. Cambridge, Mass.: Harvard University Press.

Committee on the Health and Safety Implications of Child Labor (Committee). 1998. *Protecting Youth at Work: Health, Safety, and Development of Working Children and Adolescents in the United States*. Washington: National Academy Press.

Compas, B. E., and C. L. Hammen. 1996. "Child and Adolescent Depression: Covariation and Comorbidity in Development." Pp. 225–267 in R. J. Haggerty, L. R. Sherrod, N. Garmezy, and M. Rutter, eds., *Stress, Risk, and Resilience in Children and Adolescents: Process, Mechanisms, and Interventions*. Cambridge: Cambridge University Press.

Cooney, Teresa M., and Jeylan T. Mortimer. 1999. "Family Structure Differences in the Timing of Leaving Home: Exploring Mediating Factors." *Journal of Research on Adolescence* 9: 367–393.

Csikszentmihalyi, Mihaly. 1990. *Flow: The Psychology of Optimal Experience*. New York: HarperCollins.

Csikszentmihalyi, Mihaly, and Reed Larson. 1984. *Being Adolescent*. New York: Basic Books.

Csikszentmihalyi, Mihaly, and Jennifer Schmidt. 1998. "Stress and Resilience in Adolescence: An Evolutionary Perspective." Pp. 1–17 in Kathryn Borman and Barbara Schneider, eds., *The Adolescent Years: Social Influences and Educational Challenges*. Ninety-seventh Yearbook of the National Society for the Study of Education. Part I. Chicago: University of Chicago Press.

Curtis, James E., Edward Grabb, and Douglas Baer. 1992. "Voluntary Association Membership in Fifteen Countries." *American Sociological Review* 57: 139–152.

D'Amico, R. J. 1984. "Does Employment during High School Impair Academic Progress?" *Sociology of Education* 57: 152–164.

Davis, James A. 1964. *Great Aspirations: The Graduate School Plans of America's College Seniors*. Chicago: Aldine.

———. 1965. *Undergraduate Career Decisions: Correlates of Occupational Choice*. Chicago: Aldine.

Demos, John. 1972. *A Little Commonwealth*. New York: Oxford University Press.

Dennehy, Katherine, and Jeylan T. Mortimer. 1993. "Work and Family Orientations of Contemporary Adolescent Boys and Girls." Pp. 87–107 in Jane C. Hood, ed., *Men, Work, and Family*. Newbury Park, Calif.: Sage.

Dillman, Don A. 1983. "Mail and Other Self-Administered Questionnaires." Pp. 359–377 in Peter H. Rossi, James D. Wright, and A. B. Anderson, eds., *Handbook of Survey Research*. New York: Academic Press.

Dornbusch, Sanford M. 1994. "Off the Track." Presidential Address, Society for Research on Adolescence, Annual Meeting, San Diego.

Dreeben, Robert. 1968. *On What Is Learned in School*. Reading, Mass.: Addison-Wesley.

Ebata, Aaron T., Anne C. Petersen, and John J. Conger. 1990. "The Development of Psychopathology in Adolescence." Pp. 308–333 in Jon Rolf, Ann S. Masten, Dante Cicchetti, Keith H. Nuechterlein, and Sheldon Weintraub, eds., *Risk and Protective Factors in the Development of Psychopathology*. New York: Cambridge University Press.

Eccles, Jacquelynne S., Sarah Lord, and Christy Miller Buchanan. 1996. "School Transitions in Early Adolescence: What Are We Doing to Our Young People?" Pp. 251–284 in Julia A. Graber, Jeanne Brooks-Gunn, and Anne C. Petersen, eds., *Transitions through Adolescence: Interpersonal Domains and Context*. Mahwah, N.J.: Lawrence Erlbaum.

Elder, Glen H., Jr. 1974. *Children of the Great Depression*. Chicago: University of Chicago Press.

Elder, Glen H., Jr., and Rand D. Conger. 2000. *Children of the Land: Adversity and Success in Rural America*. Chicago: University of Chicago Press.

Entwisle, Doris R., Karl L. Alexander, and Linda Steffel Olson. 1998. "Early Work Histories of Urban Youth." *American Sociological Review* 65: 279–297.

Erikson, Erik H. 1959. *Identity and the Life-cycle*. New York: International Universities Press.

———. 1963. *Childhood and Society*. 2nd ed. New York: Norton.

———. 1968. *Identity, Youth, and Crisis*. New York: Norton.

Feather, N. T., and G. E. O'Brien. 1986. "A Longitudinal Study of the Effects of Employment and Unemployment on School-leavers." *Journal of Occupational Psychology* 59: 121–144.

Finch, Michael D., and Jeylan T. Mortimer. 1985. "Adolescent Work Hours and the Process of Achievement." Pp. 171–196 in *Research in Sociology of Education and Socialization,* vol. 5. Greenwich, Conn.: JAI Press.

Finch, Michael D., Michael J. Shanahan, Jeylan T. Mortimer, and Seongryeol Ryu. 1991. "Work Experience and Control Orientation in Adolescence." *American Sociological Review* 56: 597–611.

Freedman, Audrey. 1996. "Contingent Work and the Role of Labor Market Intermediaries." Pp. 177–199 in Garth Mangum and Stephen Mangum, eds., *Of Heart and Mind: Social Policy Essays in Honor of Sar A. Levitan.* Kalamazoo: W. E. Upjohn Institute for Employment Research.

Freeman, R. B., and D. A. Wise. 1979. *Youth Unemployment.* Cambridge, Mass.: National Bureau of Economic Research.

French, John R. P., Robert D. Caplan, and R. Van Harrison. 1982. *The Mechanisms of Job Stress and Strain.* New York: Wiley.

Fuji Survey. 1992. *Voices of Young America.* New York: Edelman.

Furstenberg, Frank F., Jr., Jeanne Brooks-Gunn, and S. P. Morgan. 1987. *Adolescent Mothers in Later Life.* New York: Cambridge University Press.

Furstenberg, Frank F., Jr., Thomas D. Cook, Jacquelynne Eccles, Glen H. Elder Jr., and Arnold Sameroff. 1999. *Managing to Make It.* Chicago: University of Chicago Press.

Fussell, Elizabeth. 2002. "Youth in Aging Societies." Pp. 18–51 in Jeylan T. Mortimer and Reed Larson, eds., *The Changing Adolescent Experience: Societal Trends and the Transition to Adulthood.* New York: Cambridge University Press.

Gager, Constance T., Teresa M. Cooney, and Kathleen Thiede Call. 1999. "The Effects of Family Characteristics and Time Use on Teenagers' Household Labor." *Journal of Marriage and the Family* 61: 982–994.

Gamst, Frederick C., ed. 1995. *Meanings of Work: Considerations for the Twenty-First Century.* Albany: State University of New York Press.

Gecas, Viktor, and Michael L. Schwalbe. 1986. "Parental Behavior and Adolescent Self-Esteem." *Journal of Marriage and the Family* 48: 37–46.

Gilligan, Carol. 1982. *In a Different Voice: Psychological Theory and Women's Development.* Cambridge, Mass.: Harvard University Press.

Ginzberg, E., S. W. Ginsberg, S. Axelrad, and J. L. Herman. 1951. *Occupational Choice: An Approach to a General Theory.* New York: Columbia University Press.

Goldstein, Bernard, and Jack Oldham. 1979. *Children and Work: A Study of Socialization.* New Brunswick, N.J.: Transaction.

Goodnow, J. J. 1988. "Children's Household Work: Its Nature and Functions." *Psychological Bulletin* 103: 5–26.

Gottfredson, D. C. 1985. "Youth Employment, Crime, and Schooling:

A Longitudinal Study of a National Sample." *Developmental Psychology* 21: 419–432.

Gottfredson, Michael, and Travis Hirschi. 1990. *A General Theory of Crime.* Stanford: Stanford University Press.

Grabowski, Lorie Schabo, Kathleen Thiede Call, and Jeylan T. Mortimer. 2001. "Global and Economic Self-Efficacy in the Attainment Process." *Social Psychology Quarterly* 64: 164–179.

Graff, Harvey J. 1995. *Conflicting Paths: Growing Up in America.* Cambridge, Mass.: Harvard University Press.

Granovetter, Mark S. 1974. *Getting a Job.* Cambridge, Mass.: Harvard University Press.

Greenberger, Ellen. 1984. "Defining Psychosocial Maturity." Pp. 3–39 in Paul Karoly and John J. Steffen, eds., *Adolescent Behavior Disorders: Foundations and Contemporary Concerns.* Lexington, Mass.: Lexington Books.

———— 1988. "Working in Teenage America." Pp. 21–50 in Jeylan T. Mortimer and Kathryn M. Borman, eds., *Work Experience and Psychological Development through the Life Span.* Boulder: Westview.

Greenberger, Ellen, and Laurence Steinberg. 1983. "Sex Differences in Early Labor Force Experience: Harbinger of Things to Come." *Social Forces* 62: 467–486.

———— 1986. *When Teenagers Work: The Psychological and Social Costs of Adolescent Employment.* New York: Basic Books.

Greenberger, Ellen, Laurence Steinberg, Alan Vaux, and Sharon McAuliffe. 1980. "Adolescents Who Work: Effects of Part-time Employment on Family and Peer Relations." *Journal of Youth and Adolescence* 9: 189–202.

Greene, William H. 1995. *LIMDEP Version 7.0: User's Manual and Reference Guide.* Bellport, N.Y.: EconoMetric Software.

Hagan, John. 1991. "Destiny and Drift: Subcultural Preferences, Status Attainments, and the Risks and Rewards of Youth." *American Sociological Review* 56: 567–582.

———— 1998. "Life Course Capitalization and Adolescent Behavioral Development." Pp. 499–517 in Richard Jessor, ed., *New Perspectives on Adolescent Risk Behavior.* Cambridge: Cambridge University Press.

Hagan, John, and Blair Wheaton. 1993. "The Search for Adolescent Role Exits and the Transition to Adulthood." *Social Forces* 71: 955–980.

Hall, G. Stanley. 1904. *Adolescence: Its Psychology and Its Relations to Physiology, Anthropology, Sociology, Sex, Crime, Religion, and Education.* Vol. 1. New York: D. Appleton.

Hall, Richard H. 1969. *Occupations and the Social Structure.* Englewood, N.J.: Prentice-Hall.

———— 1994. *Sociology of Work: Perspectives, Analyses, and Issues*. Thousand Oaks, Calif.: Pine Forge Press.

Hamilton, Mary Agnes, and Stephen F. Hamilton. 1997. *Learning Well at Work: Choices for Quality*. Washington: National School-to-Work Office.

Hamilton, Stephen F. 1990. *Apprenticeship for Adulthood: Preparing Youth for the Future*. New York: Free Press.

———— 1999. "What Work Fosters Adolescent Development?" Pp. 160–167 in Booth, Crouter, and Shanahan, eds., 1999.

Hamilton, Stephen F., and Wolfgang Lempert. 1996. "The Impact of Apprenticeship on Youth: A Prospective Analysis." *Journal of Research on Adolescence* 6: 427–455.

Hamilton, V. L., W. S. Hoffman, C. L. Broman, and D. Rauma. 1991. "Aftermath: A Panel Study of Unemployment and Mental Health among Autoworkers." Manuscript.

Hansen, David M., Jeylan T. Mortimer, and Helga Krüger. 2001. "Adolescent Part-time Employment in the United States and Germany: Diverse Outcomes, Contexts, and Pathways." Pp. 121–138 in Christopher Pole, Phillip Mizen, and Angela Bolton, eds., *Hidden Hands: International Perspectives on Children's Work and Labour*. London: Routledge Falmer.

Hardy, Melissa A. 1993. *Regression with Dummy Variables: Quantitative Applications in the Social Sciences*. Series 93. Newbury Park, Calif.: Sage.

Hareven, Tamara K. 1982. *Family Time and Industrial Time: The Relationship between the Family and Work in a New England Industrial Community*. Cambridge: Cambridge University Press.

Heckhausen, Jutta. 1999. *Developmental Regulation in Adulthood: Age Normative and Sociocultural Constraints as Adaptive Challenges*. New York: Cambridge University Press.

Heckman, James J. 1996. "What Should Be Our Human Capital Investment Policy?" Pp. 323–342 in Garth Mangum and Stephen Mangum, eds., *Of Heart and Mind: Social Policy Essays in Honor of Sar A. Levitan*. Kalamazoo: W. E. Upjohn Institute for Employment Research.

Heinz, Walter R., Udo Kelle, Andreas Witzel, and Jens Zinn. 1998. "Vocational Training and Career Development in Germany: Results from a Longitudinal Study." *International Journal of Behavioral Development* 22 (1): 77–101.

Hochschild, Arlie Russell. 1989. *The Second Shift*. New York: Avon.

———— 1997. *The Time Bind: When Work Becomes Home and Home Becomes Work*. New York: Henry Holt.

Hotz, V. Joseph, Lixin Colin Xu, Marta Tienda, and Avner Ahituv. Forthcoming. "Are There Returns to the Wages of Young Men from Working While in School?" Forthcoming in *Review of Economics and Statistics*.

Jessor, Richard, John E. Donovan, and Frances M. Costa. 1991. *Beyond Adolescence: Problem Behavior and Young Adult Development*. Cambridge: Cambridge University Press.

Johansson, Gunn, and Gunner Aronsson. 1991. "Psychosocial Factors in the Workplace." Pp. 179–197 in G. M. Green and F. Baker, eds., *Work, Health, and Productivity*. New York: Oxford University Press.

Johnson, Monica Kirkpatrick, Timothy Beebe, Jeylan T. Mortimer, and Mark Snyder. 1998. "Volunteerism in Adolescence: A Process Perspective." *Journal of Research on Adolescence* 8: 309–332.

Johnson, Monica Kirkpatrick, and Jeylan T. Mortimer. 2000. "Work-Family Orientations and Attainments in the Early Life Course." Pp. 215–248 in Toby L. Parcel and Daniel B. Cornfield, eds., *Work and Family: Research Informing Policy*. Thousand Oaks, Calif.: Sage.

Johnson, Monica Kirkpatrick, Sabrina Oesterle, and Jeylan T. Mortimer. 2001. "Adolescents' Anticipations of Work-Family Conflict in a Changing Societal Context." Pp. 233–261 in Sandra L. Hofferth and Timothy J. Owens, eds., *Children at the Millennium: Where Have We Come From, Where Are We Going?* vol. 6: *Advances in Life Course Research*. Greenwich, Conn.: JAI Press.

Jordaan, Jean Pierre, and Donald E. Super. 1974. "The Prediction of Early Adult Vocational Behavior." Pp. 108–130 in David F. Ricks, Alexander Thomas, and Merrill Roff, eds., *Life History Research in Psychopathology*, vol. 3. Minneapolis: University of Minnesota Press.

Jöreskog, Karl, and Dag Sörbom. 1989. *LISREL 7: User's Reference Guide*. Chicago: Scientific Software.

Kablaoui, B. N., and A. Pautler. 1991. "The Effects of Part-time Work Experience on High School Students." *Journal of Career Development* 17: 195–211.

Kahn, Robert. 1981. *Work and Health*. New York: Wiley.

Kalleberg, Arne, Barbara F. Reskin, and Ken Hudson. 2000. "Bad Jobs in America: Standard and Nonstandard Employment Relations and Job Quality in the United States." *American Sociological Review* 65: 256–278.

Kalleberg, Arne L., and Kathryn Schmidt. 1996. "Contingency Workers and Contingent Work: Part-Time, Temporary, and Subcontracting Employment Relations in U.S. Organizations." Pp. 253–275 in Arne L. Kalleberg, David Knoke, Peter V. Marsden, and Joe L. Spaeth, eds., *Organizations in America: A Portrait of their Structures and Human Resource Practices*. Newbury Park, Calif.: Sage.

Keniston, Kenneth. 1968. *Young Radicals: Notes on Committed Youth*. New York: Harcourt, Brace and World.

Kerckhoff, Alan C. 2002. "The Transition from School to Work." In Jeylan T. Mortimer and Reed Larson, eds., *The Changing Adolescent Experience: Societal Trends and the Transition to Adulthood*. New York: Cambridge University Press.

Kerckhoff, Alan C., and Lorraine Bell. 1998. "Hidden Capital: Vocational Credentials and Attainment in the United States." *Sociology of Education* 71: 152–174.

Kett, Joseph F. 1971. "Adolescence and Youth in Nineteenth-Century America." *Journal of Interdisciplinary History* 2: 283–298.

——— 1978. "Curing the Disease of Precocity." *American Journal of Sociology* 84: S183-S211.

Klein, Hugh. 1990. "Adolescence, Youth, and Young Adulthood: Rethinking Current Conceptualizations of Life Stage." *Youth and Society:* 21: 446–471.

Kohli, M. 1985. "The World We Forgot: A Historical Review of the Life Course." Pp. 271–303 in V. W. Marshall, ed., *Later Life: The Social Psychology of Aging*. Beverly Hills: Sage.

Kohn, Melvin L. 1969. *Class and Conformity: A Study in Values*. Homewood, Ind.: Dorsey.

Kohn, Melvin L., and Carrie Schoenbach. 1983. "Class, Stratification, and Psychological Functioning." Pp. 154–189 in Kohn and Schooler, 1983.

Kohn, Melvin L., and Carmi Schooler. 1974. *Study of Occupations: Child Version*. Chicago: National Opinion Research Center, University of Chicago.

——— 1983. *Work and Personality: An Inquiry into the Impact of Social Stratification*. Norwood, N.J.: Ablex.

Larson, Reed, and Maryse H. Richards. 1994. *Divergent Realities: The Emotional Lives of Mothers, Fathers, and Adolescents*. New York: Basic Books.

Leidner, Robin. 1993. *Fast Food, Fast Talk: Service Work and the Routinization of Everyday Life*. Berkeley: University of California Press.

Lewin-Epstein, Noah. 1981. *Youth Employment during High School*. Washington: National Center for Educational Statistics.

Lillydahl, Jane H. 1990. "Academic Achievement and Part-time Employment of High School Students." *Journal of Economic Education* 21: 307–316.

Lorence, Jon, and Jeylan T. Mortimer. 1985. "Job Involvement through the Life Course: A Panel Study of Three Age Groups." *American Sociological Review* 50: 618–638.

Lowe, Graham S., and Harvey Krahn. 1992. "Do Part-Time Jobs Improve the Labor Market Chances of High School Graduates?" Pp. 131–141 in B. D. Warme, ed., *Working Part-time: Risks and Opportunities.* New York: Praeger.

Mainquist, S., and D. Eichorn. 1989. "Competence in Work Settings." Pp. 327–367 in David Stern and Dorothy Eichorn, eds., *Adolescence and Work: Influences of Social Structure, Labor Markets, and Culture.* Hillsdale, N.J.: Lawrence Erlbaum.

Manning, Wendy D. 1990. "Parenting Employed Teenagers." *Youth and Society* 22: 184–200.

Marini, Margaret Mooney, Pi-Ling Fan, Erica Finley, and Ann M. Beutel. 1996. "Gender and Job Values." *Sociology of Education* 69: 49–65.

Markus, Hazel, Susan Cross, and Elissa Wurf. 1990. "The Role of the Self-system in Competence." Pp. 205–226 in R. J. Sternberg and J. Kolligan Jr., eds., *Competence Considered.* New Haven: Yale University Press.

Markus, Hazel, and P. Nurius. 1986. "Possible Selves." *American Psychologist* 41: 954–969.

Marsh, Herbert E. 1991. "Employment during High School: Character Building or a Subversion of Academic Goals." *Sociology of Education* 64: 172–189.

Marshall, Ray. 1994. "Job and Skill Demands in the New Economy." Pp. 21–57 in Lewis C. Solmon and Alec R. Levenson, eds., *Labor Markets, Employment Policy, and Job Creation.* Boulder: Westview.

Masten, Ann S., and Norman Garmezy. 1985. "Risk, Vulnerability, and Protective Factors in Developmental Psychopathology." In B. B. Lahey and A. E. Kazdin, eds., *Advances in Clinical Child Psychology,* vol. 8. New York: Plenum.

McAdam, Doug. 1988. *Freedom Summer.* New York: Oxford University Press.

McHale, S. M., W. T. Bartko, A. C. Crouter, and M. Perry-Jenkins. 1990. "Children's Housework and Psychosocial Functioning: The Mediating Effects of Parents' Sex-Role Behaviors and Attitudes." *Child Development* 61: 1413–26.

McLanahan, Sara S., and Gary D. Sandefur. 1994. *Growing Up with a Single Parent.* Cambridge, Mass.: Harvard University Press.

McLeod, Jane D., and Ronald C. Kessler. 1990. "Socioeconomic Status Differences in Vulnerability to Undesirable Life Events." *Journal of Health and Social Behavior* 31: 162–172.

McMorris, Barbara J., and Christopher Uggen. 1998. "Alcohol and Employment in the Transition to Adulthood." Paper presented at the Annual Meeting of the American Society of Criminology, Washington.

————. 2000. "Alcohol and Employment in the Transition to Adulthood." *Journal of Health and Social Behavior* 41(3): 276–294.

McNeil, Linda. 1984. *Lowering Expectations: The Impact of Student Employment on Classroom Knowledge.* Madison: Wisconsin Center for Educational Research.

Meyer, R. M., and D. A. Wise. 1982. "High School Preparation and Early Labor Force Experience." Pp. 277–347 in R. B. Freeman and D. A. Wise, eds., *The Youth Labor Problem: Its Nature, Causes, and Consequences.* Chicago: University of Chicago Press.

Mihalic, S. W., and D. Elliott. 1997. "Short- and Long-term Consequences of Adolescent Work." *Youth and Society* 28 (4): 464–498.

Miller, Joanne. 1988. "Jobs and Work." Pp. 327–359 in Neil J. Smelser, ed., *Handbook of Sociology.* Newbury Park, Calif.: Sage.

Miller, Joanne, Carmi Schooler, Melvin L. Kohn, and Karen A. Miller. 1983. "Women and Work: The Psychological Effects of Occupational Conditions." Pp. 195–216 in Kohn and Schooler, 1983.

Miller, Joanne, and S. Yung. 1990. "The Role of Allowances in Adolescent Socialization." *Youth and Society* 22: 137–159.

Mincer, Jacob. 1958. "Investment in Human Capital and Personal Income Distribution." *Journal of Political Economy* 66 (Aug.): 281–302.

Minnesota Department of Education. 1992. *Minnesota Student Survey 1989–1992: Reflections of Social Change.* St. Paul.

Mischel, Lawrence, Jared Bernstein, and John Schmitt. 1999. *The State of Working America, 1998–99.* Ithaca: ILR Press.

Modell, John. 1979. "Changing Risks, Changing Adaptations: American Families in the Nineteenth and Twentieth Centuries." Pp. 119–144 in Allan J. Lichtman and John R. Challinor, eds., *Kin and Communities: Families in America.* Washington: Smithsonian Institution Press.

———— 1989. *Into One's Own: From Youth to Adulthood in the United States, 1920–1975.* Berkeley: University of California Press.

Mortimer, Jeylan T. 1994. "Individual Differences as Precursors of Youth Unemployment." Pp. 172–198 in Anne C. Petersen and Jeylan T. Mortimer, eds., *Youth Unemployment and Society.* Cambridge: Cambridge University Press.

Mortimer, Jeylan T., Katherine Dennehy, Chaimun Lee, and Michael D. Finch. 1994. "Economic Socialization in the American Family: The Prevalence, Distribution, and Consequences of Allowance Arrangements." *Family Relations* 43: 23–29.

Mortimer, Jeylan T., and Michael D. Finch. 1986. "The Development of Self-Esteem in the Early Work Career." *Work and Occupations* 13(2): 217–239.

———— eds. 1996. *Adolescents, Work, and Family: An Intergenerational Developmental Analysis.* Newbury Park, Calif.: Sage.

Mortimer, Jeylan T., Michael D. Finch, Katherine Dennehy, Chaimun Lee, and Timothy Beebe. 1994. "Work Experience in Adolescence." *Journal of Vocational Education Research* 19: 39–70.

Mortimer, Jeylan T., Michael D. Finch, and Geoffrey Maruyama. 1988. "Work Experience and Job Satisfaction: Variation by Age and Gender." Pp. 109–155 in Jeylan T. Mortimer and Kathryn Borman, eds., *Work Experience and Psychological Development through the Life Span.* Boulder: Westview.

Mortimer, Jeylan T., Michael D. Finch, Timothy J. Owens, and Michael Shanahan. 1990. "Gender and Work in Adolescence." *Youth and Society* 22: 201–224.

Mortimer, Jeylan T., Michael D. Finch, Seongryeol Ryu, Michael J. Shanahan, and Kathleen Thiede Call. 1996. "The Effects of Work Intensity on Adolescent Mental Health, Achievement and Behavioral Adjustment: New Evidence from a Prospective Study." *Child Development* 67: 1243–61.

Mortimer, Jeylan T., Michael D. Finch, Michael Shanahan, and Seongryeol Ryu. 1992. "Work Experience, Mental Health and Behavioral Adjustment in Adolescence." *Journal of Research on Adolescence* 2: 25–57.

Mortimer, Jeylan T., Carolyn Harley, and Pamela J. Aronson. 1999. "How Do Prior Experiences in the Workplace Set the Stage for Transitions to Adulthood?" Pp. 131–159 in Booth, Crouter, and Shanahan, eds., 1999.

Mortimer, Jeylan T., Carolyn Harley, and Jeremy Staff. 2002. "The Quality of Part-Time Work and Youth Mental Health." *Work and Occupations* 29: 166–197.

Mortimer, Jeylan T., and Monica Kirkpatrick Johnson. 1998a. "New Perspectives on Adolescent Work and the Transition to Adulthood." Pp. 425–496 in Richard Jessor, ed., *New Perspectives on Adolescent Risk Behavior.* New York: Cambridge University Press.

———— 1998b. "Adolescent Part-time Work and Educational Achievement." Pp. 183–206 in Kathryn Borman and Barbara Schneider, eds., *The Adolescent Years: Social Influences and Educational Challenges.* Chicago: National Society for the Study of Education.

———— 1999. "Adolescent Part-time Work and Post-secondary Transition Pathways: A Longitudinal Study of Youth in St. Paul, Minnesota (U.S.)." Pp. 111–148 in Walter Heinz, ed., *From Education to Work: Cross National Perspectives.* New York: Cambridge University Press.

Mortimer, Jeylan T., and Helga Krüger. 2000. "Transition from School to

Work in the United States and Germany: Formal Pathways Matter."
Pp. 475–497 in Maureen Hallinan, ed., *Handbook of the Sociology of Education*. New York: Plenum.

Mortimer, Jeylan T., and Donald S. Kumka. 1982. "A Further Examination of the 'Occupational Linkage Hypothesis'." *Sociological Quarterly* 23: 3–16.

Mortimer, Jeylan T., and Jon Lorence. 1979a. "Work Experience and Occupational Value Socialization: A Longitudinal Study." *American Journal of Sociology* 84: 1361–85.

———. 1979b. "Occupational Experience and the Self-Concept: A Longitudinal Study." *Social Psychology Quarterly* 42: 307–323.

———. 1995. "Social Psychology of Work." Pp. 497–523 in Karen S. Cook, Gary Alan Fine, and James S. House, eds., *Sociological Perspectives on Social Psychology*. Boston: Allyn and Bacon.

Mortimer, Jeylan T., Jon Lorence, and Donald Kumka. 1986. *Work, Family, and Personality: Transition to Adulthood*. Norwood, N.J.: Ablex.

Mortimer, Jeylan T., Sabrina Oesterle, and Helga Krüger. Forthcoming. "Age Norms, Institutional Structures, and the Timing of Markers of Transition to Adulthood." In Hans Bertram, ed., *Comparative Studies of the Life Course and Life Styles in the United States and Germany*. *American Behavioral Scientist*, special issue.

Mortimer, Jeylan T., Ellen Efron Pimentel, Seongryeol Ryu, Katherine Nash, and Chaimun Lee. 1996. "Part-Time Work and Occupational Value Formation in Adolescence." *Social Forces* 74: 1405–18.

Mortimer, Jeylan T., and Michael Shanahan. 1991. "Adolescent Work Experience and Relations with Peers." Paper presented at the American Sociological Association Annual Meeting, Cincinnati.

———. 1994. "Adolescent Work Experience and Family Relationships." *Work and Occupations* 21: 369–384.

Mortimer, Jeylan T., Michael Shanahan, and Seongryeol Ryu. 1993. Pp. 304–326 in Rainer K. Silbereisen and Eberhard Todt, eds., *Adolescence in Context: The Interplay of Family, School, Peers, and Work in Adjustment*. New York: Springer-Verlag.

Mortimer, Jeylan T., Melanie J. Zimmer-Gembeck, Mikki Holmes, and Michael J. Shanahan. 2002. "The Process of Occupational Decision-Making: Patterns during the Transition to Adulthood." *Journal of Vocational Behavior* 61: 1–27.

National Center for Educational Statistics. 1997. *Education Statistics on Disk*, 1996 ed. Washington: U.S. Department of Education.

Newcomb, Michael D., and Peter M. Bentler. 1988. *Consequences of Adolescent Drug Use: Impact on the Lives of Young Adults*. Newbury Park, Calif.: Sage.

Newman, Katherine S. 1996. "Working Poor: Low-Wage Employment in the Lives of Harlem Youth." Pp. 323–343 in Julia A. Graber, Jeanne Brooks-Gunn, and Anne C. Petersen, eds., *Transitions through Adolescence: Interpersonal Domains and Context*. Mahwah, N.J.: Lawrence Erlbaum.

——— 1999. *No Shame in My Game*. New York: Knopf and Russell Sage Foundation.

Nurius, Paula. 1991. "Possible Selves and Social Support: Social Cognitive Resources for Coping and Striving." Pp. 239–258 in Judith A. Howard and Peter L. Callero, eds., *The Self-Society Dynamic: Cognition, Emotion, and Action*. Cambridge: Cambridge University Press.

O'Brien, G. E., and N. T. Feather. 1990. "The Relative Effects of Unemployment and the Quality of Employment on the Affect, Work Values, and Personal Control of Adolescents." *Journal of Occupational Psychology* 63: 151–165.

Oesterle, Sabrina, Monica Kirkpatrick Johnson, and Jeylan T. Mortimer. 1998. "Volunteerism during the Transition into Adulthood." Paper presented at the Annual Meeting of the American Sociological Association, San Francisco.

Osgood, D. Wayne. 1999. "Having the Time of Their Lives: All Work and No Play?" Pp. 176–186 in Booth, Crouter, and Shanahan, eds., 1999.

Osterman, Paul. 1980. *Getting Started: The Youth Labor Market*. Cambridge, Mass.: MIT Press.

——— 1989. "The Job Market for Adolescents." In David Stern and Dorothy Eichorn, eds., *Adolescence and Work: Influences of Social Structure, Labor Markets, and Culture*. Hillsdale, N.J.: Lawrence Erlbaum.

Panel on Youth of the President's Science Advisory Committee. 1974. *Youth: Transition to Adulthood*. Chicago: University of Chicago Press.

Pearlin, Leonard I., Elizabeth G. Menaghan, Morton A. Lieberman, and Joseph T. Mullan. 1981. "The Stress Process." *Journal of Health and Social Behavior* 22: 337–356.

Phillips, Sarah, and Kent L. Sandstrom. 1990. "Parental Attitudes towards Youth Work." *Youth and Society* 22: 160–183.

Pimentel, Ellen Efron. 1996. "Effects of Adolescent Achievement and Family Goals on the Early Adult Transition." Pp. 191–220 in Mortimer and Finch, eds., 1996.

Ploeger, Matthew. 1997. "Youth Employment and Delinquency: Reconsidering a Problematic Relationship" *Criminology* 35 (4): 659–675.

Putnam, Robert D. 1995. "Bowling Alone: America's Declining Social Capital." *Journal of Democracy* 6: 65–78.

——— 1996. "The Strange Disappearance of Civic America." *American Prospect* 24: 34–48.

Raskoff, S., and Sundeen, R. 1994. "The Ties That Bond: Teenage Volunteers in the United States." Paper presented at the International Sociological Association meetings, Bielefeld, Germany.

Reich, Robert. 1991. *The Work of Nations: Preparing Ourselves for 21st-Century Capitalism.* New York: Knopf.

Reiter, Ester. 1991. *Making Fast Food: From the Frying Pan into the Fire.* Montreal: McGill-Queen's University Press.

Reskin, Barbara. 1993. "Sex Segregation in the Workplace." *Annual Review of Sociology* 19: 241–270.

Resnick, Michael D., Peters S. Bearman, Robert W. Blum, Karl E. Bauman, Kathleen M. Harris, Jo Jones, Joyce Tabor, Trish Beuhring, Renee E. Sieving, Marcia Shew, Marjorie Ireland, Linda Bearinger, and J. Richard Udry. 1997. "Protecting Adolescents from Harm: Findings from the National Longitudinal Study on Adolescent Health. *JAMA* 278 (10): 823–832.

Rindfuss, Ronald R., Elizabeth C. Cooksey, and Rebecca L. Sutterlin. 1999. "Young Adult Occupational Achievement: Early Expectations versus Behavioral Reality." *Work and Occupations* 26: 220–263.

Rindfuss, Ronald R., C. Gray Swicegood, and Rachel Rosenfeld. 1987. "Disorder in the Life Course: How Common and Does It Matter?" *American Sociological Review* 52: 785–801.

Rosenbaum, James E., Takehiko Kariya, Rick Settersten, and Tony Maier. 1990. "Market and Network Theories of the Transition from High School to Work: Their Application to Industrialized Societies." *Annual Review of Sociology* 16: 263–299.

Rosenberg, Morris. 1965. *Society and the Adolescent Self-Image.* Princeton: Princeton University Press.

Rossi, Alice. 1989. "A Life-Course Approach to Gender, Aging, and Intergenerational Relations." Pp. 207–263 in K. Warner Schaie and Carmi Schooler, eds., *Social Structure and Aging.* Hillsdale, N.J.: Lawrence Erlbaum.

Ruhm, Christopher J. 1995. "The Extent and Consequences of High School Employment." *Journal of Labor Research* 16 (3): 293–303.

——— 1997. "Is High School Employment Consumption or Investment?" *Journal of Labor Economics* 15 (4): 735–776.

Ruscoe, Gordon, Jack C. Morgan, and Cynthia Peebles. 1996. "Students Who Work." *Adolescence* 31: 625–632.

Rutter, Michael. 1985. "Resilience in the Face of Adversity: Protective Factors and Resistance to Psychiatric Disorder." *British Journal of Psychiatry* 147: 598–611.

Ryu, Seongryeol, and Jeylan T. Mortimer. 1996. "The 'Occupational Linkage Hypothesis' Applied to Occupational Value Formation in Adolescence." Pp. 167–190 in Mortimer and Finch, eds., 1996.

Sampson, Robert J., and John Laub. 1993. *Crime in the Making: Pathways and Turning Points through Life.* Cambridge, Mass.: Harvard University Press.

Schill, W. J., R. M. McCartin, and K. Meyer. 1985. "Youth Employment: Its Relationship to Academic and Family Variables." *Journal of Vocational Behavior* 26: 155–163.

Schneider, Barbara, and David Stevenson. 1999. *The Ambitious Generation: America's Teenagers, Motivated but Directionless.* New Haven: Yale University Press.

Schoenhals, Mark, Marta Tienda, and Barbara Schneider. 1998. "The Educational and Personal Consequences of Adolescent Employment." *Social Forces* 77: 723–762.

Schooler, Carmi, Melvin L. Kohn, Karen A. Miller, and Joanne Miller. 1983. "Housework as Work." Pp. 242–260 in Kohn and Schooler, eds., 1983.

Schor, Juliet B. 1998. *The Overspent American: Upscaling, Downshifting, and the New Consumer.* New York: Basic Books.

Schulenberg, John, and Jerald G. Bachman. 1993. "Long Hours on the Job? Not So Bad for Some Types of Jobs: The Quality of Work and Substance Use, Affect, and Stress." Paper presented at the Biennial Meeting of the Society for Research on Child Development. New Orleans.

Schulenberg, John, Jerald G. Bachman, Lloyd D. Johnston, and Patrick M. O'Malley. 1995. "American Adolescents' Views on Family and Work: Historical Trends from 1976–1992." Pp. 37–64 in Peter Noack, Manfred Hofer, and James Youniss, eds., *Psychological Responses to Social Change: Human Development in Changing Environments.* New York: Walter de Gruyter.

Schuman, Howard. 1995. "Attitudes, Beliefs, and Behavior." Pp. 68–89 in Karen S. Cook, Gary Alan Fine, and James S. House, eds., *Sociological Perspectives on Social Psychology.* Boston: Allyn and Bacon.

Shanahan, Michael J. 1992. "High School Work Experiences and Depressed Mood." Paper presented at the 1992 American Sociological Association Meetings, Pittsburgh.

——— 2000a. "Pathways to Adulthood in Changing Societies: Variability and Mechanisms in Life Course Perspective." *Annual Review of Sociology* 26: 667–692.

——— 2000b. "Adolescence." Pp. 1–18 in Edgar Borgatta and Rhonda J. V. Montgomery, eds., *Encyclopedia of Sociology,* 2nd ed., vol. 1. New York: Macmillan.

Shanahan, Michael J., Glen H. Elder Jr., Margaret Burchinal, and Rand D. Conger. 1996. "Adolescent Earnings and Relationships with Parents: The Work-Family Nexus in Urban and Rural Ecologies." Pp. 97–128 in Mortimer and Finch, eds., 1996.

Shanahan, Michael J., Glen H. Elder Jr., and Richard A. Miech. 1997. "History and Agency in Men's Lives: Pathways to Achievement in Cohort Perspective." *Sociology of Education* 70: 54–67.

Shanahan, Michael J., Michael D. Finch, Jeylan T. Mortimer, and Seongryeol Ryu. 1991. "Adolescent Work Experience and Depressive Affect." *Social Psychology Quarterly* 54: 299–317.

Shanahan, Michael J., and Brian P. Flaherty. 2000. "Time Use in Adolescence and the Transition to Adulthood." Paper presented at the 7th Biennial Conference of the European Association for Research on Adolescence, Jena, Germany.

———— 2001. "Dynamic Patterns of Time Use in Adolescence." *Child Development* 72: 385–401.

Shanahan, Michael J., and Jeylan T. Mortimer. 1996. "Understanding the Positive Consequences of Psychosocial Stress." Pp. 189–209 in Barry Markovsky, Michael Lovaglia, and Robin Simon, eds., *Advances in Group Processes,* vol. 13. Greenwich, Conn.: JAI Press.

Simmons, Roberta G., and Dale A. Blyth. 1987. *Moving into Adolescence: The Impact of Pubertal Change and School Context.* Hawthorne, N.Y.: Aldine de Gruyter.

Smelser, Neil J. 1959. *Social Change and the Industrial Revolution.* Chicago: University of Chicago Press.

Smelser, Neil J., and Sydney Halpern. 1978. "The Historical Triangulation of Family, Economy, and Education." *American Journal of Sociology* 84: S288–S315.

Smith, Thomas Ewin. 1992. "Time Use and Change in Academic Achievement: A Longitudinal Follow-Up." *Journal of Youth and Adolescence* 21: 725–747.

Spain, Daphne, and Suzanne M. Bianchi. 1996. *Balancing Act: Motherhood, Marriage, and Employment among American Women.* New York: Russell Sage Foundation.

Spenner, Kenneth I., and Luther B. Otto. 1985. "Work and Self-Concept: Selection and Socialization in the Early Career." Pp. 197–235 in Alan C. Kerckhoff, ed., *Research in Sociology of Education and Socialization,* vol. 5. Greenwich, Conn.: JAI Press.

Steel, Lauri. 1991. "Early Work Experience among White and Non-white Youths: Implications for Subsequent Enrollment and Employment." *Youth and Society* 22: 419–447.

Steinberg, Laurence. 1990. "Autonomy, Conflict, and Harmony in the Family Relationship." Pp. 255–276 in Shirley Feldman and G. Elliott, eds., *At the Threshold: The Developing Adolescent.* Cambridge, Mass.: Harvard University Press.

Steinberg, Laurence, and Shelli Avenevoli. 1998. "Disengagement from School and Problem Behavior in Adolescence: A Developmental-Contextual Analysis of the Influences of Family and Part-time Work." Pp. 392–424 in Richard Jessor, ed., *New Perspectives on Adolescent Risk Behavior.* New York: Cambridge University Press.

Steinberg, Laurence, and Elizabeth Cauffman. 1995. "The Impact of Employment on Adolescent Development." *Annals of Child Development* 11: 131–166.

Steinberg, Laurence, and Sanford M. Dornbusch. 1991. "Negative Correlates of Part-time Employment during Adolescence: Replication and Elaboration." *Developmental Psychology* 27: 304–313.

Steinberg, Laurence, S. Fegley, and Sanford M. Dornbusch. 1993. "Negative Impact of Part-time Work on Adolescent Adjustment: Evidence from a Longitudinal Study." *Developmental Psychology* 29: 171–180.

Steinberg, Laurence, Ellen Greenberger, Laurie Garduque, and Sharon McAuliffe. 1982a. "High-School Students in the Labor Force: Some Costs and Benefits to Schooling and Learning." *Educational Evaluation and Policy Analysis* 4: 363–372.

Steinberg, Laurence, Ellen Greenberger, L. Garduque, M. Ruggiero, and Alan Vaux. 1982b. "Effects of Working on Adolescent Development." *Developmental Psychology* 18: 385–395.

Steinberg, Laurence, and A. Levine. 1990. *You and Your Adolescent.* New York: Harper and Row.

Stephenson, Stanley P., Jr. 1981. "In-School Labour Force Status and Post-School Wage Rates of Young Men." *Applied Economics* 13: 279–302.

Stern, David, and Yoshi-Fumi Nakata. 1989. "Characteristics of High School Students, Paid Jobs, and Employment Experience after Graduation." Pp. 189–234 in David Stern and Dorothy Eichorn, eds., *Adolescence and Work: Influences of Social Structure, Labor Markets, and Culture.* Hillsdale, N.J.: Lawrence Erlbaum.

Stevens, Constance J., Laura A. Puchtell, Seongryeol Ryu, and Jeylan T. Mortimer. 1992. "Adolescent Work and Boys' and Girls' Orientations to the Future." *Sociological Quarterly* 33: 153–169.

Stevens, Gillian, and Elizabeth Hoisington. 1987. "Occupational Prestige and the 1980 U.S. Labor Force." *Social Science Research* 16: 74–105.

Stone, James R., III, and Jeylan T. Mortimer. 1998. "The Effect of Adolescent Employment on Vocational Development: Public and Educational Policy Implications." *Journal of Vocational Behavior* 53: 184–214.

Stone, James R., III, David Stern, Charles Hopkins, and Martin McMillion.

1990. "Adolescents' Perceptions of Their Work: School Supervised and Non-School Supervised." *Journal of Vocational Education Research* 15: 31–53.

Sullivan, Mercer L. 1996. "Developmental Transitions in Poor Youth: Delinquency and Crime." Pp. 141–164 in Julia A. Graber, Jeanne Brooks-Gunn, and Anne C. Petersen, eds., *Transitions through Adolescence: Interpersonal Domains and Context*. Mahwah, N.J.: Lawrence Erlbaum.

Super, D. E., R. Starishevsky, N. Matlin, and J. P. Jordaan. 1963. *Career Development: Self-Concept Theory*. New York: CEEB Research Monograph 4.

Tanner, Julian, and Harvey Krahn. 1991. "Part-Time Work and Deviance among High School Seniors." *Canadian Journal of Sociology* 16: 281–302.

Tienda, Marta, and Avner Ahituv. 1996. "Ethnic Differences in School Departure: Does Youth Employment Promote or Undermine Educational Attainment?" Pp. 93–108 in Garth Mangum and Stephen Mangum, eds., *Of Heart and Mind: Social Policy Essays in Honor of Sar A. Levitan*. Kalamazoo: W. E. Upjohn Institute for Employment Research.

Uggen, Christopher, and Jennifer Janikula. 1999. "Volunteerism and Arrest in the Transition to Adulthood." *Social Forces* 78: 331–362.

U.S. Bureau of the Census. 1982. *Census of Population and Housing, 1980*. Summary tape file 3 (Technical Documentation). Washington: Government Printing Office.

U.S. Department of Labor. 1977. *Dictionary of Occupational Titles*. 4th ed. Washington: Government Printing Office.

——— 1986. *Dictionary of Occupational Titles*. 4th ed., Supplement. Washington: Government Printing Office.

Van Maanen, John, and Edgar Schein. 1979. "Toward a Theory of Organizational Socialization." *Research in Organizational Behavior* 1: 209–264.

Vondracek, Fred W., Richard M. Lerner, and John E. Schulenberg. 1986. *Career Development: A Life-Span Developmental Approach*. Hillsdale, N.J.: Lawrence Erlbaum.

Ware, John E., Jr., Shawn A. Johnston, Allyson Davies-Avery, and Robert H. Brook. 1979. "Current HIS Mental Health Battery." Pp. 94–105 in *Conceptualization and Measurement of Health for Adults in the Health Insurance Study*, vol. 3: *Mental Health*. Santa Monica: Rand Corporation.

Warren, John Robert, Paul C. LePore, and Robert D. Mare. 2000. "Employment during High School: Consequences for Students' Grades in Academic Courses." *American Educational Research Journal* 37: 943–969.

Weinberger, Daniel A., Steven K. Tublin, Martin E. Ford, and S. Shirley

Feldman. 1990. "Preadolescents' Social-Emotional Adjustment and Selective Attrition in Family Research." *Child Development* 61:1374–86.

White, L. K., and D. B. Brinkerhoff. 1981. "Children's Work in the Family: Its Significance and Meaning." *Journal of Marriage and the Family* 43: 789–798.

Wilson, William Julius. 1987. *The Truly Disadvantaged: The Inner City, the Underclass, and Public Policy.* Chicago: University of Chicago Press.

Winefield, A. H., and M. Tiggemann. 1985. "Psychological Correlates of Employment and Unemployment: Effects, Predisposing Factors, and Sex Differences." *Journal of Occupational Psychology* 58: 229–242.

Wofford, S. 1988. "A Preliminary Analysis of the Relationship between Employment and Delinquency/Crime for Adolescents and Young Adults." National Youth Survey 50. Boulder: Institute of Behavioral Science, University of Colorado.

Wright, J. P., Frank T. Cullen, and N. Williams. 1997. "Working While in School and Delinquent Involvement: Implications for Social Policy." *Crime and Delinquency* 43: 203–221.

Yamoor, Catherine, and Jeylan T. Mortimer. 1990. "An Investigation of Age and Gender Differences in the Effects of Employment on Adolescent Achievement and Well-being." *Youth and Society* 22: 225–240.

Yates, M., and Youniss, James. 1996. "Community Service and Political-Moral Identity in Adolescents." *Journal of Research on Adolescence* 6: 271–284.

Youniss, J., J. A. McLellan, and M. Yates. 1997. "What We Know about Generating Civic Identity." *American Behavioral Scientist* 40: 620–631.

Zelizer, Viviana A. 1985. *Pricing the Priceless Child: The Changing Social Value of Children.* New York: Basic Books.